ROYAL INSTITUTE OF PHILOSOPHY LECTURES

VOLUME SIX · 1971–1972

PHILOSOPHY AND THE ARTS

ROYAL INSTITUTE OF PHILOSOPHY LECTURES

VOLUME SIX · 1971–1972

PHILOSOPHY AND
THE ARTS

MACMILLAN

First published 1973 by
THE MACMILLAN PRESS LTD
London and Basingstoke
Associated companies in New York Dublin
Melbourne Johannesburg and Madras

SBN 333 13203 3

Printed in Great Britain by
T. & A. CONSTABLE LTD, EDINBURGH

111.85
R888

CONTENTS

LIST OF PLATES

between pages 104 and 105

FOREWORD

Nonsense, I said; there were aesthetic standards which had nothing to do with a society's pleasure and understanding. Much very bad art had given great pleasure for a limited amount of time to particular societies – for instance, Pre-Raphaelite painting and verse. That didn't stop it being unspeakable. It was the aesthetic quality of a work which mattered. . . .

Charles wished I'd stick to the novel, and the contemporary novel at that. Now that philosophy had abdicated its traditional role as explicator of the mysteries of life, the novel had taken over. Novels were written and read for what sense they made of the world; that was their true importance. They were immediate. . . .

Such wild assertions, gleefully proclaimed, echoed through the beechwood and over the fields as we tramped about denouncing each other's views. It was wonderful – and terribly muddled. We kept switching positions, adopting ideas which we'd just ridiculed, not really knowing what we were saying or why we were saying it. I was very glad that none of my Oxford friends, with their minds full of logical scalpels, could hear us.

JULIAN MITCHELL, *The Undiscovered Country*, p. 133

I. LEARNING FROM LITERATURE AND ART

IT WAS reading Julian Mitchell's semi-autobiographical novel, *The Undiscovered Country*, together with the experience, new to me, of working in close collaboration with teachers of art history, history, literature and music (in trying to produce an 'interdisciplinary' Foundation Course for the Arts Faculty in The Open University) that led me to choose aesthetics as the theme for the 1971–2 session of Royal Institute of Philosophy lectures. Aesthetics was *my* 'undiscovered country'; and I looked forward with some eagerness to finding out what issues excited, and divided, people working in this field.

My first invitation was to Julian Mitchell himself. What did he mean by novels making sense of the world, I asked. He braved the

logical scalpels, not in Oxford, but at 14 Gordon Square in Blooms-
bury, London, to give his answer. 'We read to gain new information
about life . . . by imagining ourselves into situations we haven't
been present at, or which have never taken place at all, and by
imagining ourselves to be people other than ourselves', he says (p. 10).
But what *sort* of information, and *how* does our imagination work,
when we read a novel, so as to give us this new information? Indeed,
doesn't the word 'information' load the dice in favour of what might
be called 'factual' truths, as opposed to 'moral' ones? Are not the
'truths' really moral ones?

He says as much. Fiction is 'a means of moral instruction'. Moreover, 'it's not only a unique way of understanding other individuals
– an activity which seems to me moral in its own right – but also, of
course, a way of understanding individuals in relation to each other'.

Mitchell is engagingly modest about his ability to explain what
sort of truths moral truths are, and what the nature is of the 'imaginative process' whereby, in reading fiction, we 'enter into' other
people. 'I do realise', he says 'that I'm using words like truth and
knowledge and imagination in ways which would never do for a
philosopher. My excuse is that I'm providing contexts for these
words which philosophers can then examine. For if we can only
understand words in their contexts, the philosophical nagging as to
their meaning must follow not precede the usage.'

What, then, has 'philosophical nagging' to offer on these
questions?

According to Richard Beardsmore, Lecturer in Philosophy at the
University College of North Wales, 'philosophers like R. M. Hare'
assume 'that since what we learn from reading a novel or a poem is
manifestly not to be explained as a list of facts, it must be explicable in
terms of a list of principles of conduct'. He, on the contrary, holds
'that there are types of learning, understanding and knowledge
which cannot be understood as *either* the knowledge of facts *or* the
grasp of principles or techniques' (p. 29).[1]

Suppose someone finds 'a new meaning in life' by reading a novel.
What is wrong with saying that what has happened is that he has
learnt new principles of conduct?

---

[1] The reference to 'techniques' is puzzling. When Hare writes of reading novels as
'an adjunct to moral thought' (*Freedom and Reason*, p. 183) surely he is not equating
what one learns from reading novels with acquiring techniques of some sort. But
Beardsmore evidently thinks he is, for he takes what Gilbert Ryle says – about
knowing *how* (to fish, shoot, make jokes, etc.) not being a matter of knowing *that*
something is the case – to be the inspiration for Hare's view about what we may
learn from reading a novel.

Beardsmore says that what is wrong with this is that principles of conduct can be learnt in any number of ways. But when we speak of a novel or a poem bringing a man to see what is possible for him,

> we can no longer conceive of these possibilities existing independently of the way in which he was brought to recognise them. If asked what he has learnt from the novel or the poem, the man may tell me to read it more carefully. But if this is unsuccessful, then he will not offer an alternative statement of the work. For what it has to tell us is internally related to the work itself.

Beardsmore is here attacking what has been called 'the heresy of paraphrase',[1] the theory that *what* a novel or poem has to tell us is one thing, its 'sense', and *how* it tells us it is another, the manner in which the sense is expressed. The opposing theory, which Beardsmore holds, is that the sort of 'truth' that belongs to a novel or poem is inseparable from the actual language used.

I am reminded by all this of something J. M. Cameron said about the poetic representation of feelings, in his inaugural lecture, 'Poetry and Dialectic', at Leeds in 1960.[2]

> The consolation of the poetic representation of human love is that it reveals to us that condition of feeling we share with others – it gives us 'the image of man and nature' – but not, or not wholly, as articulated in the common run of concepts, but as articulated in a particular concrete representation that speaks to us and for us in our individual situation, and only *through* this to and for our common humanity. It belongs to the poetic representation that it is wholly individual, these words in this order, and that no paraphrase can be given; so that although we know that this poem that speaks to us and for us speaks also to and for others, it is still as though it speaks to us alone.

The examples Beardsmore gives of situations in which literature may be said to be responsible for a change in a man's life by enabling him, as he puts it, 'to see what is possible for him' are, he realises, mostly ones in which it would be appropriate to talk of a *moral* change. (And Mitchell called fiction 'a means of moral instruction'.) But if this is so, how can 'the heresy of paraphrase' be avoided? For doesn't a moral belief involve a moral principle or rule, and are not rules precisely the sort of things that *can* be learnt, and formulated, independently of the situations to which they are applied? Moreover,

---

[1] Richard Wollheim, *Art and its Objects* (Penguin Books, 1970) section 49.
[2] J. M. Cameron, *The Night Battle* (Burns and Oates, 1962) pp. 119–49.

in expressing a moral belief are we not implicitly claiming the
assent of *any* reasonable person? In short, how can Beardsmore, once
the confusion of moral principles and Rylean 'know-how' techniques
is sorted out, avoid agreeing with 'philosophers like R. M. Hare'
about what we learn from a novel?

D. Z. Phillips, Professor of Philosophy at the University College
of Swansea, comes to his rescue with a frontal attack on the conception of moral philosophy as the discovery of 'rules as to how *people*
in *general* ought to act'. His own view is that

> what is and what is not morally important cannot be determined
> independently of the variety of issues that present themselves. It
> cannot be determined in general in terms of an abstracted notion
> of reasonableness.

By 'an abstracted notion of reasonableness' he means the notion of
reasonableness involved in the idea that there is a criterion of right
and wrong independent of all the heterogeneous conceptions of
what is worthwhile in life. There are different 'moral perspectives',
and it is a mistake to see changes in moral perspectives 'as the rejection and replacing of hypotheses or policies within a single framework within which moral beliefs must be determined'.

The term 'perspective', in this connection, was explained by Peter
Winch in his inaugural lecture, 'Moral Integrity', at London, in
1968[1]:

> If we wish to understand the moral character of a particular man
> and his acts it is, often at any rate, not enough to notice that for
> such and such reasons he chooses a given course of action from
> among those he considers as alternatives. It may be at least as
> important to notice *what he considers the alternatives to be* and, what is
> closely connected, what are the reasons he considers it relevant
> to deploy in deciding between them. Thus one kind of difference
> between two men is that in which, agreeing about what the issues
> are with which their identical situations present them, they
> decide differently in the light of those issues. But an even more
> important difference is that in which they cannot even agree in
> their descriptions of the situation and in their account of the issues
> raised by it. For one man, for instance, a situation will raise a
> moral issue; for another it will not.
>
> Let me express this point by saying that a situation, the issues
> which it raises and the kind of reason which is appropriate to a
> discussion of those issues, involves a certain perspective. If I had

[1] Blackwell, 1968, p. 10.

to say shortly how I take the agent in the situation to be related to such a perspective I should say that the agent *is* the perspective.

Perhaps we can use Winch's final, rather cryptic, remark to take us further in our understanding of what Julian Mitchell says about the imaginative process whereby, in reading fiction, we can 'enter into' other people. If people *are* perspectives then 'entering into' other people must be a matter of our somehow acquiring new perspectives. Somehow, but how? What precisely is the 'imaginative process'?

J. M. Cameron says that the poetic representation of human love 'reveals to us that condition of feeling we share with others . . . as articulated in a particular concrete representation that speaks to us and for us in our individual situation'. I suppose that this process of revelation through articulation falls under the heading of 'how to acquire new perspectives on life'. (Perhaps Winch and Phillips would call the new perspectives 'moral' ones.[1]) But how does the 'articulation' work, and what sort of 'new information about life' (Mitchell's phrase) does it provide?

John Casey, Fellow of Gonville and Caius College, Cambridge, writes:

> Now I think we want to say . . . that successful expressions – such as works of art – can clarify a feeling, while at the same time leaving it as in some sense the same feeling that it was *before* it was clarified or articulated. This would, further, allow us to say what most people who take the arts seriously would want to say – that art is a form of knowledge, but knowledge of something other than fact.

This raises fascinating, and far-reaching, questions, to answer which Casey, like O. K. Bouwsma,[2] has to consider how it is that not only human behaviour, but also works of art, can be said to be expressive of feeling. Bouwsma tackled the question 'How can music be sad?' But Casey goes beyond this, to reflect on the *function* of the artist. The artist – the poet, say – 'can create new possibilities of feeling'. To see how, one has to reject the philosophical tradition of dualism, according to which the connection between what men feel and how they express their feelings is merely contingent, but without going

---

[1] I think that for Winch one of the main problems, if not *the* problem, in moral philosophy is that of the meaning of 'moral'. See his 'Human Nature', in *The Proper Study: Royal Institute of Philosophy Lectures*, vol. 4, 1969–70.

[2] 'The Expression Theory of Art', in *Philosophical Analysis*, ed. Max Black (Cornell University Press, 1950).

to the opposite extreme, which would not allow a place for the concept of more or less adequate expressions of the *same* feeling.

Is creating new possibilities of feeling – replacing inadequate, corrupt, or insincere modes of expression with more adequate ones – primarily a moral achievement? Casey thinks not. 'It is, rather, a triumph of imagination.' But he does not say why it should not be regarded as both.

Something rather closer to what Mitchell may have in mind when he says that, in reading fiction, we can 'enter into' other people, is described by R. K. Elliott, Senior Lecturer in the University of London Institute of Education, in his paper 'Imagination in the Experience of Art'. When contemplating Chagall's picture, *The Falling Angel*, he says, it may seem to the observer that there is movement in the picture itself.

> An image of movement comes momentarily into contact with the depicted angel, but he cannot hold it there long enough to be quite sure it was ever present at all. . . . A sort of struggle ensues between the real and the imaginal for possession of the visual impression. . . . The only solution is for Imagination to set the percipient free from his role as spectator, and enable him to experience the depicted movement in his own person, while at the same time preserving him in his spectatorial role in order that perception of the stimulating work shall be continuous. This is accomplished by the emergence of an imaginal self or ego which enters into the world of the work, most commonly by identifying itself with some depicted person.

Elliott's aim is to defend the aesthetic relevance of this type of experience against 'the presupposition that the only consummatory experiences of Art are strictly perceptual ones'.[1] 'It may be', he says, 'that a work of art is precisely the kind of thing which calls for imaginal and personal response. One might say that that is its essence and its life, and that the objectivist aesthetic extols not the work itself but its husk or corpse'.

This raises two questions: 'What are "strictly perceptual" experiences, as opposed to those involving an "imaginal and personal response"?' and 'What sort of thing is a "work of art"?' Let us consider them in turn.

In the second section, 'Learning to See', of his paper, 'Representation and Conceptual Change', Andrew Harrison, Lecturer in

---

[1] The notion of consummation is also implicit in his paper 'The Critic and the Lover of Art' in *Linguistic Analysis and Phenomenology*, ed. Wolfe Mays and S. C. Brown (Macmillan, 1972).

Philosophy at the University of Bristol, is concerned with how one learns to see natural objects with a view to drawing them. To say that this is done by learning to attend to the visual aspects an object really presents is to assume first, that visual representation works by visual reproduction, and second, 'that it not only makes sense to say that such and such is how an object really looks, but that if we clear our minds of cant, that is to say, learn to pay attention to what we really see as opposed to what we think that we see, we shall in so far as we are normal human beings equipped with normal vision, all come to notice the same thing'. If these assumptions were justified then we could 'just recognise' that something is a drawing or painting of something else – by seeing that the visual appearance of the one is the same as the visual aspect of the other. But we can't. We have to learn to 'read' a drawing as a drawing of something, and

> to 'read' a drawing as a drawing of something presupposes an elaborate background of mental habits, assumptions, and mental sets that have to be learnt, even if they have been in some cases learnt so readily that we are not aware of having done so.

Harrison goes on to say that the sense of learning to see, in which to learn to draw is to learn to see, 'occupies an uneasy borderline between a perceptual skill and a conceptual skill'. I think he would be bound to question the notion of a 'strictly perceptual' experience of art.

He concludes his paper with 'some indication of how the conceptual influence of a picture may operate quite specifically and non-generally'. Casey had remarked on how the poet 'can create new possibilities of feeling'. He can give us a more adequate mode of expressing such a feeling as grief, for example. Harrison invites us to consider Picasso's 1937 etching of a Weeping Woman.

> Its effect is to shift our conception of weeping, of outraged female grief, and the outrage of such grief, by the method of representation employed. . . . It shows us the form of a possible experience, something we may not have attended to in this form hitherto. This is a genuine shift in, or addition to our concept of grief, but it is not an addition to any theory of grief.

What was it Casey said? 'Art is a form of knowledge, but knowledge of something other than fact.' But if not of fact, then of what? Is it really knowledge when I hear the sadness in music, when there is a shift in my concept of grief on reading a poem or seeing a picture –

or merely a matter of the application of a name? I am reminded of
something John Wisdom once said[1]:

> *But the line between a question of fact and a question of decision as to the*
> *application of a name is not so simple as this way of putting things*
> *suggests.* . . . 'A difference as to the facts', 'a discovery', 'a revela-
> tion', these phrases cover many things. Discoveries have been
> made not only by Christopher Columbus and Pasteur, but by
> Tolstoy and Dostoievsky and Freud. Things are revealed to us
> not only by the scientists with microscopes, but also by the poets,
> the prophets, and the painters.

I mentioned earlier the question as to how it is that not only human
behaviour, but also works of art, can be said to be expressive of
feeling. I referred to Bouwsma's paper on 'The Expression Theory of
Art', and said that Casey goes on to describe how the artist 'can
create new possibilities of feeling'. Casey, like Cameron,[2] holds that
the question Bouwsma tackled is one which arises within the philosophical tradition of dualism, and that one way to answer it is to
reject that tradition.

J. O. Urmson, Fellow of Corpus Christi College, Oxford, tries to
answer the question without going into its philosophical context.
He can accept neither that to call a piece of music sad is to say that
it expresses the sadness of its composer, nor that it is to say that it
causes sadness in the hearer. It is not a matter of resemblance either:
'sad music does not much resemble the sounds that people make to
express their sadness, which are typically disagreeable and even

---

[1] 'Gods', *Proc. Arist. Soc.*, 1944, reprinted in John Wisdom, *Philosophy and Psycho-
analysis* (Blackwell, 1953) pp. 152, 154.

[2] *The Night Battle*, p. 142:
   One of the reasons we may have for ascribing truth to a poetic representation
is that it reveals to us the character of our inner feelings and dispositions; and by
this I do not mean that it describes accurately inner feelings and dispositions of
which we could give an account independently of the poetic representation. For
reasons I have already given, it will not do to say that the truth of the poem lies
in its 'matching' a state of affairs of which we have prior and independent
knowledge.
   We have the idea that the inner life may be described through introspection.
We habitually talk of our feelings, passions, dispositions, capacities, in terms
that suggest that introspection is to the mind and heart what sight and the other
senses are to the world of nature. It is one of the great and, I believe,
permanent advances recently made by philosophers in this country to have
shown that this account, the monstrous offspring of Cartesian dualism and
British empiricism, is impossible. The confusions in the account are legion and
they provided the later Wittgenstein with many of the problems that are
central to his *Philosophical Investigations*, a rich mine whence many lesser
philosophers have carried away their portions of precious ore.

raucous'. It is, he concludes, 'a special case of the very pervasive ascription of characteristics across the boundaries of the sense-modalities and across the boundaries between sensible and non-sensible characteristics'. Some terms, which have their primary use in one sphere, present themselves to us as appropriately used in another, and so one talks of a sweet girl, a bitter quarrel, a dark deed, a bright pupil, sad music. But *why* do they so present them-selves? 'The appropriateness', Urmson says, 'is intrinsic, rather than depending on some extrinsic causal relation or other associative principle.' He says that it is unplausible to hypothesise any special aesthetic explanation of this.

I think that Casey, on the other hand, might say that, in the case of 'feeling' words applied to works of art, the appropriateness not being extrinsic is a function of the relation of mind and matter not being as Descartes held it to be. But whether or not this is an 'aesthetic' explanation, I don't know. In some regions the border between philosophy of mind and aesthetics is not clearly marked.

2. WHAT IS A 'WORK OF ART'?

David Pole, Lecturer in Philosophy at King's College, London, calls works of art 'presentational objects', a term which, he says, he has stolen from Professor Wollheim. Wollheim[1] contrasts with the view that works of art are physical objects the views (i) that 'the work of art is non-physical in that it is something mental or even ethereal' (the Ideal theory), and (ii) that 'the work of art differs from physical objects, not in the sense that it is imperceptible, but because it has only sensible properties; it has no properties (for instance dispositional or historical) that are not open to direct or immediate observation' (the Presentational theory).

Apart from the usual problem, which Wollheim mentions, of knowing what 'direct or immediate observation' is, I can understand this. Someone who holds the Presentational theory of works of art will *not* hold, for example, that works of art, as such, have a place in history, or are to be evaluated as solving problems in the history of art. Pole holds that they *do* have a place in history, etc., and yet says that he holds that works of art *are* 'presentational objects'. He is not using the term 'presentational object' as Wollheim is. He is using it, he says, as a convenient formula to summarise the platitude that works of art 'are known, viewed and valued as we all very famil-iarly understand them to be known, viewed and valued'. Pole says

---

[1] Richard Wollheim, *Art and its Objects* (Penguin Books, 1970) section 21. See also sections 24 and 33.

that Wollheim advocates the view that works of art, with certain
qualifications, are to be identified with physical things. He finds the
whole notion a perplexing one, and asks: 'What sort of identity can
be in question?'

I don't think Pole and Wollheim differ on this as much as Pole
thinks.[1] In the penultimate section (64) of his book Wollheim writes:

> It needs however at this stage to be pointed out that the arguments
> in the opening sections are less conclusive than perhaps they
> appeared to be. Certainly some conventional arguments to the
> effect that (certain) works are not (are not identical with)
> physical objects were disposed of. But it could be wrong to think
> that it follows from this that (certain) works of art are (are
> identical with) physical objects. The difficulty here lies in the
> highly elusive notion of 'identity', the analysis of which belongs
> to the more intricate part of general philosophy.

Pole holds that works of art have a 'quasi-propositional' character:
they are like theories in that they can be called good or bad; they
are intrinsically objects of assessment; and their 'merits, or demerits,
are their own, and not alterable with their creator's intentions'.

Saying that works of art have a quasi-propositional character is
like saying that in some sense a work of art says something to its
beholder. But not in the sense that what it says could be paraphrased.
(But let's not go into that again.) The question is: what is the criterion
of what it says? That is, is 'what it says' what the artist intended it to
say? Or what it was taken to say by contemporaries of the artist?
Or what it says to any Tom, Dick or Harry, with or without an
educated eye, who happens to see it?

I'm not sure that this exhausts the possibilities. That is, I think
that if a painting says one thing, something rather profound, to one
person, and nothing, or something much less profound, to another,
then there is the possibility of the first person's getting the second to
see what he sees in the picture, this not being a matter of discovering
either the artist's intentions *or* something about the painting's place
in history. Taste in art isn't like taste in food (and perhaps even taste
in food isn't like what some philosophers say it is).

To say that taste in art isn't like taste in food might be taken to be a
way of saying that beauty isn't merely subjective (whatever that

[1] Moreover Wollheim, like Pole, recognises the importance of the art-history
context of works of art. In section 59 he refers to a 'consideration, whose consequences are far-reaching indeed. And that is that in many instances the kind of
order that is sought by the artist depends from historical precedents: that is, he will
assemble his elements in ways that self-consciously react against, or overtly
presuppose, arrangements that have already been tried out within the tradition'.

means). Oliver Johnson, Professor of Philosophy at the University of California, Riverside, has an argument that is intended to show that beauty *is* subjective, but that nevertheless we can make 'stable judgments of aesthetic quality'. The argument goes like this:

(*a*) It has been maintained that beauty is objective, in the literal sense that it is an attribute of the 'object' we call beautiful.

(*b*) We call an object beautiful because of its secondary qualities.[1]

But,

(*c*) Secondary qualities are subjective.

Therefore,

(*d*) Beauty is subjective.

Now,

(*e*) Although secondary qualities are subjective, normal observers (i.e. people who aren't colour-blind, etc.) interpret received stimuli in similar ways. This provides us with a standard of normality in terms of which we can make judgments, such as that a traffic light is red.

And,

(*f*) Although the apprehension of beauty involves a more complex mechanism than that of simple sense perception, a rough analogy can be drawn from our experience of secondary qualities to that of beauty.

Therefore,

(*g*) We can use parallel reasoning in order to establish stable standards for the beautiful.

There are a number of questions that can be asked about this argument. Don't we sometimes call an object beautiful because of its primary qualities? If so, would it follow that the beauty it had was objective? Is Locke's argument for colours, etc., being 'nothing in the objects themselves' valid?[2] If it is valid – that is, if colours are

---

[1] John Locke (*An Essay Concerning Human Understanding* (1690) bk II, ch. viii) distinguished between qualities which are 'utterly inseparable from the body', such as solidity, extension, figure, motion or rest, and number, which he called 'primary qualities', and ones 'which in truth are nothing in the objects themselves but powers to produce various sensations in us by their primary qualities', such as colours, sounds, and tastes, which he called secondary qualities.

[2] It is interesting to note that David Pole is as sure that red apples are red as Oliver Johnson is that they are not. See p. 153.

subjective – how can we ever know that normal observers 'interpret received stimuli in similar ways'? Or doesn't it matter, provided they use the same word for the same things? If I say the top traffic light is green I am, flatly, wrong; if I say that something is beautiful, and am alone in this judgment, does it follow that I am, flatly, wrong?

I only wish I had the space to try to answer some of these questions. Pole, I imagine, would add to the list one about the first premiss of the argument: Is it not a mistake to identify the object we call beautiful with a physical thing? His answer, supported by the Wittgensteinian aphorism that 'grammar tells us what kind of object anything is', would be that it *is* a mistake. I don't think Johnson could follow him in this answer.

With Pole's view may be contrasted the theory that the term 'work of art' is used honorifically, a theory defended in this volume by Cyril Barrett, Lecturer in Philosophy at the University of Warwick. Barrett argues that supposedly neutral definitions of 'work of art' (such as Weitz's: 'some sort of artifact, made by human skill, ingenuity and imagination, which embodies in its sensuous, public medium certain distinguishable elements and relations') are really honorific. To call something a work of imagination, for instance, commits us to passing a favourable judgment on it. It is in keeping with this theory that, to the possible embarrassment of customs officials, the application of the term 'work of art' should fluctuate with fluctuations of taste. Until a neutral account of value judgments can be given, Barrett says, no neutral definition of 'work of art' will be forthcoming, and (with his tongue in his cheek?) that he has reason to believe that such an event is not likely in our lifetime. It doesn't follow, says Barrett, from 'work of art' being used honorifically that 'bad work of art' is self-contradictory, because we employ different interrelated criteria. As of a tennis player with a bad style but who won matches, one might want to say that a work was, for technical reasons, bad, but nevertheless, for other reasons, a work of art.

Pole denies that the merits or demerits of a work of art are 'alterable with their creator's intentions'. If he means by this that one should not evaluate a work of art in terms of its being, or not being, a successful fulfilment of the artist's prior intention, then Colin Lyas, Lecturer in Philosophy at the University of Lancaster, could agree with him. But to say this is not to say that it is improper to use of works of art terms like 'perceptive', 'ironic', 'courageous', 'shallow', 'vulgar' or 'heavy-handed'. These qualities in the work of art reflect the personality of the artist. Lyas argues that knowledge of, and reference to, a work being intentional cannot be irrelevant to criticism since 'the only difference between a work of art and a natural object is that intentional human activity is involved in the making of art'. (We shall come back to this.)

Why should anyone hold it to be improper to use personal terms in criticism, once the difference is pointed out between this and 'the intentional fallacy'? It might be said that the critic should concentrate on what is public, the work itself, and ignore the private mind of the artist. But this, Lyas says, would be to be misled by a dualistic view of the relation between mental and non-mental phenomena. Here, he says, the philosophy of art and the philosophy of mind come together:

> . . . if it is possible to replace a dualism of persons and behaviour with the monism of 'persons behaving', it may be possible to replace the dualism of artist and work by a monism of an artist showing himself in the response articulated by the work. If this is so then *in* talking of the work itself we may well be talking of the artist.

In other words, I suppose, we can regard the work of art as an extension of the artist's behaviour, and personal terms as referring to this behaviour and not, inferentially, to an elusive Cartesian soul.[1]

With the paper by Martin Dodsworth, Lecturer in English at Royal Holloway College, London, we return to criticism of Wollheim's *Art and its Objects*. Dodsworth's own view is that '*genre* is part of the way we talk about art, but not a necessary part of the way we experience art'. Wollheim, he thinks, 'mistakes as something necessary to an understanding of the novel a phenomenon that could only be necessary to an understanding of the historical circumstances of its composition'. This can be taken as having a bearing on the Presentational theory. Wollheim holds that it is incompatible with the Presentational theory that we must bring to our perception of a work of art the recognition that it is a work of art. If to experience a work of art as such we need to recognise its *genre*, then since such recognition exemplifies recognition that the work is a work of art, the Presentational theory must be false. Dodsworth does not wish to defend the Presentational theory, but does not go along with this one of Wollheim's reasons for rejecting it.

His concluding note is critical: 'We may agree with Professor Wollheim that art is a complex concept, and yet feel that he adds unnecessarily to its complexity.'

Against this it might be argued that some of Wollheim's distinctions help to make the question 'What is a "work of art"?' *less*

[1] Cf. Wollheim, section 18.

complex. For instance when, in reply to the question 'Are works of art physical objects?', he distinguishes between 'Are works of art *physical* objects?' and 'Are they physical *objects?*'[1] this is a simplifying move. It allows us to affirm that they are physical rather than mental, at the same time as denying that they are particular physical things.

3. ART AND NATURE

'The only difference between a work of art and a natural object is that intentional human activity is involved in the making of art' (Colin Lyas). By 'making' Lyas means something like painting or sculpturing – using one's hands. He would not count the intentional human act of regarding as art something that was not so made – e.g. a sea-cleaned branch of pine on an Oregon beach – as falling under his description of a necessary condition of something being art. In other words he would reject a possibility Wollheim mentions,[2] that we should define the notion of art in terms of an attitude – the aesthetic attitude – we can take to things that were made for some quite utilitarian end, such as Lewisham Borough Council drains, or simply 'chosen' or 'found'. This is a possibility that Andrew Forge however is prepared to entertain. R. W. Hepburn, Professor of Philosophy at Edinburgh University, does so with reservations. 'Philosophy cannot legislate against the possibility that significant art may emerge, and may have emerged, from non-purposive activities', but 'it is not as mere occurrences that art-productions are appraised and appreciated'. Saying that art is of natural origin, or that the artist is a channel for natural forces, leaves it unclear how art is to be appraised and appreciated.

Another meaning that can be given to the question 'How are art and nature to be distinguished?' relates to the way in which art determines how we see things.

Forge contrasts the way in which eighteenth-century country gentlemen would see nature as art, using amber-coloured reducing lenses, with the way in which he may see a plane tree as if he were in an Impressionist picture, or the vertical stripe in a bathroom curtain as if it had meaning and intention ('and although I reflect that this is absurd, the impression remains'). 'In the eighteenth century example', he says, 'we can be fairly clear about the boundaries within which the nature into art game was being played out.' It is the other examples that puzzle him. He can see, and ignore, the curtain simply as a curtain; or he can see it in this other, art-

---

[1] Wollheim, op. cit., section 20. See also section 55 ff.
[2] Wollheim, section 40.

conditioned, way. Granted that the curtain's having meaning and intention is a function of his way of looking at it, is not the same true of its simply being a curtain? 'Does it mean that "nature" is in the way that I look too, and that the contrast art/nature has somehow broken down?'

I don't think it does mean that the art/nature contrast has broken down, any more than the fact of our hearing music as sad means that the sentient/non-sentient contrast has broken down. We can still distinguish between the 'natural' curtain and the curtain with 'meaning and intention' (it is the former we send to the laundry, dye, and shorten) just as we can distinguish between a sad person and sad music (sympathy is appropriate to one but not to the other). But to say this is not to deny the implications of Forge's observation about the artistic vision being continuous with the natural one.

One implication Hepburn mentions, in section 4 of his paper, must serve to round off this foreword, by reminding us of issues touched on earlier.

> To have one's view of nature part-determined by art is also to have one's sense of self, one's posture *vis-à-vis* nature determined as well. Seeing nature in the light of art has a *reflexive* aspect. . . . What we call the *'inner'* life is substantially constituted by the images, metaphors, analogies we draw from external nature and re-apply to the articulating of our emotions, feelings, attitudes. And the stock of images of nature on which we thus draw is itself, in part, the product of art.[1]

Next year's lectures will all be on the philosophy of Wittgenstein.

GODFREY VESEY

Honorary Director
The Royal Institute of Philosophy

Professor of Philosophy
The Open University

[1] On the analogical character of the language of introspection see J. N. Findlay, 'Recommendations regarding the Language of Introspection', in H. D. Lewis (ed.), *Clarity is not enough* (Allen and Unwin, 1963).

1

TRUTH AND FICTION

Julian Mitchell

1. As I'm a writer, I'll begin with a story. It's not, I'm sorry to say, one of my own – I wish it were – but it *is* very philosophical. It's by the great blind Argentinian, Jorge Luis Borges, and it's called 'Funes the Memorious'. Somewhere in a marshy province of Uruguay, Borges comes across a young man called Funes who has gone into an extraordinary mental state after a crippling fall from a horse. He is quite unable to forget anything that has ever happened to him in his physical or mental life. He 'not only remembered every leaf on every tree of every wood, but even every one of the times he had perceived or imagined it' – and with exceptional vividness. In an attempt to manage this colossal burden, Funes thinks about classifying and reducing his memories to some practical order. But 'two considerations dissuaded him: the thought that the task was interminable, and the thought that it was useless. He knew that at the hour of his death he would scarcely have finished classifying even all the memories of his childhood.'

Borges suggests that because of his astonishing gift – or rather, as I said, burden – Funes 'was not very capable of thought. To think is to forget a difference, to generalise, to abstract. In the overly replete world of Funes there were nothing but details, almost contiguous details.' The details are, finally, unbearable: Funes finds it very hard to sleep and, not long after Borges's meeting with him, dies, aged 21, of a pulmonary congestion which I think we can safely assume to be a physical metaphor for congestion of the memory.

Borges is often called a metaphysical writer, though not in the sense that we use to describe John Donne as a metaphysical poet. His stories are often only metaphors or conceits, as this one is –

though I find it appropriately unforgettable. But metaphysical or not, the story rests on what seems to be a physical fact. The human mind cannot store more than a limited number of memories, and wouldn't be at all functional if it stored everything. Repleteness would lead to congestion, as Borges says. We all forget, I believe, even those of us with prodigious powers of recall, far more than we remember. I don't think I can prove this, because it's impossible to say how much we've repressed rather than forgotten – how much, that is, we *have* remembered or stored, but which our sub-consciouses won't allow us to recall. But if I understand the theory of repression, it is that we repress memories which are for one reason or another significant. Insignificant experiences aren't remembered for more than a very short time after they occur. If this is so, and even adding, which is impossible, the repressed to the unrepressed, we only remember a small part of all our physical and mental experience. And when Borges says we wouldn't be able to think unless we had what is almost a positive power of forgetting, he's surely right. I think our minds virtually edit our experience as it's happening. We classify and reduce it all the time. The process of thinking is, among other things, one of selection. We simply couldn't cope with the whole truth of our lives every hour of every day.

Not of course that our memories tell us the whole truth even about the past experiences we do remember. Memory is not only selective, but also subjective. What we remember, or what our subconsciouses permit us to remember, is only one version of an event, a single viewpoint. The whole truth, in fact, is unattainable and, though it may in certain circumstances be a useful ideal, it is for most practical purposes not even that. Yet we obviously need truth of some kind to get along in life at all. But what kind? How partial a truth do we consider adequate for which circumstances? What kinds of selection and qualification do we allow while still describing a version of an event as 'true'? I shan't attempt to answer these questions, which seem very large to me indeed. But they do underlie everything I shall be saying.

It seems to me that though for many purposes we judge truth by our own direct subjective experience, we rely – and by the nature of things have to rely – far more on indirect experience. For instance, we all know, or think we know, about the daily events of the world because we read newspapers or listen to the radio or watch television, all of which describe, with varying degrees of accuracy, what's going on. The accuracy of the information depends on a large number of things: the accuracy of the subjective reporters, to start with, then the decisions of the news editors, who have to judge whether or not something's important and whether or not it's likely to interest the particular audience of the particular paper or programme. There is both conscious and unconscious censorship. There are scarcely relevant factors like the look of the news item on the page, or the availability of film or tape. As a result, what we actually get from the information media is only the shaped and trimmed tip of the vast mound of daily news and rubbish. And none of it is our direct experience. It's obvious, I think, that we can't possibly experience directly more than a tiny number of the things we need to know as ordinary citizens. Society couldn't exist unless we took a very great deal about life on trust from other people.

The nature of this trust varies, I think, from individual to individual. Some of us are very much more critical than others, obviously. Some of us are, sadly, paranoid and won't accept anything. Some of us are aware that our direct experience is just as subjective as everyone else's, and fall into despondency. Mostly, though, we learn from our direct and subjective experience of the world how to estimate the information we're given, to judge whom and what we can trust, and we choose our papers and programmes accordingly. Temperament obviously comes in here. And there are areas perhaps, where we never quite trust anyone, even the more or less sane of us, because no certain judgments can be made in them. For instance – religion. I think the history of religion demonstrates that people have always had reservations about what they will take on trust even from the most militant of churches – the more militant the church, in fact, the more argument about fundamentals. Heresy and schism are always signs that someone somewhere has been doing some thinking for himself about matters which must be uncertain.

But of course there are large areas of life in which we do accept the information we're given without hesitation. We believe signposts: some of us, alas, believe advertisements. Only highly educated sceptics question the whole version of world affairs put out by capitalist or socialist information media. And even the most truculent sceptic, like the solipsist, has to make practical concessions to his theory in order to live. Though very attractive to people who find the world distasteful and disappointing for whatever psychological reason, total scepticism in fact too shallowly assumes the impossibility of making reasoned judgments. If direct objective knowledge *was* the only kind for making reasoned judgments, the absolute sceptic would be right, of course: but it simply isn't. We have subjective direct experience, and we have indirect experience, and we have imagination, working on both. It is, I believe, by using our imaginations that we can come to reasoned and reasonable opinions. Indeed, it's what we do every day. It's what we mean by being informed of the world at large.

What do I mean by imagination? I hope that will become clear. Basically, I conceive it as an essential human faculty, without which the human race would probably never have advanced beyond its most primitive stage. It feeds not only on direct and indirect experience, perceived through our other faculties, but on its own experience as well. This imaginative experience can be called unreal and untrue, but I believe it to be enormously important, that without it we couldn't know, or think we know, more than a tiny amount about the world. It is entirely subjective, yet we use it to judge the truth. And it brings me to the subject of fiction.

2. There isn't, I'm sorry to say, much written in English, at least in Britain, about the fundamental nature of literature – or if there is, it hasn't been read by many writers, critics, or English teachers. There is still an all too common notion about that literature, indeed all art, is somehow a matter of pure instinct, that it's created by geniuses who have no more idea of what they're doing than most passengers on aeroplanes have about theory of jet propulsion. Painters, poets, sculptors, novelists, composers – they all soar into the empyrean, puffed there by the muse, carrying neither parachute nor insurance against the goddess's possible loss of interest. This romantic and intellectually lazy idea explains perhaps why there's so much sloppy art about. It's also, I think, simply untrue. Most good artists do think profoundly about their art, about its essential nature, its social function and of course its practice. Often, though, they're afraid to admit it. Partly, perhaps, because the aristocratic amateur tradition is still so socially powerful in England: it just doesn't do to talk about such things. And partly it may be that artists are unsure of themselves in academic discussion: with some reason, seeing how vicious it can be. It may also be because artists are unwilling to come to definite conclusions. The internal debate is a way of keeping intellectually and aesthetically fit rather than a way of establishing permanent opinions – flexibility can be important.

However, I'd like to make one large assertion about literature in general before getting down to some particular ones about fiction. Literature, I believe, has always been the least pure of the arts. Walter Pater said that all art aspires towards the condition of music – meaning that in music alone there is a complete identification of form and content. Literature, I'd say, aspires least of all. Where an abstract sculpture or painting or piece of music can, at least in theory, refer to nothing, words, which writers are obliged to use, never fail to have a sense linking them to things in the real world. Not that people haven't tried to make them do so. One can think of the experiments of Gertrude Stein: of the vigorous contemporary school of concrete poetry: of Kurt Schwitters's extraordinary solo perform-ance of human sounds. But none of these attempts succeeds or, I believe, could ever hope to succeed for the simple reason that human sounds always convey some human meaning, intentional or not; and even strictly meaningless assemblies of letters, hardly worthy of the name 'words' at all, will suggest some meaning to a reader. The human mind is looking for meanings all the time, and however much it may irritate avant-garde artists, no one has yet thought up a literary way of stopping it finding them.

In literature, art and life can never be entirely separated. There is no purely literary criticism, and if there were we would rightly call it trivial. We are always interested in what is being said as well as the way it's expressed. The most beautifully formal writing can be the least interesting, the clumsiest can absorb us. Of course in the best writing form and content do perfectly combine: but I think it's impossible for them to be one and the same thing. Where the other arts in this century have concerned themselves more and more with formal ideas – with how we hear and how we see – literature remains necessarily committed to how we live rather than to how we perceive our lives.

I wonder if it isn't because literature is so concerned with life and society that the one branch of it which doesn't deal with real life and real society is sometimes considered the least important. Many people who read books think history, for instance, is much more valuable than fiction, which they superficially disdain on the grounds that it isn't true. To read novels, they think, is to lapse from high seriousness. Reading history or biography or autobiography, they believe they are learning about life, while from fiction they can only learn about fiction. I believe this is to misunderstand both life and fiction, yet the argument is, for a practising novelist, distressingly common in England – partly no doubt because of the absence of writing about the nature of literary experience which I've mentioned.

Whatever the reason, the argument against fiction has largely been allowed to go by default. Poets, more formal creatures anyway, have sometimes tried to explain what they think they're doing, but there's hardly a novelist of stature who's so much as admitted to noticing what's going on. For all I know, there may have been philosophers considering the issue, but their speculations don't seem to have reached the reading public. And as for literary critics – well, I shall take some pleasure in being unfair. I think most literary criticism is genuinely trivial. It's about placing one book or author in relation to another; it's about literary history; it's about symbols and myths and God knows what; everything except the reasons for reading and writing fiction at all. Myself, I prefer the sports news to knowing that Professor X has had new thoughts about James's influence on Conrad. Useful though the book or article may be in advancing Professor X's career, it's unlikely to help me understand either James or Conrad better. Of course there is undoubtedly useful criticism, the kind which explains things one needs to know, which helps one to read a particular book with more appreciation – explicatory criticism. I have nothing against footnotes as such. And literary history has its place in the history of ideas. But all too often criticism is simply an adjunct to the teaching of literature as a school or university subject. And though I don't deny that we all need help, that intelligent reading is something one has to learn how to do, just like intelligent looking or listening, I feel that critics are too easily satisfied to do no more than, as it were, take us through the set books. Adult readers can justifiably ask for something more. Why *should* a serious man or woman bother to read a novel? What is there about the experience of reading fiction which is valuable or unique or both? How does our imaginative experience affect our ways of perceiving the real world?

Such questions aren't very hard, really. But they particularly need asking and answering now. It is a much asserted historical fact that the literary media have in many ways been replaced by the visual and audio-visual. But have they been completely superseded, as some people maintain? Or does the novel still have a special function? I believe it does.

3. The argument that fiction is trivial because not true has been advanced by philosophers, I'm sorry to say, as well as by crass and ignorant philistines. At least, I think the late Dr Joad was considered a philosopher, and he certainly believed that there were so many facts about the world one ought to know that there was no time for reading fiction at all. That at any rate was what he told a well-known actor at a party, and the actor swears he hasn't read a novel since. I know of no other quite so dismaying an example of the instant and lasting effect of philosophy on a non-philosophical mind. Of course I do see that it all depends on what one means by philosophy. I think what I mean is good reasoning, and I believe that Dr Joad's argument can be shown to be badly reasoned as well as philistine.

There are several kinds of literature, but there's a commonly made distinction among them between those which are meant to be read as true, and those which are not. Novels are understood by the reader, on the whole, to be not true – that is, they are not about real people or events. Though this omits the common and puzzling case of the autobiographical novel, I think we can agree that at least in theory this is what we assume, just as we assume that history and autobiography *are* about real people and events. Here again, I must make an immediate qualification: there are all too many examples of alleged history whose authors know perfectly well that what they have written isn't true from any point of view, objective or subjective, their own or anyone else's. There is the obvious example of the endless writing and rewriting of Soviet encyclopaedias, in which the truth simply is not. And there are and have always been pious liars writing hagiography for their churches, and Grub Street hacks puffing politicians. For all writers of this sort of thing truth is a highly volatile and relative concept. But I think we can, without being entirely naïve, assume a genuine desire among at least some historians to tell the truth as objectively as they can, even if we and they are aware that it's only the truth as they, with their individual prejudices, happen to see it. Even so, it's extraordinary what enormous differences of interpretation can be put by separate scholars on the same document, even when it's considered within a generally agreed context.

In fact I wonder if we can talk about the truth of written history at all. The writing is fraught by so many and such invincible difficulties. There is the arbitrary selection of evidence made by time: there are the deliberate falsifications of the dead, who so often lived with an anxious eye on their future reputations. Fame has been the spur for art, perhaps: it's also led to a great deal of tampering with the facts. I'd like to take a specific case to demonstrate how little we know about the truth of past events – one of the most celebrated occasions in all English history, an apparently documented fact known to every man, woman and child in the country, and celebrated too in the other sense, with bonfires and fireworks. I mean of course the Gunpowder Plot of 1605. I recently read all the relevant books on this subject, thinking that what actually happened must be pretty well established by now. Nothing could be further from objective truth. The evidence was certainly and heavily doctored at the time by interested parties. A good deal was falsified to confuse any investigator of that period or this; much more was destroyed. Time has helped the falsifiers by obliterating much of what they didn't. What remains often makes no sense without its vanished context. There is, it's true, the official government version of the Plot, put out shortly after the event: but it's the most blatant propaganda, and cannot be trusted except in its reporting of the prosecution speeches at the conspirators' trial. The Plot was so useful an excuse for the government of James I to increase its persecution of Catholics, in fact, that some modern catholic historians, going far beyond their seventeenth century counterparts, suggest there was no Plot at all, that the whole thing was a brilliant fabrication by Robert Cecil, the Earl of Salisbury. This last view is extreme, but it's not entirely implausible: it can't be completely ruled out. Thus one of the most popularly famous events in English history *may* have been one of the biggest and most popular non-events. We shall certainly never know now. And not only because the event or non-event took place so long ago. It is almost never possible to establish the truth about a particular historical event – the whole truth, that is. Consider the assassinations of President Kennedy and Lee Harvey Oswald. Will we ever be sure we know the truth about either of those? No wonder historians prefer to deal with generalisations, with developments and trends. Too much contiguous detail leads to hopeless historical congestion: too little to insuperable doubt.

Knowing all these difficulties as we do, I think it must be clear that we don't, after all, read history as though it were true. We read it with the idea very much in our minds that we are reading a possible version only – we read it, in fact, critically. And the more professional a historian, the more critically, I'd say, he reads. It's only stupid and slovenly readers who allow themselves to imagine that history is somehow true. Not that it's bunk, therefore – it isn't. It's an attempt to reconstruct the past as probably as possible: that is, the kind of history I've been talking about – there are obviously other kinds, less concerned with reconstruction, more with interpretation. But that brings me to yet another objection to the idea of historical truth. The study of written history shows us how impossible it is for any historian to free himself from the prejudices and unconsidered attitudes of his class, nationality and period. Probability is judged differently from generation to generation. A historian is part of his own times' history, and it always shows. So – the idea that historians can aspire to giving us more than a partial and impermanent probable truth about the past simply won't hold up.

And if this is true of historians, men and women who are genuinely attempting to establish a reasonably accurate version of events – what is to be said about autobiographers? They, it would seem, really are writing the truth, their evidence is direct, not indirect, they know what they're talking about. But surely, much of what they write, like much of what passes for history, is manifestly dishonest –

generals selectively quoting despatches for the sake of their reputations, suppressing this, neglecting that, over-emphasising the other,
sometimes simply lying. (Though not often: there's usually another
general to catch the first one out, it's too risky.) Actresses, for seekers
after truth, are notoriously unreliable about dates and plays in
which they did *not* have the leading role. Show jumpers and racing
drivers might, to all intents and purposes, be horses and cars – the
human side of their lives is usually ignored altogether. Of course,
since the purpose of such autobiographers is self-advertisement or
financial gain, there is bound to be a great deal of omission, false
colouring and simplification. Not to show the subject in the most
flattering light would be foolish. Though the lie direct is usually
avoided, as I've said, all the other kinds of lie are employed with
more or less conscious ruthlessness.

So much must be obvious. But there are more important objections to the idea that autobiography is true in any useful sense –
even autobiography written with the same earnest desire for truth
we've granted some historians. There is the fact I mentioned at
the beginning – the partiality and selectivity of the conscious human
memory. Much of what must be for anyone his most significant
experience is literally unavailable to him as an autobiographer,
because it's repressed. And then, even if he is scrupulous as well as
earnest, no one can get over the impossibility of being objective
about himself. Just as much evasion, omission and distortion is
practised subconsciously by the would-be honest writer as by the
conscious liar. There is yet another objection: one of the purposes
of writing one's life story is to justify it, to make sense of it: but
one's life may not be justified or sensible. In any case, who is one
to say? All in all, I'm not sure that a historian isn't more likely
to get the facts of a man's life straight than the man himself. I
think I've indicated sufficiently how unstraight I think that's likely
to be.

But there is one thing to be said for autobiography over history,
whatever its accuracy or truth. It can't help giving us the flavour of
the writer, it can't help telling us a great deal about his personality.
The omissions are very revealing, the distortions don't so much
conceal the facts as throw light on the man who makes them.
Because, just as with history, few of us are fooled by the claim to truth.
We read autobiography only incidentally, I believe, for the facts:
it's the way they're told that interests us. We don't read along the
lines, but between them. Ah, yes, we say to ourselves, she says she
felt this, but from the way she says it you can tell what she really
felt was that – *that's* what she's like, not what she wants people to

B

think at all. And we read like this because the only reason for reading autobiography is to know what it felt or feels like to be someone else. I exaggerate a little, perhaps: we do like a good plot to a life, too. But what really interests, I'm sure, is the personality behind it. We judge the writer on the page, I think, very much as if he were telling his story in real life: we watch for tell-tale gestures, a shifty eye: we listen for false notes, lapses of tone, traces of accent. We read about real people, in fact, exactly the same way as we read about fictional ones. And how do we do it? How do we watch and listen to black marks on a white page? By using the faculty of imagination, by re-creating the person, real or fictional, live or dead, in our own heads, judging him as we go along by what we know directly and indirectly about life, and by what we've learnt through imagination alone. The imagination is a highly critical as well as a highly creative faculty.

The purpose of reading literature, which is a complex imaginative process, seems to me the same whether we're reading history, auto-biography or fiction. We read to gain new information about life. And we do this by imagining ourselves into situations we haven't been present at, or which have never taken place at all, and by imagining ourselves to be people other than ourselves, real or fictional. It makes very little difference to us, I believe, whether we're concerned with real or fictional situations and people: the value lies in the imaginative process. I should qualify this by saying that we read for some kinds of information which don't require much use of imagination as well. If we want to know about the growth of the wine trade in Bordeaux between January and February 1346, for instance: but if we want to know what it was like to be a Bordeaux wine-merchant that winter, then we have to start imagining.

Having said that all kinds of literature are more or less the same as far as we're concerned, at least fundamentally, I must add that of course in practice they have marked differences. Perhaps the single most important distinguishing element in fiction is the greater freedom it gives to the reader's imagination. Since novels don't pretend to be true in the ways that history and autobiography some-times pretend, the reader doesn't have to worry about whether the dates and statistics are correct or correctly interpreted, or whether or not the evidence has been twisted. He can concentrate on people about whom all the relevant facts – which of course aren't real facts – can be accepted on trust. It doesn't mean the novel reader is less critical – on the contrary, he demands a much higher standard of – what is it to be called? Psychological truth? Human truth?

Imaginative truth? Whatever we decide to call it, I think it's clear that we do consider fiction to be very much concerned with something called truth.

4. I must pause here to say that I do realise that I'm using words like truth and knowledge and imagination in ways which would never do for a philosopher. My excuse is that I'm providing contexts for these words which philosophers can then examine. For if we can only understand words in their contexts, the philosophical nagging as to their meaning must follow not precede the usage.

Furthermore it's the ambiguity of our notions of truth and knowledge that interests me: that for instance we *can* call true a book which we know perfectly well is neither true nor false. I think writers probably prefer their concepts to be ambiguous, to be rich in meanings, even self-contradictory except in their precise contexts. And I think I may think that the ambiguity and confusion we have about some of these ideas are fundamental.

5. It seems to me that we can, from observation, have a very good idea of someone's general character; we can, if you like, predict with a high degree of accuracy how that person is likely to behave in given circumstances. But observation can't tell us what it's like to be someone else, to feel and think and remember in another person's head. We can only imagine it. And our imaginations have a number of obvious limitations – of age, sex, race, education and so on. We all know how little we know of our neighbours. One can even be married to someone for many years without ever having an accurate idea of what's going on in her or his head. An extreme form of this ignorance can be found perhaps in the common adolescent fear that one is a freak, completely different from the whole of the rest of the human race. Turned in on himself, the adolescent finds it impossible to see himself in others. It could be that his problem, at least in part, is that he isn't using his imagination on other people, only on himself. Learning to see others in oneself is as important as trying to see oneself in others. In any case, the problem is certainly one of imaginative failure. It *is* an extreme example, though. In the many daily occurrences when we need to see things from someone else's viewpoint if we're to manage socially, most of us do.

In all this it seems impossible to avoid using the metaphor of sight. It's plain that we can't literally ever see through someone else's eyes, except after a corneal graft: and that isn't what we mean. It's true too that we can't prove beyond doubt that our visual perceptions are even of the same order as anyone else's. But 'seeing' is certainly what we think we do when we imagine ourselves to be someone else.

We learn to do it, I believe, very young, with the first stories we're told, often with pictures we look at, while a fond parent dotingly reads the text. All stories are about people, even those about gods and animals: the gods and animals, I mean, are always created in entirely anthropomorphic terms. As early as nursery rhymes we start learning to identify with the characters. If I may give a subjective example, which wasn't, I hope, as traumatic as it sounds, I remember shrinking with fear as the farmer's wife came after the three blind mice with the carving knife, and – a mouse again – running up the grandfather clock we had, which promptly struck one. I think I remember imagining how nice it would be to be able to run vertically up something; and I still connect the face of that clock with a mouse. Of course, my memory may be quite false, an adult romanticisation of childhood – a common occurrence, and one which I should have added to the list of other objections to the evidence of memory. But I think most people would admit to similar experiences, and I think they're observable in children themselves.

As we get older, our stories become more realistic and more complex. We lose interest in the anthropomorphic elephants and bears, we start – at least boys start – going on adventures. The total absorption in narrative to which a child can give himself is often nostalgically recalled by those who would like to be able to lose their adult selves in the same way. And it's true that complete giving of oneself to an imaginary world, the excitement, the identification, aren't recapturable. But the loss is inevitable, a part of normal growth: adult reading is an altogether richer experience. Novels for grown-ups absorb us in another way: we not only enter imaginary worlds, we think about them at the same time, we judge what's being said and how it's said: far from being unable to put the book down, we frequently do so and reflect on what we're reading. Where a child can't bear to be stopped before he's reached the end, we like the idea of letting the book grow slowly inside us. We don't lose ourselves – should adults ever lose themselves? We bring our complex minds, full of complex knowledge of the world, to equally complex fictions.

Ideally, reader and writer engage through the printed pages of the book in a lively debate about the most serious issues of the mind, spirit and heart, imagined through particular individuals in particular situations. Nothing is now taken on trust as a child takes Babar or Rupert Bear: the reader is meeting and enjoying an emotional and intellectual challenge. He is having his experience enlarged, and he wants to make sure that what he's being told is true and valuable. Yet he is still using the same mind's eye he used as a child to imagine himself into the personalities of other people.

This process is sometimes called 'identification', but I don't think that's a very satisfactory word. For one thing, though children may identify themselves with the characters in books, adults do so very charily, if at all. We don't lose our own identities, I mean, and we don't merge our personalities into those of the people we're reading about: we remain ourselves. At least, I believe we do. There are considerable difficulties here, to do with the power of the written word to *change* us at all. Though one's opinions can, of course, be changed by one's reading, I'm not sure what it would mean to say someone's personality had been changed by any external stimulus. What reading can and does do, is make us sympathetic to other people's ways of seeing the world, make us feel with them. But sympathy has been such an abused word, I don't think it will quite do, any more than identification. Perhaps there is no word to describe our 'entering into' a character without 'becoming' him, our understanding him by feeling with him.

It could be argued – it probably has been argued by Dr Joad – that clinical psychology provides a more useful means of understanding other human beings than this imaginative process involved with fiction – even though Freud and Jung both used literary sources so freely to describe the neuroses they investigated. Psychology does offer immensely detailed studies of individual cases, often with all the narrative drive of a good thriller – will the patient recover or won't he? Will the good doctor uncover the lost trauma in time? (Sound of galloping horses, excited strumming on the piano.) With analysis lasting so long, I've often thought it must be like an endlessly fascinating serial – at least for the patient. But do case studies really help us to understand people in the same way as fiction? Surely not. For one thing, they are *cases*. Their description is deliberately as objective as possible in the approved scientific manner; and the more objective the description, the less room for imaginative speculation, and the less opportunity for us to put our subjective knowledge of the world to work on it. For another, it seems to me that psychiatrists, psychologists, psychoanalysts and psychotherapists, whatever the quarrels among them (and they are fierce), are all trying to be like scientists in another way – they are looking for general rules about human behaviour. Novelists aren't trying to do that at all: they may be trying to make statements about the human condition, sometimes, but they would never try and draw up rules as to how human beings will react to that condition. If there *were* discoverable rules, I rather think fiction and imagination would both perish. But if there are, the only ones so far discovered are so general, permit so much variation, that the practice of clinical psychology offers no challenge to that of fiction. One reason for this must be that, as hardly can be denied, clinical psychology and psychiatry do tend to deal only with a very small and unusual section of society. Though it has been valuably established that there is no such thing as normality in human behaviour, it can still be maintained with a fair degree of reason that abnormality is not the common human state. Yet it's abnormality, neurosis and psychosis which psychiatry and the other related disciplines study – for the very best medical and financial reasons. People who lead nearly normal lives, or at least those who think they do, don't go to the analyst, they beat their wives; or if they are wives, their children. And among his many cases, the doctor is likely to want to write up his most extreme rather than his most average cases, because they're usually more interesting: the average ones just go into statistics. The psychological case-study, then, though it may tell us a great deal, doesn't tell us much about what it's like to be the patient: only what the case is. I think our reading of such studies is more like our reading of history than our reading of fiction. If we want to have an explanation of neurosis or madness, then of course we go to the books containing such studies. If we want to know what it's like to be neurotic or mad, we read diaries or novels. There are all too many to choose from – though I withdraw that: if one person in ten in our society receives treatment for mental illness at some time or another in his life, then we need all the novels about madness we have, and more, if we're to make the imaginative effort necessary to understand our relatives and friends.

Which brings me to perhaps my main point: fiction has, I believe, a very important social function, and has always had it. I don't mean only the novel – a recent and quite possibly decaying form – but fiction: the imagining of unreal worlds full of truth and meaning, and the conveying of them to others, who recreate them in their own imaginations. I don't know when the first story was told – but I suppose it was thousands of years before the invention of writing. The first stories of our culture, apart from the Bible ones, are, I take it, Homer's; and I take it too that Homer was a travelling story-teller of the sort still to be found in backward countries. In the Djma-el-fna, for instance, the great square of Marrakech in Morocco, you can usually see a man squatting with a book open in his hand. He's surrounded by a circle of squatting listeners, with another circle standing behind them, and more people pressing behind *them*. He's telling a story. The book is entirely for show – a prop at which he occasionally jabs a finger, though he never turns a page. He knows his stories by heart, and I dare say he makes up new bits as he goes along, varying the stories according to audience demand and reaction and size. But they are old stories, which he presumably learnt from someone else. His audience is rapt, hanging on every word. He is – a story-teller. Of course Homer may not have been like that at all, but that's how I imagine him, and his audience. I'm sure you could watch his Greeks imagining the characters and events of the story just as you can watch the modern Moroccans: you can literally see them doing it, it shows on the faces. As it may even show on ours when we're reading a novel – so long, of course, as there's no one else in the room.

Much is made these days of the 'special' quality of reading – how we do it alone, how we can put a book down and go away and come back, and so on. I'll come back to that later. Now I want to say that there doesn't seem to me any fundamental difference between hearing a story and reading it as far as the actual work of imagining is concerned. The fact that you can cheat by looking ahead in a book, or re-read, is beside the point. Both in listening and reading our imaginations are extremely active, both creatively and critically. And it's for that reason, I believe, that fiction has from earliest times been a means of moral instruction. It's not only a unique way of understanding other individuals – an activity which seems to me moral in its own right – but also of course a way of understanding individuals in relation to each other. Fiction offers a way of conveying social as well as personal experience through the imagination. One of the means by which it does this calls for particular attention – its use of time.

6. Time isn't a very easy subject. Borges, the Argentinian writer whose story I quoted at the beginning, includes among his works 'A New Refutation of Time', which is even more philosophical than 'Funes the Memorious'. I'm not going to attempt anything nearly so rash. But perhaps time in fiction isn't the kind Borges wants to refute, anyway.

There are, in fact, several times to be considered. There are the reader's times: the time he takes to read a book – not usually an unbroken span: the time he reflects on it: the time the fiction persists in his imagination and his memory: the time of life he reads it. Then there are the times of the fiction: the time at which it was written, inevitably reflected in style if not always in content: the time-span within the work: the characters' times within this time.

One of the great advantages of the novel as a narrative form has been its freedom to move about in time, to refer backwards and forwards with the greatest ease. In this it resembles the working of our memories. The writer can make his characters remember relevant information, if he chooses, just as our memories can summon it up. And if the characters lack information about the past which is relevant to their story, the writer can simply tell us what they don't know. In a way, the writer is like an ideal memory, providing us with all and only the information we need as readers. His selection of events, though of course subjective, *appears* objective to the reader, who trusts his judgment on what is and isn't important. An interesting exception to this is the detective story, where it's an understood convention that the writer and reader are engaged in a battle of wits, the reader trying to guess what the author is concealing. There are almost rules as to what is and isn't fair. But the detective story is a very minor, trivial, and almost abstract genre. In the novel proper the convention is that the author gives us the relevant information and has freedom to tell us things his characters don't know.

At least, this is true of the third-person narrator, the godlike author who knows all and is somewhat out of fashion, for very good reasons which I can't go into here. But even the first-person narrator, very much more restricted though he must be, is written by an invisible author who decides what information we shall have about him, and what he shall pass on. The author remains fairly godlike. And in any case, he always has complete freedom of time – to start at the end, in the middle, at the beginning, and to leap about with all the illogic of daily life. One of the greatest and least recognised of English novels, *The Good Soldier*, by Ford Madox Ford, which is told in the first person, moves so much about in time that it takes a critic several pages simply to put things in their linear order – time thoroughly wasted, needless to say. The freedom to move in time is put to unforgettable use, to imitate the way our own minds move from subject to subject as though time didn't exist at all.

I suppose that's false: our minds exist in time, and receive new perceptions in a linear way, and they age too. But it seems to me we think in a continuous present. We think, that is, 'I am', not, 'I was a second ago, I shall be in another second'. When we remember, we don't think 'I felt', we feel again. It's in this continuous present – which I realise I haven't described very well, but don't see how to describe any better – that the imagination works as we read: the characters are as alive to us as we are ourselves. Yet because of the ability of fiction to move about in time, we are also aware of the characters' pasts, parts of which have been equally alive, and are again when we recall or re-read them. We may even know what's going to happen to them, have looked into their futures and felt them alive in them. We feel we know them, ultimately, from the cradle to the grave – if it's that sort of book, of course: there are other books where we only know about forty-eight hours in the characters' lives altogether. But we can know everything, birth and death, all between the pages of a book, in the short or long time it takes us to read it.

I believe this is how we remember people in real life – only more so. In real life we know people from time to time; but few people all the time and intensely. Memories fade. The pages of a book may fade, but not the characters portrayed in them. Fiction is a way – or it can be a way – of knowing the whole lives of people, of compressing information by compressing time. Life can't equal that at all. The information isn't only about people, as I've said already: because individuals live in societies and are part of the history of their times, fiction compresses information about society and social movements too. Many of the great nineteenth-century novels, it's interesting to note, are set in the past: *Middlemarch* for instance and *War and Peace*. George Eliot especially, it seems to me, was trying to illuminate the present in which she wrote by understanding the whole lives of people in the not very distant past – the Wesleyan movement, the Reform movement and the societies which produced them, also produced her age. Even James Joyce's *Ulysses* is set in the past, though only a single day of it.

I think the reason for this interest in the past among the great novelists is the desire to describe something which is whole, something completed and graspable, which can be imagined back to life, to the continuous present in our heads. Things have changed a good deal since George Eliot of course, and the continuous present used so beautifully by Joyce has become a conventional narrative device itself. The tendency in fiction has been to move away from the historical to the psychological, to describe states of mind rather than societies, to concern itself with what's called inner space rather than external reality. Very often a contemporary novel will invite the reader into a character's head and consider that sufficient – the knowing of that one person is enough. But the ability to move about in time – even out of time, one might say, when it comes to the reveries of Samuel Beckett – this ability, and the ability to compress time, make fiction still an enormously important source of the imaginative experience I spoke of earlier.

7. I'd like to make a few points now about the importance of reading and the novel in a period when our sources of imaginative experience

have become largely visual. It's true that we still have newspapers and magazines and that a great deal of information still has to be conveyed in words alone – in manuals and textbooks and instruction booklets – all those things which manufacturers have the cheek to call 'literature'. But the purely imaginative experience of most western people, at least, now comes predominantly from the television set and the cinema. I don't know if much scientific work has been done on the different ways our imaginations respond to different kinds of perception: if it hasn't, it should be. What seems clear to me, though not to many of the propagandists of the audio-visual revolution, is that the audio-visual hasn't *replaced* the literary experience. I believe it works in a different way altogether. It may have taken over, but it isn't doing the same thing. And if its take-over were to become complete it would be, I think, a disaster.

Of course it's not in dispute that the great technological advances of the last fifty years – there wasn't even radio fifty years ago – have vastly increased the amount of audio-visual as opposed to literary information available to us. But what is audio-visual information? By its nature, it seems to me, it can only be externally descriptive. That it does external descriptions far better than the written word I don't for a moment deny. The complete decline in portrait painting since the invention of the camera offers a devastating parallel from art: there is no competition. In the novel we no longer find the great set-pieces of topography which were virtually required writing in the nineteenth century – it's impossible to imagine the Brontës or Hardy except in terms of landscape, for instance. But now we have far less of the external world altogether. I suspect we may have far less sheer narrative than there used to be, too, though it's impossible to prove, and in the trashy novel it's true that narrative remains essential – James Bond novels are read by cinema-sized audiences as well as seen by them. I think, though, that for sheer story-telling the visual media are simply more efficient than the literary.

Some people regard the take-over of information about the external world as a loss to the novel. I don't. It may even be a gain – though to talk in such terms isn't very helpful. The novel has never been a strictly defined form: all that's happened, I believe, is a new adaptation to new needs. One result of the changes is that novels are now, as a general rule, much shorter than they used to be – sad for those who like a thousand-page wallow, but not for those like me who read with what seems increasing slowness. However, the more serious point is that external descriptions in novels have never worked like those in television or the cinema. To take a celebrated example: most readers of Jane Austen have very vivid pictures in their minds of what her characters look like and what sort of rooms they live in. And when I say pictures, I mean pictures. One has only to adapt a Jane Austen novel for television, to show actresses and actors – whose faces are their own, of course – playing the parts, and there is immediate indignation. 'His face should be redder', 'Her mouth is too big' – the criticisms are physiognomically detailed, and prove to my satisfaction, if to no one else's, that the phrase 'the mind's eye' does very accurately describe how at least we think we imaginatively 'see'. Jane Austen's readers are convinced they know exactly what all the characters look like. And the interesting thing is that they can't agree among themselves, because Jane Austen hardly tells us. Her descriptions are often brief and unhelpful, such as that someone has 'lost her bloom'. Unhelpful, that is, for a casting director, for anyone looking for precise instructions: but very helpful to the imagination, which thrives on suggestion. I believe the imagination can be shown here to be bringing experience of all kinds to re-create a character. The sharp pictures we have in our mind's eye are not Jane Austen's creations but our own.

The suggestiveness, the vagueness, of Jane Austen's physical descriptions and our imaginative response to them illustrate, I think, the significant difference between our imaginative use of things read and things seen. A film or television play presents us with a wealth of accurate detail – more than we ever consciously take in, in fact. If you look at a set for a television play, you find the most scrupulous care is taken over tiny details which will scarcely be visible on the screen – mantel ornaments, for instance. It's the same with the outward appearances of the characters: we know them down to the last pore and pubic hair. Our imaginations are left with almost nothing to do. We sit passively and watch, absorbing sensations at a predetermined speed. We can't stop and go for a walk and come back to pick up the story where we left off: if we stop watching, that's it – we never find out what happened. A simple interruption, like a telephone call, can ruin a television play for us: it scarcely interrupts the reading of a novel at all.

The visual media therefore seem to me altogether more passive, imaginatively speaking, than fiction. There is far less active imaginative work required, far less of that creativity which makes reading a novel such a special pleasure and so – as I hope I've argued – socially useful too. I don't mean that we don't feel with people in films and television – obviously we do. But I think we see them much more externally, we feel for their observed situations: we don't feel what it's like to be them in those situations. We imagine *ourselves* in the situations, I believe, rather than the characters. We are much more of an audience, as in the theatre. Now I don't see anything inferior or superior in these other forms of imaginative information. All I'm saying is, they're different. And I don't think they've replaced, or can replace, the imaginative experience of reading fiction – especially that 'entering into' other people I've tried to describe, and which for me is the essential element of fiction. I believe we shall always need to know what it's like to be someone else. And I don't think the visual media will ever be able to get under the skin of human beings in the same way. Because however much we observe, with all the patience in the world, feelings and thoughts, the sense of oneself as a self, will never be visible. The kind of thinking aloud which is used in films and television to overcome their inadequacy here is manifestly inferior to the many means of fiction.

Then there is also the question I've gone into already – the question of time, and the fullness of character which fiction can create by its freedom to move back and forth. The visual media simply can't compete here: four hours is very long for a film – inordinately long, most people would say. So there is that temporal limitation, to start with. Then there's the problem – virtually insuperable – of successful casting: you'd need at least half a dozen actors to do the whole life of someone properly. I suppose television serials come nearest to the novel – and are usually adapted from novels, of course. But paradoxically, they suffer from not being long enough – two half-hour or fifty-minute episodes a week at most, each with its need for dramatic climax, a need which comes to seem increasingly arbitrary and unsatisfying. One of the great advantages of the novel is that it can have great long sections in which it lies almost fallow, with nothing very much happening at all. It can re-create the great lulls of life in a few pages. These, for commercial reasons, are absolutely forbidden to films and television. There's much else forbidden by the financial structures of the visual media, which I won't go into. But there's one last point I'd like to make which almost brings me back to the subject of truth.

The writer of a novel is most unlikely to receive as much reward from his book as he would for the same subject treated as a TV play: certainly not nearly as much as he would for a film – though it's true, of course, that a novel contains the possibility of TV and film adaptation. The novelist is never going to be read by a tenth of the people who would see the play or a hundredth, perhaps, of those who might see the film. These are serious considerations for any writer. But it isn't only idealism which keeps the novel going. There is also autonomy. When you read a book – at least if it's not one of the ones carefully manufactured in a publisher's office – you're reading what the writer wanted you to read. Well – no writer is ever completely satisfied, I suppose, but you're reading what he's finally decided may appear. There are no actors or directors or producers or cameramen or vision mixers or dubbers or art directors or script editors or designers or hairstylists or make-up artists or scene-shifters or grips or cigarettes by Abdulla – a nostalgic touch for older theatre-goers there – to get between the print and the reader. What the writer has imagined, well or ill, is his own. That his version of the truth is highly personal, completely subjective, is part of its point, part of the understanding between reader and writer. There is no pretence of objectivity. The camera, by its very mechanical nature, can't help pretending all the time, as all those people I mentioned decide where it's to point and when.

8. A final point before I sum up. It can be objected to my claims for the unreal truth of fiction that it is not only unverifiable, but that it's so subjective it must vary widely from reader to reader. I concede that, and more. It varies within each reader too. We're all, I'm sure, familiar with the experience of re-reading a book and finding it quite different from what we remembered. It may be that we didn't know how to read it first time – it was too advanced or we were too backward. I read *War and Peace* when I was fourteen, for instance, and it can't possibly have meant much to me. And it may be that we resisted the book or embraced it too warmly for some psychological reason: or because we were being taught it for an exam – a hatred of literature is forced on so many young people, I seriously think that literature shouldn't be examined at all.

It seems clear that the reason why a book so often seems different on re-reading can't be that it *is* different in any important sense. It's only that it's different to us. So it must be we who have changed. And of course we have. I said earlier that the interrelation between life and literature was fundamental. We bring a great deal to our reading – our total experience of life, direct, indirect and imaginative. And that naturally grows as we grow. Very often – indeed I'd say most often – the reason a re-reading surprises us with pleasure or disappoints us is that we are, simply, older. When we're young we are literally incapable of responding fully to the most subtle and complex works – *Middlemarch* or *King Lear*. (The idiocy of our literary education is plain, I think, from the fact that I did *King Lear* for A-levels; I consider I'm only just beginning to understand it now.) Equally, the books which seemed wonderful at nineteen can seem very jejune later on – Aldous Huxley, for instance. Because one's first discovery of a truth *is* wonderful, doesn't make that truth less common. Later, when we understand it all too well, it may even seem trivial.

If this is so, and surely it is, is there any point in talking about truth and fiction at all?

9. I hope I've argued convincingly that the personal and social function of fiction is significant, even vital: that the imaginative process of 'entering into' an imaginary character is not only an entertaining pleasure but a unique way of extending our knowledge by extending our imaginative understanding of other human beings. Since it is impossible literally to go inside another man's head to find out what he's thinking and feeling, we have to use our imaginations. And fiction teaches us how to do this from a very early age. Furthermore, fiction can condense whole lives to manageable proportions, so that we can understand them and their relation to their societies.

I've also argued that in our actual reading we don't regard the distinctions between fiction and other literary forms as very important: and specifically the distinction between the alleged truth of autobiography and the obviously fictional quality of fiction. We do all reading, I've tried to say, to gain what I've called imaginative experience, because the world is too vast and complex for us possibly to experience more than fragments of it directly. And we continually criticise all literature by our experience of life, direct and indirect and imaginative, because it's impossible for us to judge literature by purely formal concepts; and anyway we don't want to.

Right at the beginning I argued that the whole truth is unattainable, and asked what kinds of qualification and selection we permitted while still describing an event as true. It seems to me that we talk all the time about the truth of our impressions. And we obtain impressions through our perceptual apparatus. What I've been saying all along really is that imagination is a way of perceiving. It doesn't have a physical shape, like a nose or an eye, but it's no accident that we refer so often to 'the mind's eye'. And if we can talk about the truth and falsehood of other impressions, then we can talk of the truth and falsehood of imaginative ones, too. As far as fiction is concerned, I believe this is what we do when we call books good or bad. What we mean is, the novel creates a true or false impression. And we judge truth and falsehood in fiction as we judge it in everything else – by our total experience of life. We judge books by life and other books: we judge life by books and other life. Fiction can be as true as anything else.

2

LEARNING FROM A NOVEL

R. W. Beardsmore

THERE is always a danger in philosophy, that what is intended initially as simply one explanation of some form of activity, should come to be regarded as the only possible form of explanation. Nor does this danger seem to be diminished where a philosopher's aim is itself that of attacking limited notions of what is possible as an explanation. This is one, though not the only, reason why it is often the case that what at first appears as a revolutionary and illuminating solution of certain philosophical difficulties, later gives rise to even more intractable problems of its own.

When Gilbert Ryle wrote *The Concept of Mind*, he numbered among his aims that of curing what he saw as a traditional obsession among philosophers with propositional knowledge as the form of knowledge *par excellence*. More generally, he wished to attack a limited view of the nature of qualities of mind, the view that all intelligent activity, all forms of learning, knowledge, understanding were to be explained as forms of intellectual activity, as different species of knowledge that something is the case.

> There are many activities which directly display qualities of mind, yet are neither themselves intellectual operations nor yet effects of intellectual operations. Intelligent practice is not a step-child of theory.[1]

Intelligent practice is not a matter of propositional knowledge, of 'knowledge that' at all. It is a matter of 'knowledge how'. To speak of a man's powers of reasoning, his knowledge of football or his skill at cards is not to refer to a list of facts which he possesses. Rather it is

[1] *The Concept of Mind* (Hutchinson, 1949) p. 26.

to credit him with the ability to perform tasks in accordance with certain rules of procedure. Knowledge how is exercised in the observance of these rules. Its absence lies in their breach.

With the distinction between knowledge how and knowledge that in his hands, Ryle proceeds to wreak havoc among traditional theories of knowledge, the will, emotion and the intellect. And in this he has been both praised and condemned. But it is not to my purpose in this paper either to praise or to condemn Ryle's application of the distinction. Nor, at least in one sense, shall I be concerned to criticise the distinction itself. Despite suggestions to the contrary, Ryle's contrast between propositional and executive knowledge may be a perfectly illuminating account of the differences between certain cases of learning, discovering, understanding. My objection is that it has been presented as more than that. What should be a flexible distinction between certain forms which intelligence may take has, in the hands of certain philosophers, shown signs of hardening into a rigid dichotomy. There are indications that the disjunction 'either knowledge how or knowledge that', 'either theoretical or practical' is itself tending to become a model for the form which any example of knowledge or understanding *must* take, so that philosophers like R. M. Hare[1] are now found assuming that since, for example, what we learn from reading a novel or a poem is manifestly not to be explained as a list of facts, it must be explicable in terms of a list of principles of conduct.

In this paper I shall try to show that such attempted explanations inevitably lead to failure. The dichotomy of knowledge how and knowledge that, at least in the form given by Ryle, is unable to account for certain cases with which we are all perfectly familiar. In particular I shall suggest that the case which I have just mentioned is of this sort, and that an unbiased study of what it means to speak of a man's learning from literature leads to the destruction of the dichotomy in question.

1. The seeds of this destruction are to be found in the account given by Ryle himself, particularly in the account of what is variously termed 'executive' knowledge, 'practical' knowledge, and 'knowledge how'. As we have seen, it is a pervasive theme of Ryle's book that intelligence is to be explained not (or at least not primarily) as the knowledge or ignorance of this or that truth, but as the possession of 'know-how'. Of course, in itself this is sufficiently vague, but it can, I think, be rendered more precise if we turn our attention to a collection of terms which feature predominantly in

[1] *Freedom and Reason* (Oxford, 1963) ch. 9.

Ryle's account of knowledge how. I have in mind his equation of 'acting intelligently' with 'acting efficiently', 'skilfully', 'methodically', 'shrewdly', 'competently', his failure to distinguish between 'teaching' or 'education' and 'training', his continual reference to the different forms of intelligence as 'skills' or 'competences', and so on. For what is obvious about these ways of speaking is that they are most naturally used when what we are discussing is a man's mastery of a method or technique, that is, his ability to employ a set of established procedures in order to bring about certain pre-determined results. Thus, to take what is obviously one of Ryle's central examples, the intelligent marksman, the man who knows how to shoot accurately, is not someone who can call to mind numerous facts about the use of small arms, but someone who shoots according to the rules. And when we speak of rules in these sorts of context, what we are thinking of are primary recipes for achievement within the sphere of activity in question—that is to say, rules of skill. What we expect from a crack shot is perfect technique.

That Ryle's is an adequate account of the sort of intelligence manifested in some forms of activity is of course undeniable. It is, for the most part, a good account of his own central examples, of those with which he chooses to deal in any detail. But it is I think evident that the account is in many cases not being offered by Ryle as merely an analysis of certain forms of intelligent activity but as an account of the nature of intelligent activity itself. Were this not made clear in a series of explicit statements of quite unrestricted generality – 'Intelligence lies . . . in the ability or inability to do certain things', 'Understanding is a part of knowing how' – it would nevertheless be apparent from the examples to which the account is successively applied – pruning trees, tying a reef knot, having skill at cards or prudence in investment, planning military strategy, obeying one's conscience, writing poetry, and so on. Thus, when on page twenty-eight Ryle asks rhetorically, 'What is involved in our descriptions of people as knowing how to make and appreciate jokes, to talk grammatically, to play chess, to fish, or to argue?' his question at least suggests that there is *one* thing involved in these different activities, that *one* model will serve to explain the type of excellence appropriate to each of them. And on the face of it, this might not seem particularly plausible. For why *should* it be assumed that what is to be found in the ability to make or appreciate jokes will also be found in the ability to talk grammatically or the ability to fish? Indeed at first sight it might appear that one thing which characterises the ability to make jokes, that is to say originality or creativity, is fairly conspicuously lacking from a mastery of English

grammar or skill with a fishing rod. Normally success in either of
the latter activities depends on the agent's acting in pretty firmly
established ways. A man will not be said to speak grammatically
until he constructs sentences in *precisely* the ways laid down by
certain authorities, teachers, parents or perhaps television news-
readers. And it would be the height of irrationality for an angler
to think of departing from the traditional techniques at least until
he had acquired very considerable understanding of, or competence
in those techniques. The techniques might, it is true, be poor ones.
Still, it would be quite irrational for anyone to *begin* by assuming
this to be so.

With a joke it is quite different. One of Whistler's barbed wise-
cracks once elicited from the young Oscar Wilde the admiring
response, 'I wish I'd said that'. It is said that Whistler, who had no
great regard for Wilde, replied grimly, 'You will, Oscar, you will.'
I do not know what Whistler's original remark was, or the context
in which it was made. But presumably one important aspect of it
lay in its unpredictability. Just this quality would be what was
lacking from Wilde's subsequent plagiarisms. Wilde, Whistler
was implying, was the sort of man who would turn original remarks
into clichés. By contrast, Whistler's reputation for wit rested upon
his ability to avoid well-trodden conversational paths, his ability to
turn a conversation in unexpected directions. One might say that
Whistler's remarks were humorous at least in part because they
went beyond any of the rules governing polite conversation.

Unlike the ability to fish or to speak grammatically, the possession
of a sense of humour does not seem to rest on the mastery of established rules or techniques. Indeed, the fact that it is natural to
speak of the 'rules of grammar' though not of the 'rules of humour',
of the 'rules of fishing' but of the 'ability to make jokes' rather than
the 'rules for making jokes' should give pause for thought here. For
it is worth noting that though Ryle makes considerable capital from
the initial implausibility of supposing that the wit simply knows
certain facts of which his audience is unaware, precisely such an
implausibility is to be found in the suggestion that he alone has been
initiated into some method, some set of rules which they have not
mastered. To talk grammatically or to fish competently is to obey
established rules in a way that making or appreciating jokes conspicuously is not.

Now Ryle, obsessed as he is to fit any form of intelligent activity
into his preconceived model of 'executive knowledge' is forced to
deny just these sorts of difference. This is especially apparent in a
passage which might at first seem to point the opposite conclusion.

The wit, when challenged to cite the maxims, or canons, by which he constructs and appreciates jokes, is unable to answer. He knows how to make good jokes and how to detect bad ones, but he cannot tell us or himself any recipes for them.[1]

One might be forgiven for supposing that in this passage Ryle is in fact denying that there are any such recipes. But this would be a mistake. For according to Ryle the reason why the wit is unable when challenged to cite the rules of wit is not that there are no such rules but that they are unformulated. And this of course is a possible case. As Ryle remarks elsewhere, methodologies presuppose an application of the methods of which they are the products. It is possible for a man to fish according to the principles formulated in Walton's *Compleat Angler* without himself being able to formulate them. What is curious is that Ryle seems automatically to assume that what is true here of fishing will also be true of humour, that whenever an activity is carried on without reference to rules this will be merely because the rules are (as yet) unformulated, and to ignore a rather more obvious possibility, namely that the wit is unable to formulate the principles of humour for the simple reason that there is nothing to formulate.

Now, one reason for Ryle's failure to consider this possibility lies in his recognition that the sphere of humour is one within which it makes sense to speak of a man's having performed correctly or incorrectly, well or badly. For one of the main attractions of the notion of a rule, as Ryle uses it, is that where it is applicable, it enables us to explain what it is for a performance to fail or succeed. Thus, for example, the marksman condemning a pupil's use of the rifle can defend or explain his judgment by an appeal to those rules contravened by his pupil's practice. So it is tempting to assume that if it is possible, as it clearly is, to identify among a comic's performances those which fail and those which succeed, if it is possible to appreciate a good joke and to distinguish it from a bad one, then here as well there must be rules, albeit unformulated, in terms of which the distinction is made.

And of course it *is* true that a knowledge of rules may also be relevant to the appreciation of humour. For a joke is made within the context of the rules governing language, and the man who fails to grasp these rules will miss the point of the joke. What does not follow is that the rules in question can be regarded as constituting a technique for appreciating jokes, or that they will be any help in explaining why one joke is good and another bad. In *Puddn'head*

[1] *The Concept of Mind*, p. 30.

Wilson Mark Twain begins his portrait of the hero of the story with
an example of the latter's 'deadpan humour':

> He made his fatal remark the first day he spent in the village,
> and it 'gaged' him. He had just made the acquaintance of a group
> of citizens when an invisible dog began to yelp and snarl and howl
> and make himself very comprehensively disagreeable, whereupon
> young Wilson said, much as one who is thinking aloud –
> 'I wish I owned half of that dog.'
> 'Why?' somebody asked.
> 'Because I would kill my half.'
> The group searched his face with curiosity, with anxiety even,
> but they found no light there, no expression that they could read.
> They fell away from him as from something uncanny, and went
> into privacy to discuss him. One said:
> ' 'Pears to be a fool.'
> ' 'Pears?' said another. '*Is*, I reckon you better say.'
> 'Said he wished he owned *half* of the dog, the idiot,' said a
> third. 'What did he reckon would become of the other half if he
> killed his half? Do you reckon he thought it would live?'[1]

The way in which language is used in Wilson's joke does stand in
some relation to certain rules, namely to the rules governing the uses
of the words 'half', 'kill', etc. One could not understand the joke
unless one understood the way in which these words are normally
used. If one wished I suppose one could say that the normal use, the
rules for their use in *other* contexts, lends itself to the sort of joke
that Wilson makes. But this is far from saying that the joke is itself
an application of these rules. Indeed Wilson's audience regard him
as an idiot precisely because his remark is so plainly *not* an application of the linguistic rules which they have all been taught, but on
the contrary breaks them. And though an understanding of these
rules is certainly relevant to an understanding of Wilson's joke,
though for example one way (and indeed so far as I can see the
only way) in which one might explain the joke to someone who
failed to understand it, would be to indicate the relationship of
Wilson's comment to the rules, ('But, don't you see? You *can't* kill
half a dog'), this can scarcely be regarded as itself a rule or method
for appreciating the joke. Wilson's audience understood this
relationship perfectly, though they were unaware that a joke had
even been made. And while a similar relationship would have been
involved if Wilson had remarked that he wished to breed half of the

[1] *Puddn'head Wilson* (Zodiac Press, 1955) p. 37.

dog or enter half of it for a dog-show, his remark would no longer have constituted a joke at all, or at best an extremely pointless one.

When Ryle speaks of the rules, maxims, canons, methods or techniques according to which jokes are constructed or appreciated then, it is by no means clear what application his remarks have. Whatever rules or principles may be relevant to the appreciation of humour, they do not themselves seem to provide a criterion for distinguishing between good and bad jokes. Nor can this conclusion be avoided by arguing, as some seem to wish to, that since the creative comic cannot be understood by reference to any established rules, then his remarks must be seen as bringing with them their own rules, or as involving an appeal to rules which he himself has invented. For this would be merely an attempt to retain the vocabulary in question where it has already been shown to be inapplicable. If on entering a restaurant I am told that the establishment has a rule against serving philosophy lecturers, then I shall probably be both surprised and displeased. But if I am then told that this is a rule which has been specially invented to suit my particular case, I shall certainly not conclude that the rule in question is one of that particular species which characterises creative acts. On the contrary, I shall assume with good reason that there is in fact no such rule and that the proprietor is simply indulging a private whim.

Ryle's own example of humour brings out certain characteristics of his philosophical procedure in *The Concept of Mind*. We have seen that, faced with any example of intelligent activity, Ryle is inclined to explain the activity as an instance of knowledge how, as the application of a method for attaining certain results, as a set of rules or principles of skill. And we have also seen that he shows precisely the same inclination even where the examples with which he is faced will not support such an interpretation but on the contrary underline its inadequacies. What we are faced with here, therefore, is explicable only as a philosophical prejudice about the nature of intelligence, a prejudice which, I have suggested, is to be seen at work in Ryle's discussion of the form of intelligence manifested in making or appreciating jokes.

Of course, in saying this I am not criticising the negative part of Ryle's thesis. I am not, for instance, suggesting that the possession of a sense of humour is explicable as a type of factual knowledge. My point is that there are types of learning, understanding and knowledge which cannot be understood as *either* the knowledge of facts *or* the grasp of principles or techniques. And I want now to turn to the main example of my paper, which, unlike those I have so far discussed, is not mentioned by Ryle except in passing. I shall try to show that this oversight is no merely contingent matter, but is on the contrary necessitated by the sort of account offered by Ryle, and to this end I shall begin by indicating certain characteristics of the types of learning, knowledge and understanding discussed in *The Concept of Mind*, which are not, I think, shared by the examples which I have in mind.

2. When a man learns a fact or a technique, learns that something is the case or learns how to perform some task, then what he learns is only contingently related to the source of his information. For example, he learns the history of the Trade Union movement from a course of lectures, where he might have learned the same facts from a history book. Or he is taught to mend a fuse while apprenticed to an electrician, where a do-it-yourself manual could have imparted the same technique. In a way it is even a matter of indifference for what is learnt whether a man is taught by a good or bad teacher. Presumably we shall not be inclined to describe a teacher as good unless pupils tend to learn more thoroughly under his guidance, remember what he has taught them more easily. Nevertheless, there is no contradiction in the assertion that though my first history teacher was a wonderful teacher, he did not impart to me as much information as did the unimaginative drudge who succeeded him. And in neither case need an account of what I have learned involve a reference either to my teacher or to anything which he has said to me. Indeed, it is often true of these sorts of learning (what Ryle continually suggests is true of *all* learning) that a pupil's proficiency depends at least in part on his *ceasing* to pay attention to his teacher's precise words. If he has been well taught, he will have learnt to concentrate on the activity in which he is engaged, rather than on describing that activity. So that, if asked to put the knowledge he has acquired into words, he may even be unable to do so.

Let us now contrast this with a rather different case. Let us imagine a man who finds that his life has gone sour on him. By this I do not mean that he regrets the particular course which his life has taken, so that a change in his fortune might immediately bring about a new perspective, but rather that he fails to see interest or significance in anything. Like Mill in his youth, he has 'worn out all pleasures' and feels that 'life, to all who possess the good things of it, must necessarily be a vapid, uninteresting thing'.[1]

Such a man may ask himself or others how he can go on living. But it is important for my purpose to notice that this question is unlikely to be a request either for information, or for some method

[1] J. S. Mill, *Autobiography* (The World's Classics, 1924) p. 124.

of overcoming his difficulties. This is connected with the point that unlike problems relating to the acquisition of knowledge or the mastery of a technique, problems about the meaning of life are personal problems not general ones. There is, for example, no such thing as 'finding meaning in someone's life for him' as we may speak of obtaining information for someone, nor would it show much intelligence in the face of such problems to reply, 'Well, you'll just have to try to snap out of it', or 'Why don't you take up golf?' Such remarks would have a sense only where one suspected that the man in question was insincere, or perhaps deceiving himself about the depth of his problem. They would not be ways of dealing with a serious case of despair.

Nevertheless I do not think it senseless to speak of ways in which such despair might be overcome. Let us suppose, for example, that by chance the man in my example one day picks up a novel or a poem. Absorbed by what he reads he goes on, reads it again, possibly many times. And afterwards he is no longer inclined to think or speak of the world in the same way. The significance which events have for him is changed, and he now finds a new meaning in life. Perhaps he is inclined to say, 'I never thought that it could be possible to get much out of this life, but Wordsworth or Tolstoi has shown me that it is'.

Now it seems to me clear that this example differs quite radically from the examples of learning which I have mentioned so far, the learning of facts or of techniques. For though we may speak in this case also of the man having learnt something – of his having learnt what life is really like, or of his having learnt that certain things are possible for him – it no longer makes much sense to speak of alternative ways of learning these things. If someone teaches me that it is possible to drive a car up a wall, say by a discussion of the laws of gravity and the principles of the internal combustion engine, then he may change my ideas of what is possible in this way. But just the same change might have been brought about in another way, for instance by his driving the car up a wall in front of my very eyes. On the other hand, though we may speak of a novel or a poem's bringing a man to see what is possible for him, we can no longer conceive of these possibilities existing independently of the way in which he was brought to recognise them. If asked what he has learned from the novel or the poem, the man may tell me to read it more carefully. Or he may read it himself, emphasising what he takes to be the correct expression. But if this is unsuccessful, then he will not offer an alternative statement of the work. For what it has to tell us is internally related to the work itself.

Precisely what this claim amounts to can be seen in another
rather more specific case. In his autobiography, Edwin Muir recalls
how a poem[1] once broke the hold which certain memories had over
him. As a child he had been chased home under humiliating circumstances by a school-friend, and had thereafter been unable to think
of the incident without shame and terror.

> I got rid of that terror almost thirty years later in a poem
> describing Achilles chasing Hector round Troy. . . . The poem
> cleared my conscience. I saw that my shame was a fantastically
> elongated shadow of a childish moment imperfectly remembered
> . . . and I could at last see the incident whole by seeing it as
> happening, on a great and tragic scale, to someone else. After I
> had written the poem the flight itself was changed, and with that
> my feelings towards it.[2]

This differs from my earlier example in that the agent learns from
creation rather than contemplation, but the cases are similar in
that in both a man is brought to see a new significance in his life.
I speak of an agent's seeing a new significance 'in *his* life' rather than
'in life' or 'in the world', because, at least in the case of Muir, I
think that this is more natural. But I doubt whether the distinction
could be pressed very far. In a radio discussion Dylan Thomas once
remarked that 'A good poem helps to change the shape and significance of the universe, helps to extend everyone's knowledge of
himself and the world around him'.[3] But to suppose that understanding the world around one and understanding oneself or one's
own life can be regarded as distinct in this context would show a
failure to grasp Thomas's point. Part of what would be meant by
speaking of Muir's having learned from writing *Ballad of Hector in
Hades*, would be that the poem made a difference to *his* life, made
a difference to the significance which he attached to the incident
from his childhood for instance. Nor could this change be understood except by reference to the sort of man Muir was, to the
difficulties and problems in his life, and to the sort of understanding
which he brought to the poem.

This understanding is something which will differ with different
people. It may even be completely absent, for the sort of learning
which is involved here is not possible for everyone. I do not mean
that not everyone is capable of writing poetry though that is of
course true, but rather that the way in which literature con-

---

[1] Ballad of Hector in Hades.
[2] *An Autobiography* (The Hogarth Press, 1954) p. 43.
[3] On Poetry: A Discussion, in *Encounter*, 1954.

tributes to a man's understanding depends partly at least on what he brings to the study of a novel or a poem. This is why it may deepen one man's understanding where it says nothing at all to another. 'Lessing', Goethe is reported to have said, 'was of the very highest understanding and only one equally great could learn of him. To a half faculty he was dangerous.'[1] On a rather more mundane plane, parents and teachers may wonder whether a play or a novel is not beyond the grasp of a child of a certain age, while recognising that it would present no difficulties for older children.

Yet though people may differ in what, if anything, they learn from the same work of literature, it does not follow that what is learnt can be specified independently of the work itself, though this is a tempting conclusion. To see why the temptation should be resisted, we must recognise that the sort of learning from literature which I have mentioned is possible only where the poem or the novel is good of its kind. The man in my first example would not have spoken of coming to see a new significance in his life, had he regarded what he read as an artistic failure. Muir's poem could not have brought him an insight into his childhood cowardice, had it not been an example of artistic care, had he not laboured over the form of the poem. For its form of expression, the vividness or power of the language in a poem, is bound up with what enables us to learn from it.

The same is not true of the forms of learning on which Ryle concentrates. For here the linguistic formulation, the way in which things are said, does not have the importance which it does with a work of literature. Of course, this does not mean that it has *no* importance. If a pupil is to benefit from his teaching, it is important that he should be given correct information, or that the principles which he is taught should be adequate to the situation which he is likely to face. But when one speaks of a piece of information as false or of the statement of a maxim or principle as inadequate, then one rejects a form of words because, though they *might* be used to make a true assertion, *as it happens* they are being used to make a false one. If someone tells me that the President of the United States is a Red Indian, or that it is advisable to swim the breast stroke with one's legs motionless, then I shall reject what he says, not on the grounds that it would be a misleading account of any conceivable situation, but on the grounds that it is inapplicable to a particular situation, namely that in which we find ourselves. The man tells me something. But he tells me something which, it so happens, is false.

[1] Eckermann, *Conversations of Goethe*, p. 110.

These sorts of considerations will not take us far if we are trying to explain what, if anything, it means to speak of truth or falsity in literature. For here the particular words which are used have an importance which they do not in the statement of facts or of rules. When a man formulates a principle incorrectly, asserts for example that gooseberry bushes should be planted 3′ 6″ apart, we may be inclined to say that, though wrong, what he says is not far wrong. 'Actually', we reply, 'they should be planted 4′ apart, but still, what you say is close enough.' But though a man's understanding of literature may come out in the way he reads to his wife or children, if he misreads a line of poetry, say, and when corrected, replies, 'Oh well, I wasn't far out', we shall have difficulty in seeing how he could ever have got anything from it. Our inclination would be to say that he had missed the point of the line. A man who appreciates the truth in a poem, shows a concern with the particular words which the poet uses. For him it is not merely a contingent matter that these words are capable of telling him something.

In the same way, the falsity in a poem or a novel is something which comes out in the writer's style, in its tendency to run to cliché for instance, or in the use of phrases simply for cheap effects. Muir speaks of the way in which a man's understanding may be corrupted by literature. 'There is', he tells us, 'as well as exquisite wit, a sickly, graveyard strain in Heine's poetry. It was this that attracted me now. I battened on tombs and shrouds.'[1] But when he comes to characterise the falsity in Heine's thought, he does not present us with some statement or some principle which he regards as mistaken. Rather it is Heine's style, the repetitive nature of his poems which he emphasises.

> The word *einsam* ('lonely') recurs over and over again in Heine's poetry; the lonely cottage, the lonely man in his grave, the lonely pine-tree, and always the lonely Heine. I steeped myself in that sweet poison.[2]

One might contrast what Muir says here with the way in which for example, people speak of the harmful effects of television violence. It is sometimes said that the portrayal of violence in people's homes will eventually prove harmful to them. But I do not imagine that anyone has ever supposed this to be the only way in which such corruption can be brought about. Television violence is generally supposed to corrupt in much the same way as exposure to, say, real-life violence, or as violence in the cinema. But when Muir

---

[1] *An Autobiography*, p. 144.
[2] Ibid., p. 146.

spoke of the way in which a study of Heine's writings might corrupt or cheapen a man's understanding of death, and later went on to contrast him with Baudelaire, 'a man who was genuinely possessed by death and not merely coquetting with the shroud and the tomb'[1] he did not have in mind something which might have been induced by different means. The falsity of Heine's thought, its capacity for corruption, was a falsity in the way he wrote, the falsity of a writer who thinks in stereotypes ('the shroud and the tomb'), whose words and phrases have lost their force through constant repetition in literary contexts. It was presumably this force which he *found* in Baudelaire. I think that this would be what was meant if one spoke of the truth in the latter's work.

Certainly it is this sense of 'truth' and 'falsity' of which Joyce Cary is thinking when he says that a man who reads a great novel like *Lord Jim* must feel, 'That is important, that is true', and then contrasts this sense with the sense in which one might say, 'I suppose that is true, but I've heard it before.'[2] If the man who reads *Lord Jim* were to say, 'I suppose that is true, but I've heard it before', then he could not be speaking of artistic truth. For here what makes it true and what makes it original, memorable, striking, cannot be distinguished in this way. This would be inexplicable if we were thinking of the truth of a factual statement or of a principle or maxim, for when a man imparts information or new techniques, then what makes his words memorable or important is the context in which they occur. It is likely that a swimming instructor who emphasises a pupil's first lesson by throwing him in the deep end, will give the pupil cause to remember his words. And I shall probably remember the first man who tells me my name is to appear in the New Year's Honours Lists in a way that I shall not remember the fifth. Though both will say something equally true (or false), it is possible here to distinguish the truth of what is said and its importance, what makes the statement striking or memorable on a particular occasion. A true statement may be of the utmost importance or trivial in the extreme.

It would make no sense to speak of a trivial or everyday artistic truth. Because it is not the occasion of its utterance, but the character of the language itself which makes the poem memorable, it will still be capable of fixing our attention at other times and places. And though it is true that a man may remember his first contact with the work of Milton or Coleridge for the rest of his life, it would be a mediocre poem where what impressed him could not survive

---

[1] *An Autobiography*, p. 146.
[2] *Art and Reality* (Cambridge 1958) p. 4.

a second reading. Thomas Mann brings out how an artist's concern for the words he uses goes with what makes his work important for us:

> And a sentence which must be heard twice must be fashioned accordingly. It must – I do not speak of beauty – possess a certain high level, and symbolic suggestion, which will make it worthy to sound again in any epic future. So every point becomes a standing ground, every adjective a decision, and it is clear that such work is not to be produced off-hand.[1]

Mann was I suppose speaking here primarily of his own work. But though it would obviously be false to say that all literature displays *this* degree of care, his remarks are not merely an indication of the attitude which *he* brought to his writing. They are philosophical rather than biographical. For they indicate the *sort* of concern for detail which makes it possible for a novel to teach us something. Similarly, the failure to see what a writer has to tell you, is a failure to grasp the importance which details have in his work, a failure to see why only the particular words which he uses will do. In his first lecture on Shakespeare, Coleridge brings out perfectly how these things go hand in hand.

> I was (he says) one day admiring one of the falls of the Clyde; and ruminating upon what descriptive term could be most fully applied to it, I came to the conclusion that the epithet 'majestic' was the most appropriate. While I was still contemplating the scene a gentleman and a lady came up, neither of whose faces bore much stamp of superior intelligence and the first words the gentleman uttered were 'It is very majestic'. I was pleased to find such a confirmation of my opinion, and I complimented the speaker upon the best choice of epithet, saying that he had used the best word that could have been selected from our language. 'Yes Sir,' replied the gentleman. 'I say it is very majestic; it is sublime; it is beautiful; it is grand; it is picturesque.' 'Ay (added the lady) it is the prettiest thing I ever saw.' I own that I was not a little disconcerted.[2]

By treating the words 'majestic', 'sublime', 'picturesque', and so on, as if they were interchangeable, Coleridge's acquaintances showed their failure to understand what he himself had seen, namely that only the word 'majestic' possessed the right force to

---

[1] Quoted in D. H. Lawrence, *Selected Literary Criticism* (Heinemann, 1955) p. 126.

[2] *Seven Lectures on Shakespeare and Milton* (Chapman and Hall, 1856) p. 10.

bring out the true character of the scene before them. This is not something which one might find in another word, even in a synonym, and for this reason I think it unfortunate to try (as many writers do) to explain it as a matter of the 'associations' of words. Joyce Cary shows signs of this confusion when he notes, quite correctly, that 'the word "seaman" carries a quite different meaning from "sailor", a tougher, more versatile and grimmer meaning', but then goes on to characterise this difference as a matter of mere subjective associations. The very fact that it is possible for Cary to appeal to the difference between the words 'sailor' and 'seaman' in the way that he does, and to be confident of his example being understood, the fact that Coleridge could rely on his readers' sympathising with his consternation at the sightseers' remarks, shows that what is involved here is no merely subjective matter, not just a question of the associations which a word may happen to have for a man, but something which is part of a shared life and language. Of course, the various words which Coleridge's sightseer used may well have had similar associations for him. Probably they were all words which he associated in some vague way with impressive examples of natural beauty. But to admit this is quite compatible with the assertion that the words have nevertheless very different forces, that though in some cases their meaning is fairly close, in another sense they all have quite different meanings. In this latter sense of 'meaning' there are no synonyms. There are no synonyms for the force of a word.

When a man's contact with literature enables him to discover meaning in what had before seemed pointless and boring, when Muir's poem brought him to see his fears in proper perspective, when Coleridge settled on the epithet 'majestic' to describe the falls of the Clyde, then the new understanding involved was bound up with the way in which each came to speak of these things. Unlike the sort of learning which Ryle discusses, unlike the acquisition of factual knowledge or the mastery of a technique, what is learnt in the cases I have discussed could not have been learnt in any other way, by any alternative means. It was, for example, only when Edwin Muir found precisely the right words in which to express his fear that he came to see it in a new way.[1]

I speak here of literature bringing men to see their lives or events in their lives in a different way. And indeed this is how Muir himself speaks of his experience. Nevertheless, I should perhaps make

[1] The matter is complicated because Muir's own explanation of the situation is partly influenced by psychoanalytic theory. But I think that my own account is nevertheless for the most part correct.

it clear that in this context 'seeing' cannot be equated with perception.[1] When Muir tells us that after writing his poem he could
'at last see the incident whole by seeing it as happening, on a great
and tragic scale, to someone else', he is making a remark of a
logically quite different sort from the man who says, 'I could at
last see the needle, though without my son's sharp eyes, I might
have missed it completely.' In the latter case, the ability to see
something depends on acuteness of visual powers. It is a quality which
might be displayed by a well-trained gun dog or a hawk, though not
by a bat or by an oyster. When, on the other hand, one speaks of a
poet's ability to open one's eyes to what one had overlooked, one is
thinking of something which could happen only to a human being,
and indeed only to a human being brought up within a certain
cultural life. Within that cultural life it might happen to a blind
man.

The difference becomes apparent, if one compares the change
which I have just mentioned with another which Muir discusses
later in the book. After an unhappy period in Glasgow he had
moved to Prague, where:

> I began to learn the visible world all over again. In Glasgow
> the ugliness of everything – the walks through the slums, the
> uncongenial work – had turned me in upon myself, so that I no
> longer saw things, but was merely aware of them in a vague way.
> In Prague everything seemed to be asking me to notice it; I spent
> weeks in an orgy of looking; I saw everywhere the visible world
> before my eyes.[2]

Muir's life in Glasgow had bred in him the habit of ignoring his
surroundings. When in Prague he began to break himself of this
habit, began to 'learn the visible world all over again', the change
which came over him can be explained by saying that he now saw
things whose presence he had before failed to notice. He had failed
to notice his surroundings in Glasgow because, for fear of seeing
what was unpleasant or distasteful, he had simply refused to look.
It is easy to imagine a change of the sort which Muir mentions
being contrived in a quite different manner, perhaps by a television
documentary on the city, or even by a spell of good weather. For
the change was not a change in the significance which Muir's

---

[1] The temptation is, of course, considerably greater in respect of the visual and
plastic arts, that is, when one speaks of a painter or a sculptor bringing someone to
see something. I think that it is to be resisted equally strongly here, and for similar
reasons.

[2] *An Autobiography*, p. 189.

environment had for him. He had simply become more observant of that environment.

When he came to see his childhood terrors in proper perspective by writing of them, there is also a sense in which Muir now saw things whose presence he had before failed to notice. But this sense cannot be explained by saying that he discovered facts about the incident which he had hitherto failed to appreciate, or that he remembered new aspects which he had forgotten. Apart from the doubtful sense of speaking of a man's imparting information to himself by writing a poem, Muir makes it clear that as a biographical source the poem in question would have been quite unhelpful. 'I imagined Hector', he remarks, 'as noticing with intense, dream-like precision certain little things, not the huge simplified things which my conscious memory tells me I noticed in my own flight.'[1]

What the poem brought him to see was nothing which a television documentary on childhood or a cine-film of the incident might have shown him. Rather it was a change in the significance which the whole event came to have for him, a change bound up with the way in which he was inclined to think and speak of it. 'After I had written the poem', he tells us, 'the flight itself was changed and with it my feelings towards it.' One might speak of this as a difference in the way Muir interpreted the event or a difference in his viewpoint, were it not for the fact that normally when one speaks in this way one has an idea of some independent standpoint or state of affairs of which the different points of view or interpretations may be shown to be adequate or inadequate accounts. 'There is a lot to be said for his point of view', we say, or 'That interpretation is quite indefensible.' And to say that an interpretation is mistaken or inadequate will be to say that the state of affairs in question really possesses characteristics which the interpretation cannot explain. As we have seen, Muir *might* have spoken in this way of the change which came over him in Prague. But if writing *Ballad of Hector in Hades* had led him to condemn his earlier attitude towards his childhood as mistaken, this would not have been because the poem brought out features of his life which it could independently have been shown not to possess, but because he no longer felt any inclination to speak or think of it in the same way as before. Just as, having seen how Shakespeare expresses Romeo's love for Juliet, the way in which I have been accustomed to speak of my love for my wife may lose its hold over me, so Muir's terror lost its hold over him, when *he* learnt how to talk of it. This

[1] *An Autobiography*, p. 43.

is why what he learnt cannot be seen as a matter of either the knowledge of facts or the knowledge of a technique. What we are faced
with here is not a case of either learning how or learning that, at
least in Ryle's sense. If such a phrase is necessary, I think that this
case might best be described as a case of learning *from*.

3. So far I have discussed certain situations in which literature
may be said to be responsible for changes in men's lives, in order to
bring out the limitations in one account of the nature of learning
and knowledge. Unfortunately it might be thought that in one way
my choice of examples has been ill-considered. For it is noticeable
that for the most part they involve situations which might justifiably
be referred to as instances of moral change.

   To some extent this is of course predictable, since it is likely that
any really fundamental change in a man's life will have a moral
dimension. Nor do I think it unimportant that when men speak of
what they have learned from literature, often their discussions will
be couched in moral terms. Clearly moral considerations enter
deeply into the sort of importance which literature has for us, so that
it would be a mistake to try to explain how one can learn from
novels and poems, and then to discuss, as a quite different matter,
what it is for a man's moral understanding to be deepened.

   Nevertheless, a recognition of these points may lead to confusion.
For it may lead one to suppose that any situation where one might
speak of learning from literature will *necessarily* possess a moral
aspect, that the form of learning involved will *always* be describable
in moral terms. Thus, D. H. Lawrence has suggested that 'Every
work of art adheres to some system of morality', though he recognises
that within that morality it may constitute a revolutionary force,
may, as he says, 'contain the essential criticism of the morality to
which it adheres'.[1] And even a writer like Joyce Cary, who is unwilling to make any generalisation about the nature of art itself,
nevertheless accepts Lawrence's thesis as applied to literature.
'When we speak of the novelist and poet's revelation of truth', he
says, 'we mean that it is essentially moral, that it asserts a moral
meaning.'[2]

   These remarks do of course have some value in so far as they
indicate that morality stands in a relationship to literature which
other aspects of our lives do not. For a novel or a play may embody
a moral vision, may be spoken of as contributing to the moral life
of society, in a way in which it would make no sense to speak of its

[1] *Selected Literary Criticism*, p. 185.
[2] *Art and Reality*, p. 144.

embodying a *scientific* vision or of its contributing ideas to the
economic life of the society or to its civil engineering. But they are
confusing if they are taken to imply that literature need always
involve moral notions, and not simply because a work of literature
generally contributes to aspects of our life other than morality – to
religion, to politics, to love – but also because we can speak of
learning from a novel or a poem even where it would no longer be
helpful to speak of *any* specific form of activity to which it contributes.
When Oscar Wilde wished to indicate how art may influence
men's lives, he did not find it necessary to discuss changes in their
moral or religious ideas. But nor did he speak of *any* activity on
which the work of artists might throw new light. He spoke only of
the importance which natural beauty may have for men.

> At present people see fogs not because there are fogs, but
> because poets and painters have taught them the mysterious
> loveliness of such effects.[1]

Of course, it may be thought that this example tilts the scales
rather heavily in my own favour. For it is notorious that, for quite
bad philosophical reasons, Wilde was particularly concerned to
emphasise the independence of art and morality. Moreover, it
might well be argued that there is in any case no necessary incompatibility
between an artist's treatment of nature and his
concern with moral issues.

> Dickens, at the beginning of *Bleak House*, gives us only the
> London fog. But that fog is the keynote of the whole. It gave
> Dickens back all the time whenever he needed it, the sense of a
> dark, dirty and muddled world, of the confusion and despair
> of lost souls.[2]

Despite this, I see no reason to suppose that *any* artistic treatment
of natural beauty must be of the above sort, and to maintain that
literature always involves a moral perspective would be to run the
risk of blurring important differences. One might compare here the
sorts of cases of *moral* change which I discussed earlier with what
Ford Madox Ford found in the novels of W. H. Hudson:

> It is years and years since I first read *Nature in Downland*, yet,
> as I have already said somewhere or other, the first words that I

[1] *The Works of Oscar Wilde* (Collins, 1948) p. 986.
[2] Joyce Cary, *Art and Reality*, p. 100.

C

there read have become a part of my life. They describe how, lying on the turf on the high, sunlit down above Lewes in Sussex, Hudson looked up into the perfect, limpid blue of the sky. . . . Now that is part of my life.[1]

If one were comparing what Ford found in Hudson's novels with what, say, Muir learnt from his own poem, or from the writings of Baudelaire, then one might speak in very similar ways. One might say, for instance, that both were brought to a deeper understanding of some aspect of life, or that both came to see what the world was like. And one would emphasise that in neither case could this recognition be regarded as distinct from the way in which Ford or Muir was brought to it. Coming to see what life or the world is like cannot be compared with finding out what an ammeter is like. If I have found out what an ammeter is like, then I shall be able to tell you. 'It's a sort of metal box', I may say, 'with a dial on it.' On the other hand neither Ford not Muir could have *said* what they had learned from literature, from their own writings or from those of others. Muir did not try to explain what he found in Baudelaire, and when Ford wishes to characterise the difference which reading Hudson made to him, he says only that the first words of *Nature in Downland* have become a part of his life. I doubt whether anyone who failed to see these similarities could have understood much of what was involved in either example.

This having been said, it is then important to notice the differences. One is bound, that is, to mention that, though in the case of Muir what was learnt had a moral dimension, with Ford this was not so. Muir came to a new idea of the significance of certain events in his life which it is difficult not to see as moral. Ford simply learnt what it was like to lie on the downs, looking up at the sky, so that though he had never done this, yet 'that is I, not Hudson, looking up into the heavens'.[2] It would be absurd to suggest that this is not an important difference between the examples. But given the similarities between them already indicated, it would seem sheer philosophical prejudice to go on to argue with Lawrence and Cary that, since Hudson's novels brought about no moral change in Ford's life, Ford cannot be said to have learned from them. If one were willing to speak of learning in the case of either Ford or Muir, then I fail to see why one should not speak of it in both.

At this point I can imagine someone wishing to push the argument rather further. 'You have denied', they may say, 'that reference

[1] *The Bodley Head Ford Madox Ford* (Bodley Head, 1962–3) vol. 3, p. 297.
[2] Ibid., p. 297.

to the artistic worth of a novel or poem need necessarily involve reference to a moral vision. And you have indicated cases where a man might speak of learning from a work of literature, even though it is not possible to identify any moral aspect to what he learns. But have you gone far enough? May there not be cases in which a work of art is recognised as having artistic merit, whilst involving a corrupt or evil vision? And if you deny that this may be so, are you not then guilty of a mere philosophical prejudice of the sort which you have attacked in the views of Lawrence and Cary?

The man who asks these questions may for instance be impressed by the way in which qualities which are normally regarded as morally blameworthy may nevertheless, in the hands of a great artist, become acceptable. He may remember how Orwell, having condemned Swift for a world-view so diseased that it 'only just passes the test of sanity', was led then to admit that he regarded *Gulliver's Travels* as a 'great work of art'.

> From what I have written it may seem that I am *against* Swift, and that my object is to refute him and even to belittle him. In a political and moral sense I am against him, so far as I understand him. Yet curiously enough he is one of the writers I admire with least reserve, and *Gulliver's Travels*, in particular, is a book which it seems impossible for me to grow tired of.[1]

I doubt whether anything *general* could usefully be said about this sort of case. Clearly much will depend, with the example I have chosen, on whether Orwell is interpreted as saying on the one hand that Swift's work is good *despite* the pernicious moral viewpoint which it embodies, or on the other that it is good *as well as* pernicious or even good *in its* perniciousness. As it happens, the first interpretation does seem to some extent a plausible one. Many of Orwell's remarks indicate that he does not see himself as praising (from an artistic viewpoint) Swift's moral failings, but rather those qualities which override these failings, the 'power and simplicity of Swift's prose', for example, which he says, 'has been able to make not one but a whole series of impossible worlds more credible than the majority of history books'.[2] It would therefore seem to me correct to say that, in this respect at least, Orwell regards Swift's work as good *despite* its moral corruption. Furthermore, I think that this could be the *only* correct description of any case in which a writer's vision was

---

[1] *Inside the Whale and other essays* (Penguin Press, 1962) p. 142.
[2] p. 139.

thought of as being morally trivial in some way. For instance, a work of literature could only be good *despite* its sentimentality.

On the other hand, I should not wish to deny that there are many aspects of Orwell's discussion of which the above would not be a correct account and where it would perhaps be more appropriate to say that he finds Swift's work both artistically good *and* morally corrupt, that he responds to the expression of a moral viewpoint which he nevertheless regards as diseased and evil. What is to be noted here is that Orwell does not find Swift's viewpoint *merely* diseased and evil. He himself says that he cannot imagine himself responding to any moral position of which this was true, for example that of 'spiritualist, a Buchmanite or a member of the Ku-Klux Klan'. Swift's moral position differs from theirs in that, though it is one which most people would regard as distorted, even dangerous, it is also one which most people could imagine themselves holding. It is not merely trivial or crazy. Swift, Orwell tells us:

> remains permanently in a depressed mood which in most people is only intermittent. . . . But we all know that mood, and something in us responds to the expression of it. . . . Swift falsifies his picture of the world by refusing to see anything in human life except dirt, folly and wickedness, but the part which he abstracts from the whole does exist, and it is something which we all know about while shrinking from mentioning it.[1]

There are then two sides to Orwell's regard for Swift. To some extent he admires Swift's work in spite of its immorality. To some extent it is the immoral position embodied in Swift's work to which he responds. On the other hand, it is worth remarking that for those who mistakenly believe that *all* art embodies a moral viewpoint, there may be considerable temptation to ignore this distinction, and to suppose that however evil or even trivial a writer's moral viewpoint, it must always be by virtue of this viewpoint, rather than in spite of it, that he is admired. Thus, faced with Orwell's example, if they do not simply write it off as confused, they will be inclined to argue that since Orwell regarded Swift as a great writer, and since it is *only* in respect of the moral viewpoint which it embodies that any work can be of artistic worth, it follows that Orwell, who recognised the corruptness of Swift's moral vision, must have thought him a great writer solely by virtue of a corrupt moral vision.

The fallacy in this argument should be apparent from what I have said already. What makes a writer's work valuable for us need

---

[1] *Inside the Whale and other essays* (Penguin Press, 1962) p. 140.

not be thought of in *moral* terms at all. As a matter of fact Orwell *was* impressed by aspects of Swift's work quite unconnected with morality. Once the supposition that art must always embody moral ideas is rejected, then there is no reason why we should continue to deny that a work of literature may possess artistic excellence in spite of its embodying a morally outrageous or even trivial theme. It is just that where this is so, it will not be this aspect of the work which impresses us, but other non-moral aspects.

It should, however, be clear that my position here is to be sharply distinguished from another to which it is, at least in this respect, apparently similar. For what I have argued is that when we learn from a work of literature, then what we learn, the content of the work, is essentially bound up with the way in which the writer expresses himself, bound up, that is, with the author's style. And I have also indicated that I regard it as a mistake to assume that the content of the work will always be of a moral nature.

Now, those who do *not* reject this assumption, but are on the contrary *very* strongly influenced by it, are sometimes led to suppose that in cases where a work has apparently *no* moral content, or no moral content worthy of consideration, the artist's merit, if any, must lie simply in his style, in a sense in which style *is* distinguishable from content. Thus, for example, G. K. Chesterton, recognising that Milton was 'a man of magnificent genius', but nevertheless finding his moral vision hackneyed and unoriginal, felt himself forced to locate Milton's greatness 'in a style and a style which seems to me rather unusually separated from its substance.'[1]

The sense of 'style' which Chesterton has in mind here, the sense in which one can distinguish an artist's style from what he has to tell you, is, as his subsequent remarks make plain, simply a matter of the architecture of a poem or a novel, of its word-arrangement or rhyme-scheme. It is the sense in which schoolteachers often speak when they compare Pope's style with that of, say, Coleridge, or when they distinguish blank verse from rhyme. And indeed, a schoolteacher might bring a child to see these sorts of differences even if the child were incapable of learning anything from poetry or literature, or cared nothing for either. The teacher need only communicate certain rules or methods, need only teach the child to count the number of iambic feet in a line, or to notice how often the writer uses the word 'and'.

But, though we might say that in one sense the child understands Pope's style or understands certain stylistic differences, this would

[1] *G. K. Chesterton: A Selection from his non-fictional prose* (Faber and Faber, 1970) p. 86.

be a superficial, a trivial sense of 'style' and of 'understanding'. The child would never see what was great about Pope's writing for example, nor would he see why Pope's use of certain rhyme-schemes differed from that of mediocre, but competent, imitators. To make him alive to this difference you would have to point to far more than rules or methods. You would have to bring him to see what Pope had to say about life. A knowledge of rules and canons might enable him to recognise that the *Epistles* are written in heroic couplets, or perhaps where Pope breaks the rules of this poetic form, but if that were all that he found in Pope's style, there would be no reason why he should marvel at it (except as you might marvel at a man's skill in composing tongue-twisters). And he would never learn anything from it.

It is this last sense of 'learning' which I have tried to explain in this paper. And I have tried to show why Ryle with his emphasis on training and skills, on rules and on the transmission of techniques, does not even notice that there is such a sense. This is why I do not find it surprising that whenever Ryle refers to the appreciation of literature or poetry in *The Concept of Mind*, his references are always couched in the terminology of rules and canons. I have said that such references involve a trivial conception of style. But then, it is a limitation of the account of learning and knowledge offered by Ryle that it could not explain any sense of 'literary style' which was *not* trivial. Ryle refers somewhere to his task in the book as that of 'mapping the logical geography of the concept of mind'. It is as though, the task having been completed to Ryle's satisfaction, he and certain of his followers then proceeded to mistake the map for the country and simply forgot those places which had never been entered on the map. My suggestion is that the cases of learning from literature which I have discussed in this paper constitute just such a Shangri-la.

3

ALLEGIANCE AND CHANGE
IN MORALITY:
A STUDY IN CONTRASTS

D. Z. Phillips

I. INTRODUCTION

It has been said that the tendency to make use of examples drawn
from literature in discussing problems in moral philosophy is not
only dangerous, but needless. Dangers there certainly are, but these
have little to do with the reasons offered for the needlessness of such
examples. Examples drawn from literature, it is said, introduce an
unnecessary complexity into one's philosophising. Indeed, as Peter
Winch has pointed out, according to 'a fairly well-established . . .
tradition in recent Anglo-Saxon moral philosophy . . . it is not
merely permissible, but desirable, to take *trivial* examples. The
rationale of this view is that such examples do not generate the
emotion which is liable to surround more serious cases and thus
enable us to look more coolly at the logical issues involved',[1] and it
carries the implication that 'moral concerns can be examined quite
apart from any consideration of what it is about these concerns
which makes them important to us'.[2]

Anyone who accepts these conclusions ignores, or fails to recognise,
the tension which exists between certain ways of doing moral
philosophy and the novel. I am not suggesting that this tension
need exist or that it is inevitable. One is faced by the contrast
between complexity and simplicity: the complexity of the novel, and
the comparative simplicity of contemporary moral philosophy.
The student of moral philosophy may be surprised at the suggestion

[1] Peter Winch, 'The Universalizability of Moral Judgements', *The Monist*,
vol. 49, 1965, pp. 199–200.
[2] p. 200.

that his subject is simple; he may protest that it is difficult enough. But I am not equating simplicity with easiness. What I mean by the comparative simplicity of moral philosophy is the tendency to examine human conduct within narrow boundaries which the novelist does not hesitate to transgress. My suggestion is that in this matter it is the philosophers who exhibit this tendency who are confused, and who have much to learn from the greater complexity of the novel.

I have argued elsewhere that the ethical theories dominating contemporary moral philosophy, though different in important respects, are characterised by optimism, order and progress.[1] These characteristics make up what might be called an abstracted concept of reasonableness. In this lecture I want to explore some features of this notion of reasonableness and to contrast these with moral reasons which are rooted in the ways people live and in their conceptions of what is important in life. I shall try to bring out the nature of the contrasts by reference to some novels by Edith Wharton. The contrast depends on showing how much separates examples suggested by prevailing moral philosophies from other moral possibilities. The difficulty is in showing the force of these other possibilities. Such a showing involves an ability not given to many. The novelist with such ability brings us to see possibilities which otherwise we might not recognise.[2]

2. AN ABSTRACTED CONCEPT OF REASONABLENESS

Before turning to an examination of Edith Wharton's work, more needs to be said about the notion of reasonableness I want to criticise. At first, it may seem doubtful whether different viewpoints in contemporary moral philosophy can be seen as sharing an abstracted concept of reasonableness. After all, much seems to separate those who say that there is something called human good and harm by reference to which one can assess in general what people ought to do, and those who say, not only that each person must decide his ultimate moral principles for himself, but that anything could constitute such principles for a person. Yet the differences lessen when one is told that a person must not simply be free to choose his ultimate moral principles, but must also act rationally in doing so. This latter stipulation means, it is said, that

---

[1] 'Some Limits to Moral Endeavour', an Inaugural Lecture published by the University College of Swansea, 1971.

[2] I am grateful to Mr D. L. Sims for emphasising this point in a discussion of this paper at the University College of Swansea English Society.

the agent's principles must be such that he is prepared to abide by them himself as well as expecting other people to abide by them. Despite the fact that it is recognised that some fanatics will legislate in such a way that their principles will make them subject, in certain circumstances, to what no reasonable man would want, the general impression one receives is that there will be a large measure of agreement in men's moral principles. Because men generally want to attain and avoid the same sorts of things, their principles, it is said, framed with such consequences in view, are unlikely to show drastic divergencies. Behind this view, no less than that which makes an explicit appeal to human good and harm, is to be found the notion of what all men want, which psychologically, if not logically, tends to limit what could count as ultimate moral principles.

It is true that obstacles to the attainment of human good are recognised, but impediments, such as lack of experience and imagination, are seen as contingently related to morality. If all the facts concerning what are in people's interests were known, there would no longer be any room for disagreement about how men should conduct their lives.

Such is the philosophical neighbourhood in which an abstracted concept of reasonableness can grow. One can easily imagine a character emerging from this background. We could call him the reasonable man. Of course I am not suggesting that one could ever meet such a man. But that one could not do so is precisely the point, since the caricature is constructed on confused presuppositions which are latent in a great deal of contemporary moral philosophy. As we examine six features of the reasonable man's character, those who are acquainted with recent discussions in ethics will recognise in him, though he is nameless, a familiar friend.

The first characteristic of the reasonable man is that he has reasons for his moral allegiances. He will tell you proudly that his values are not without foundations. Since these foundations, human good and harm, serve as justifications of his allegiances, the relation between the allegiance and its grounds must be contingent. It would seem to follow that his moral principles have the status of well-tested hypotheses, well-founded generalisations, or well-grounded policies. Still, this is not something about which the reasonable man would feel apologetic. On the contrary, he will point out that if one has made a mistake in one's assessment of whether allegiance to a principle is conducive to human good, it is far better to abandon or to modify the principle than to persist in one's unreasonableness. The reasonable man is always prepared to change if called upon by reason to do so.

The second characteristic of the reasonable man follows from what I have just said. The reasonable man has reasons, not only for his allegiances, but also for his changes. If moral beliefs and actions are subject to an external measure of validity, it should not be surprising if faulty assessments are made from time to time. Change, when it comes, is justified by appeal to the same criterion that justified the prior allegiance, namely what all men want to attain and what all men want to avoid, human good and harm. Change, for the reasonable man, is always reasonable change.

The third characteristic of the reasonable man is extremely important. He believes in the unity of reason; for him, reason is one. There are many different moral beliefs, but they are all either right or wrong. This is decided by bringing them all to the bar of reason. Thus, when the reasonable man changes his beliefs, he has done so by coming to a greater appreciation of the same external measure that brought him to his initial moral beliefs.

In the light of his belief in the unity of reason we can appreciate the fourth characteristic of the reasonable man, namely that when he changes he always changes for the better. When he changes his moral beliefs he has a deeper grasp of what is and what is not reasonable, but he is still appealing to reasons of the same kind. Therefore since his change is a change within the same rational terms of reference, his change, being more reasonable than his former allegiance, is a change for the better.

Fifthly, since the reasonable man always changes for the better, the beliefs he has discarded or refused to believe in can be regarded as outmoded, outdated, inhibitions, or as irrational taboos.

Finally, the reasonable man is likely to regard wider moral changes in society, when he agrees with them, in the same way as he regards his own moral changes. Society is progressing to a more rational morality; it is coming of age, casting off its old inhibitions and taboos. Those who resist the changes he agrees with will be regarded by the reasonable man as defenders of the *status quo*, as those who do not realise that we live in a real world, as being inhibited by old taboos and bound by outworn habits and customs.

No doubt additional characteristics of the reasonable man can be thought of, but I believe the six I have outlined are sufficient to illustrate one form that an abstracted concept of reasonableness can take. Adherence to such a concept obscures the essential heterogeneity of moral beliefs and the very different account of moral allegiance which is called for, once this heterogeneity is recognised. Examples play an essential role here, since in terms of the issues they present one can show, as Winch has said, that 'The seriousness of such issues is not something we can add, or not, after the explanation of what those issues are, as a sort of emotional extra: it is something that "shows itself" . . . *in* the explanation of the issues'.[1] If this is right, then what is and what is not morally important cannot be determined independently of the variety of issues that present themselves. It cannot be determined in general in terms of an abstracted notion of reasonableness. In turning to the issues which are embodied in the novels of Edith Wharton, we shall find that the notion of reasonableness we have been discussing can claim literary critics as well as philosophers among its victims.

3. ABSTRACTION, REASONABLENESS AND THE CRITICS

Edith Wharton is concerned with allegiance and change in morality but, for her, these notions are not abstractions. On the contrary, they are rooted in the New York of the last third of the nineteenth century and the early years of the twentieth century. She depicts the upper middle-class life of New York in the 1870's and 1880's as a life dominated by a hierarchical family system. Free and undisturbed by major crises, it laid great emphasis on tradition, decorum, and honesty in business. If its mannerly code was broken, one was expected to break it without scandal. The young men of the community practised law, but in a half-hearted way which left plenty of time for frequent dinings and European excursions. Edith Wharton is alive to the force of convention in the world she depicts. Speaking of *The Age of Innocence* she says that 'What was or was not "the thing" played a part as important . . . as the inscrutable totem terrors that had ruled the destinies of (their) forefathers thousands of years ago'. She describes people as living in 'a kind of hieroglyphic world, where the real thing was never said or done or even thought, but only represented by a set of arbitrary signs'. The easiness with which this conventionality can be appreciated has blinded critics to the moral dimension in Edith Wharton's work. Guided by very different moral beliefs, critics have abstracted selective elements from the situations and made them a picture of the whole. For example, Blake Nevius, describing old New York, says that

> The real drama is played out below the surface – the impeccable, sophisticated surface – and communicates itself, if at all, to the observer by means of signs which only the initiate can read. Hence the significance, to old New York, of certain gestures by which the private drama is made public: that frightening portent of social annihilation, the 'cut': the dinner invitation from the

[1] Op. cit., p. 200.

van der Luydens, the invitation to occupy a prominent box at the opera, or the presence of Mrs Manson Mingott's carriage before the door, all signalising reinstatement; the sudden flight to Europe, which is the solution to every serious emotional crisis. These were the less arbitrary signs. By and large however the acquired manners of old New York lend themselves to what Edith Wharton termed 'an elaborate system of mystification'.[1]

Edith Wharton herself sees far more in *The Age of Innocence*. Into the society we have described comes Countess Olenska, fleeing from a broken marriage and threatening to divorce her husband. As she is an ex-member of old New York society, the influential families decide that she must be prevented from bringing scandal on herself and on them. Newland Archer is chosen to present their case to her. He is himself betrothed to May Welland in whom many critics have seen a perfect product of the society Edith Wharton was portraying. In presenting the case, however, Newland Archer's relationship with Ellen Olenska changes. What begins in criticism, ends in love. But he has put his community's case too well. He has convinced Ellen Olenska that personal happiness is not the most important thing in life. He shows her values connected with honour, time, tradition, obedience and sacrifice. Despite their love, they part. Archer marries May Welland, but even after her death when he has a chance to meet Ellen Olenska again, he lets the opportunity go by, convinced that nothing that could happen as a result of such a meeting would be as real as the considerations that parted them in the first place. The moral notions involved in the relationship between Newland Archer and Ellen Olenska are at the centre of the story.

Why have many critics distorted these moral notions in their discussions of *The Age of Innocence*? The answer lies in the fact that having already laid down what is to count as reasonable conduct, they cannot see anything in the novel other than a straightforward tale of a weak man trapped by a trivial society, unable to take the opportunity of freedom and a life worth living. There is no doubt in their minds that Newland Archer ends defeated.

Newland Archer's defeat, it is suggested, can be seen in the way meeting Ellen Olenska changed his attitude to May Welland. At first Blake Nevius tells us,

He is the willing accomplice of a society 'wholly absorbed in barricading itself against the unpleasant', and his appreciation

[1] '*On* The Age of Innocence' in *Edith Wharton: A Collection of Critical Essays*, ed. by Irving Howe (Prentice-Hall, 1962) p. 166.

of May Welland is based on this precarious ideal: 'Nothing about his betrothed pleased him more than her resolute determination to carry to its utmost limits that ritual of ignoring the "unpleasant" in which they had both been brought up.' In the story that follows Edith Wharton tries to make clear what this innocence costs. The measure of change wrought in Archer's outlook by his experience with Ellen is suggested by a sentence occurring midway in the novel, before the echo of his earlier belief has quite died away: 'Ah, no, he did not want May to have that kind of innocence, the innocence that seals the mind against imagination and the heart against experience!' . . . When he returns to May Welland, it is to the ultimate realisation that, like John Marcher in James's 'The Beast in the Jungle', he is the man 'to whom nothing was ever to happen'.[1]

The evaluations involved in this criticism are fairly obvious: it is reasonable to be open to change, experiment, challenge and novelty, and unreasonable to ignore the opportunities for these things. For similar reasons, it seems to me, Edmund Wilson describes *The Age of Innocence* as follows:

> Countess Olenska – returns to the United States to intrude upon and disturb the existence of a conservative provincial society . . . she attracts and almost captivates an intelligent man of the community who turns out, in the long run, to be unable to muster the courage to take her, and who allows her to go back to Europe.[2]

These critics ignore the moral notions involved in the relations which Edith Wharton depicts. In making the separation between Ellen Olenska and Newland Archer solely a product of weakness, Wilson is distorting the moral integrity it also exemplifies. Blake Nevius's characterisation of Newland Archer is deficient for similar reasons. In discussing them further we can see how far-reaching an influence an abstracted notion of reasonableness has had on the critics.

Wilson is wrong in thinking that Newland Archer's decision to stay in old New York is simply the result of weakness on his part. Wilson finds Newland Archer's decline after his initial protest against the old ways paralleled in Edith Wharton's later works. He claims that they 'show a dismay and a shrinking before what seemed to her the social and moral chaos of an age which was battering down the old edifice that she herself had once depicted as a prison.

[1] Ibid., pp. 168–9.
[2] Edmund Wilson, 'Justice to Edith Wharton', ibid., p. 26.

Perhaps, after all, the old mismated couples who had stayed married in deference to the decencies were better than the new divorced who were not aware of any duties at all'.[1] If Edith Wharton's view of the new is open at times to these charges, is not Wilson in danger of precisely the same deficiencies in his attitude to the old? He tends to write them off as deference to decencies, and his language implies that there is little more to be found here than sham, arid convention, and doing the done thing. When he describes Ellen Olenska's role in the novel as a narrow failure to capture one of the more intelligent of old New York's social clan, there is an unmistakable implication that if intelligence had its way, everyone would break out of the self-imposed prison they had devised for themselves. Similarly, when Nevius contrasts the protectionism, conventionalism and conformity of May Welland with the imagination, experience, protest and unpredictability offered by Ellen Olenska, there is little doubt as to which side he thinks exemplifies intelligence, and which exemplifies unthinking obedience, 'the dull unthinking round of duties', to use the description which Lionel Trilling gives to 'the morality of inertia' which he claims to find in Edith Wharton's *Ethan Frome*.[2]

Of course these critics could be right, but I am suggesting that a closer examination of Edith Wharton's best work shows that they are wrong. Furthermore, they are wrong because they are in the grip of an abstracted concept of reasonableness which here takes the form of the unwarrantable assumption that intelligence must take a specific form; one that excludes the kind of intelligence and integrity one finds in Edith Wharton's old New York. The critics are in danger of abstracting a standard of intelligence and reasonableness from the variety of such standards, and using it as a means of assessing different ways of living. In so far as they do so, they are not dissimilar to the reasonable man I characterised earlier. His first characteristic, you will recall, was his insistence that we must have reasons for our values. In relation to Edith Wharton's *The Age of Innocence* he is likely to ask for reasons for the conformity to decorum and rigid standards, and for the ignoring of opportunities for wider experience and imagination. His answer, in our time, is almost certain to be that no good reason can be found for such conformity, and that those who become its victims, like Newland Archer, are doomed to waste their lives.

'That it has all been a waste' is not an infrequent reaction on completing a reading of *The Age of Innocence*. In making such a

---

[1] Ibid., p. 29.
[2] Lionel Trilling, 'The Morality of Inertia', ibid., p. 145.

judgment high priority is given to the importance of satisfying genuine love, talking out difficulties in frank open discussion, making up one's own mind on moral issues and not paying too much attention to what one's parents or one's family have to say on the matter, and the conviction that since one only has one life to live, one should not allow its course to be determined by others. It is essential to understand that it is no part of my intention in this lecture to criticise these moral beliefs. Still less do I want to deny that people can or should criticise different attitudes in terms of them. What I am protesting against is the equation of these beliefs with intelligence as such, such that any beliefs which conflict with them are ruled out of court as moral possibilities. In this way, conflicting beliefs can be accused of lacking intelligence and reasonableness, and the illusion created that this conclusion has been reached by appeal to a norm which is independent of the moral beliefs involved. As a result of this illusion, the moral beliefs which are said to be inferior are almost certain to be ignored or distorted. Indeed, one may find it being denied that they are moral beliefs at all.

Such is the hold of an abstracted concept of reasonableness on the thinking of certain critics. Before considering the philosophical criticisms that can be made of such an influence, it is necessary to give an account of what such abstractions ignore in Edith Wharton's work, namely, the moral ideas which enter into the relationships she depicts; one must show that these are genuinely moral ideas. This can only be achieved by waiting on the novel.

4. WAITING ON THE NOVEL

Can one see more than dull unthinking conformity in Newland Archer and May Welland? I believe one can, and so do other critics of the work. Louis Auchincloss says that despite Newland Archer's decision to marry May Welland and not to elope with Ellen Olenska, 'There is no feeling, however, that Archer has condemned himself and the Countess to an unrewarding life of frustration'.[1] Why is this so? It could hardly be the case if, as we have been told, the decision was merely the product of deference to duties due to lack of nerve. There must be something more positive about the decision. The key to this is to be found in what happens when, having mechanically put the case against her divorcing her husband, Archer finds himself in love with Ellen Olenska, and pleads with her to come away with him. She has perceived a moral

---

[1] Louis Auchincloss, 'Edith Wharton and Her New Yorks', ibid., p. 38.

reality in what to him was little more than decorum. When Ellen reminds him that he is betrothed and that she is married, he replies, ' "Nonsense! It's too late for that sort of thing. We've no right to lie to other people or to ourselves" '. But Ellen Olenska is able to tell him what she has learnt from him:

'New York simply meant peace and freedom to me: it was coming home. And I was so happy at being among my own people that everyone I met seemed kind and good, and glad to see me. But from the very beginning,' she continued, 'I felt that there was no one as kind as you; no one who gave me reasons that I understood for doing what at first seemed so hard and – unnecessary. The very good people didn't convince me; I felt they'd never be tempted. But you knew; you understood; you had felt the world outside tugging at one with all its golden hands – and yet you hated the things it asks of one; you hated happiness bought by disloyalty and cruelty and indifference. That was what I'd never known before – and it's better than anything I've known.'

When Newland Archer appeals to rights, their right to happiness and the fact that May Welland has no right to ask them to forgo it, Ellen Olenska simply replies, 'Ah, you've taught me what an ugly word that is'.

It is true that for some time after his marriage Ellen is seldom out of Newland Archer's thoughts. He is desperately unhappy, and, without doubt, she is unhappy too. Yet, even so, when Archer does meet her again, it is to be told 'It was you who made me understand that under the dullness there are things so fine and sensitive and delicate that even those I most cared for in my other life look cheap by comparison'. The force with which Edith Wharton portrays the dullness and conventionality in society should not obscure the sterner stuff she also shows us. As Auchincloss says, 'This is the climax of the message: that under the thick glass of convention blooms the fine, fragile flower of patient suffering and denial. To drop out of society is as vulgar as to predominate; one must endure and properly smile'.[1] Sometimes, the propriety of the smile may all but hide the moral strength beneath it. This is so in the case of May Welland.

According to Nevius, 'May Welland personifies all the evasions and compromises of his (Archer's) clan, she is the "safe" alternative'. This, it is true, is how Newland Archer thought of his wife at many times, but it leaves out a great deal if it is meant as a final judgment

[1] Ibid., p. 38.

by the reader. After his wife's death, through his son, Archer learns
that there was more to his wife's character than he had realised.

' . . . you date, you see, dear old boy. But mother said . . . '
'Your mother?'
'Yes: the day before she died. It was when she sent for me
alone – you remember? She said she knew we were safe with you
and always would be, because once, when she asked you to,
you'd given up the thing you most wanted.'
Archer received this communication in silence . . . At length
he said in a low voice, 'She never asked me'.
'No, I forgot. You never did ask each other anything, did you?
And you never told each other anything. You just sat and watched
each other, and guessed at what was going on underneath.'

Another critic, Louis Coxe, in what I regard as the finest essay in
Irving Howe's collection, asks,

The total commitment of May to her world and to Newland
Archer: is there nothing admirable in this? Nothing of the
heroic? For I believe that if any character in this novel partakes
of the heroic nature, it is indeed May Welland, she of the pink
and white surface and the candid glance, whose capacity for
passion and sacrifice her husband never knew.[1]

Finally, are we to assume that Archer's reflections on his life,
culminating in this revelation about his wife, had no effect on him,
that the truths he had unwittingly conveyed to Ellen Olenska had
not come home to him? Hardly. At the end of the novel we see him
with another chance to meet Ellen Olenska. He thinks, fleetingly,
that even if at fifty-seven it is too late for summer dreams, it may
not be too late for friendship and comradeship. In the end however he
decides not to go up to her hotel room and remains in the park. He
has sent his son ahead of him and imagines how he will be received.

'It's more real to me here than if I went up,' he suddenly
heard himself say; and the fear lest that last shadow of reality
should lose its edge kept him rooted to his seat as the minutes
succeeded each other.
He sat for a long time on the bench in the thickening dusk, his
eyes never turning from the balcony. At length a light shone
through the windows, and a moment later a manservant came out
on the balcony, drew up the awnings, and closed the shutters.
At that, as if it had been the signal he waited for, Newland
Archer got up slowly and walked back alone to his hotel.

[1] Louis O. Coxe, 'What Edith Wharton Saw in Innocence,' ibid., p. 159.

If Archer is to think of Ellen Olenska at all now, it is in the context of the great decision she had once made, and which had governed most of his life. Is this a man 'to whom nothing was ever to happen'?

5. PHILOSOPHICAL CONSEQUENCES OF WAITING ON THE NOVEL

The philosophical consequences of waiting on Edith Wharton's novel are that the artificiality of an abstracted concept of reasonableness is revealed. The tenets of the reasonable man are shown to be equally artificial. In fact, all these tenets are reversed. Let us see how this comes about.

We have seen that Newland Archer, Ellen Olenska and May Welland, in different ways, embody the old New York morality Edith Wharton wanted to depict. But could we say, as some philosophers insist we must say, that these characters have reasons for their values? On the contrary, their values constitute their reasons. Without taking these values into account, one cannot understand their actions or even their descriptions of situations in which action is called for. Without the values which enter into it, the choice facing Ellen Olenska is unintelligible. Before Archer convinces her otherwise, the satisfaction of true love and her own happiness would have been of paramount importance to her. She would have described her elopement with Archer as a flight to freedom. But when she becomes aware of other values, values involving suffering, denial, endurance, discipline, she can no longer see things in that way. She says that her former way of looking at things is cheap by comparison. This judgment is not arrived at however by cashing the two attitudes into a common coinage by which one can be demonstrated to be cheaper than the other. This is how the reasonable man would have us argue. Ellen Olenska's judgment bears no relation to such an argument. On the contrary, her judgment about her former attitude is intelligible only in terms of the new moral perspective she comes to embrace.

What has become of the claim that one must have reasons for one's values? Of course, a person can provide moral reasons for an action in specific circumstances. Ellen Olenska claimed that Newland Archer gave her such reasons without realising it. But these are not the reasons that the reasonable man has in mind. These reasons already have a moral character, whereas he is looking for a further justification for such reasons. A natural context for such talk would be those cases where a person has hidden reasons for holding moral beliefs. A so-called allegiance to moral values may turn out to be sham, hypocrisy, pretence or self-deception. The presence of such reasons indicates that a person has a mere external relation to the values in question.

Edith Wharton depicts an external relation to values in her portrayal of Undine Spragg in *The Custom of the Country*. Undine personifies the *nouveaux riches* who were being created by the financial empires being formed in the cities of the Midwest. She comes to threaten the placid society we find in *The Age of Innocence*. Her values at any time are essentially transient, serving the constant need for new pleasures, new thrills, new conquests. Undine goes from marriage to marriage unable to share any of the genuine enthusiasms or values of her husbands, or to appreciate the traditions of the families she enters into. Her attitude can be summed up by the way she reacts to a husband's comment on her insistence on being painted by a fashionable portrait painter. The husband remarks, 'Oh, if a "smart" portrait's all you want!' to which she replies, 'I want what the others want'. With such an attitude she is condemned to perpetual rootlessness. Despite the fact that she ends up by marrying someone whose love of money and status is as all-consuming as her own, our last glimpse of her sees her regretting that as a result of her divorces she can never be the wife of an ambassador!

It is precisely because Undine Spragg has reasons for her values which are externally related to those values, that we see in her a fundamental rootlessness in which no form of decency can grow or flourish. The difference between Undine Spragg and the characters in *The Age of Innocence* we have discussed can be expressed once again by saying that whereas she has reasons for her values, their values were their reasons.

These conclusions have drastic consequences for the reasonable man's notion of moral change. For him, since the reasons for such change must be of the same kind as those which supported prior allegiances, change occurs within a unified rational system. The inadequacy of this view can be brought out by reference to one incident in *The Age of Innocence*.

Despite the fact that Archer's son reveals depths of character in his mother which his father had never appreciated, he can hardly appreciate them. For Dallas, the son, his parents' attitudes are dated, outmoded, eccentric. Louis Coxe says, rightly, that

For Dallas it would have been so simple: run away with Ellen Olenska and hang what people will say. . . . Times have changed, and in this simpler and freer world of Dallas' young manhood, there are no occasions to exercise the feelings nor nourish passion. ... Can Dallas or anyone like him begin to understand the meaning of the kind of feelings Archer has known? Have they the time? the imagination? the passion? What can the notion of a buried life mean to one who can conceive only of surface?[1]

To Dallas, the relationship between his parents is 'a deaf and dumb asylum'.

If one compares the views of Newland Archer's generation with those of his son, can one appeal to a common criterion of reasonableness which would bring out the character of the differences between them? It is difficult to see how one could do so in general. What we see is that many of the values of one generation mean little to the other. With the social changes Edith Wharton describes so well, the old values of respect for tradition, endurance, loyalty, faithfulness, and the possibility of a buried life, that is, burying one's strongest desires, are eroded by the increasing dominance of new values characterised by frankness, openness, articulate honesty, courage and experiment. A common criterion of reasonableness is not necessary in order to explain such changes. One need only bring out the content of the opposing values to show how they naturally militate against each other. To call one set of beliefs irrational often obscures what disagreement amounts to in this context; that the disagreement is itself an expression or a product of a moral judgment.

If these conclusions are correct, one can no longer believe, as the reasonable man does, in the unity of reason. Fundamental changes in moral perspectives need no longer be seen as the rejection and replacing of hypotheses or policies within a single framework within which moral beliefs must be determined. Old values do die, and new ones take their place. What separates Archer and his son is not a matter of different tentative beliefs within a common notion of reason but, rather, different ways of looking at the world, different conceptions of what is important in life.

If these differences in moral perspective are not recognised there is a danger not simply of distorting the reality of radical change, but also of misdescribing discarded beliefs as taboos and inhibitions. We see this latter danger exemplified to some extent in Dallas' mildly amused view of his parents' attitudes. With later generations, with which we are more familiar, amusement gives way to arrogance. It is assumed that earlier generations have wanted all along to be just

---

[1] Louis O. Coxe, 'What Edith Wharton Saw in Innocence', ibid., pp. 157–8.

as we are. It is often suggested that earlier generations are not really doing or believing what they think they are doing and believing. Their beliefs, it is said, form a prison which suppresses and confines their real desires.

The credibility of this view depends, to a large extent, on examples of ways of living already in decline, where nominal existence has outlived actual existence. If one thinks of lost generations, following old rules out of habit or from fear of social sanctions, alienated from their background, but unable to embrace an alternative, it is not hard to see how it can be said that these people are not at home in their world, that they are not doing what they think they are doing. In *The House of Mirth* Edith Wharton shows the empty respectability which results from the decline of old New York morality. Irving Howe describes the situation as follows:

> The action of *The House of Mirth* occurs in the first years of the twentieth century, several stages and a few decades beyond the dispossession of old New York. We barely see any representatives of the faded aristocracy; what we do see in the first half of the book are several of its distant offshoots and descendants, most of them already twisted by the vulgarity of the new bourgeoisie yet, for no very good reasons, still contemptuous of it. The standards of these characters who have any claim to the old aristocracy are not so much guides to their own conduct as strategies for the exclusion of outsiders . . . they have kept some pretence to social superiority, but very little right to it. . . .[1]

In such situations as these it can be said, with justice, that things are not what they seem. What one must not do is to generalise indiscriminately from such examples. For instance, one cannot say that what Newland Archer really wants, despite what he says and does, is what his son and his generation realise. It would be a distortion to say that Archer wants to follow his desires without a second thought in the way Dallas does. The notion of a buried life is important to Archer and determines the degree of importance he attaches to satisfying one's desires. To say that Archer must have been wanting all along what Dallas achieved, to say that anyone who loved the standards of old New York must have been deceiving himself, one would have to produce evidence of tension, self-deception or alienation. When the judgment is made in the absence of such evidence, one conception of what is worthwhile in life is being made a criterion of rationality by which all other conceptions must be judged. At this stage, a moral judgment has been changed

[1] Irving Howe, 'A Reading of The House of Mirth', ibid., p. 122.

into a metaphysical thesis about what all men want and the essence of rational conduct. No such thesis can be found in Edith Wharton. Louis Coxe says that in contrasting Newland Archer, the near-rebel, with May Welland, the total conformist,

> a lesser novelist would have been content to rest, in the mere showing of the processes by which an American with separatist tendencies is broken to harness and curb. (This corresponds to what Edmund Wilson saw in the novel.) That she does not leave it at this adds dimension to the book and to the novelist's vision. The emphasis rests finally upon the ways in which an individual, in more or less settled times, can come to identify his illusions with those of his world. The rightness or wrongness of such identification we may determine if we can, though for my part I would say that the triumph of Edith Wharton's realism strikes one as most sweeping in just her very refusal to draw any such line: she seems merely to say, that is the way things were for these people. Had you done differently, it would have been a different time, place and cast.[1]

This brings us to the last characteristic of the reasonable man, namely his tendency to see the society to which he belongs as the product of a coming of age in which old inhibitions and taboos have been cast off. The confusion is in the claim that this *must* be the case, and in the *a priori* ruling out of the possibility of decline and loss in a society. There is no confusion in the claim that a whole society could be in the grip of self-deception. Edith Wharton, in writing *The House of Mirth*, asked herself how 'could a society of irresponsible pleasure-seekers be said to have, on the "old woes of the world", any deeper bearing than the people composing such a society could guess?' She answered: 'A frivolous society can acquire dramatic significance only through what its frivolity destroys. Its tragic implication lies in its power of debasing people and ideas'. That such comments have a point is not in dispute. What is in dispute is the larger claim that the heterogeneity of morals can be reduced to some kind of rational unity.

When some beliefs and values give way to others, some may want to condemn the old ways as wrong, and even as wicked. That is their privilege. What cannot be said, in general, is that the old ways were irrational, that men had reasons for adopting them which seemed good at the time, that men discovered better reasons for rejecting them, and having thus progressed again and again, have now achieved the freedom which only reason can bring. Such wholesale

[1] Op. cit., p. 160.

judgments are invariably confused. What one can say often is that a society is better or worse than its predecessors in certain respects. Edith Wharton however shows us another possibility, namely that of refraining from such judgments and being content to observe that whereas people once thought about certain matters in a particular way, we no longer do so.

I am not suggesting that the literary judgments about Edith Wharton, which, I have claimed, many critics ignore, can be arrived at independently of the moral beliefs or sympathies of the critics. To do so would be to advocate a concept of literary criticism as abstracted as the concept of reasonableness I have been attacking. A critic must be able to sympathise with a variety of moral beliefs in order to recognise their seriousness. A critic's moral beliefs may be such, however, as to rule out certain attitudes as trivial, and a novel which gave serious attention to these would be criticised by him for this very reason.[1] If this happened with too many moral beliefs, however, the critic's narrowness would itself count against his standing as a critic.[2]

6. CONCLUSION

In the brief look we have taken at Edith Wharton's novels, we have reversed and rejected all the reasonable man's principles. If I am right in thinking that these principles underlie a great deal of contemporary moral philosophy, the reason why there should be a tension between moral philosophy and the novel is not hard to find.

I shall end as I began by calling attention to the misgivings that are felt by some philosophers about giving a detailed analysis of examples taken from literature. In his *Critique of Linguistic Philosophy*, C. W. K. Mundle is wary of what he detects as 'a method of teaching ethics (which) has become popular in parts of Wales and England. This is to read long extracts from Russian novels or Existentialist plays, describing moral dilemmas'. Mundle says that 'When well done, this is an excellent way of starting arguments about *what* you would have done in the problem situations. And, sometimes, about *why*.'[3] To this, as we have seen, Edith Wharton would reply, 'Had

[1] These points were made by Mr H. O. Mounce in the discussion referred to on p. 48 footnote 2.

[2] I have examined one example of such narrowness in 'Moral Presuppositions and Literary Judgement', *The Human World*, No. 6, 1972.

[3] C. W. K. Mundle, *A Critique of Linguistic Philosophy* (Clarendon Press, Oxford, 1970) p. 14.

you done differently, it would have been a different time, place, and cast'. Mundle's concern to determine the content and justification of moral conduct goes with his conception of moral philosophy as the discovery of 'rules as to how *people* in *general* ought to act'. After all, he argues, since all moral problems and beliefs are called 'moral', we must be concerned with the same thing in all of them.

Our discussion of Edith Wharton's work should help us to see that the question of what we mean by allegiance and change in morality does not admit of a *general* answer. The assumption that moral philosophy can provide such an answer is but another symptom of the desire for tidiness and simplicity in ethics from which attention to literature can help to deliver us. As Eugene Kamenka has said, 'The complexity of individuals and "their" interests has long been recognised in literature, especially in the novel; it is time that it was more clearly recognised in ethics'.[1]

---

[1] E. Kamenka, *Marxism and Ethics* (Macmillan 1969) p. 35.

4

THE AUTONOMY OF ART

John Casey[1]

PART I

IN his *Aesthetic* Croce makes some remarks upon the subject of sincerity:

> Artists protest vainly: 'Lasciva est nobis pagina, vita proba'. They are merely taxed (in addition) with lying and hypocrisy. How far more prudent you were, poor women of Verona, when you founded your belief that Dante had really descended to Hell upon his blackened countenance. Yours was at any rate an historical conjecture.
>
> Finally, *sincerity* imposed as a duty upon the artist (a law of ethics also said to be a law of aesthetic) rests upon another double meaning. For by sincerity may be meant, in the first place, the moral duty not to deceive one's neighbour; and in that case it is foreign to the artist. For indeed he deceives no one, since he gives form to what is already in his soul. He would only deceive if he were to betray his duty as an artist by failing to execute his task in its essential nature. If lies and deceit are in his soul, then the form which he gives to these things cannot be deceit or lies, precisely because it is aesthetic. If an artist be a charlatan, a liar, or a miscreant, he purifies his other self by reflecting it in art. If by sincerity be meant, in the second place, fulness and truth of expression, it is clear that this second sense has no relation to the ethical concept. The law, called both ethical and aesthetic, reveals itself here as nothing but a word used by both Ethics and Aesthetic (pp. 53–4).

[1] I am grateful to Dr J. E. J. Altham for criticisms. I am particularly indebted to Mr Roger Scruton for much helpful criticism, and for letting me make use of an unpublished manuscript, from which I derived several helpful suggestions. I am grateful to the University of Bristol for an invitation to lecture which resulted in an earlier version of the present paper.

In this passage Croce commits himself to a form of the doctrine that art is 'autonomous'. Many critics and aestheticians, especially in the nineteenth and twentieth centuries, have argued in favour of this doctrine.

In fact it would be misleading to speak as though there were a single doctrine. Art has been held to be autonomous in many senses, and even if the doctrine is true when interpreted one way, there are other ways of interpreting it such that it is certainly false. Some people have thought for instance that there is a distinct category of aesthetic experience, distinct from every other sort of experience, yet somehow essential to our understanding of works of art. Again it is sometimes said[1] that to describe the aesthetic character of something is to engage in an activity quite different from any other sort of describing. Works of art have an aesthetic character quite distinct from their character as physical objects, or as patterns of sound and meaning. Aesthetic properties – properties such as features of expression – are a distinct kind of property. They are properties essential to an object regarded as a work of art, but are logically unrelated to any other properties it might have.

This view of autonomy – which seems to be close to Croce's remarks about sincerity – often goes with another, as it did for Croce. This third view is perhaps the most familiar, and is a characteristic doctrine of what is in America called 'the New Criticism'. This doctrine holds that in trying to understand a work of art we cannot make use of facts external to the work itself – facts of biography, convention and (perhaps) intention. Such facts would be irrelevant to appreciation or criticism. This theory of autonomy runs together a lot of different ideas, and I shall not be able to discuss it properly now. Indeed, it seems to me that the very important question of how far art is autonomous in this third sense remains very obscure until we have become clearer about whether it is autonomous in the second sense. So I shall mostly concentrate on this second sense.

It is worth mentioning, that although it is because of its connection with the third sense – the New Criticism sense – that Croce's theory might seem to have a renewed importance, its real interest probably derives from its connection with the notion of autonomy in the *first* sense – the autonomy of aesthetic experience. Partly through the influence of Kant and Schopenhauer, it is this notion of autonomy which has preoccupied aestheticians in modern times. The 'aesthetic attitude' has sometimes been thought of as one of 'pure contemplation' quite remote from 'practical attitudes', and hence not vulner-

[1] See F. Sibley, *Philosophical Review*, 1959 and 1965.

able to moral or for that matter political considerations. This view of art has probably made some contribution to the modern orthodoxy which tends to regard the direction or censorship of works of art not merely as foolish or immoral, but as in some fundamental sense futile and misconceived. And of course in the nineteenth century a theory of the autonomy of art became a reply to the hostility or philistinism of bourgeois, industrial society and indeed to the whole doctrine of Utilitarianism. This was deepened – particularly by Matthew Arnold – to become a theory of Culture, a quasi-ethical doctrine which held that an humane artistic and literary tradition must stand in opposition to the utilitarian values of philistine society. In this form the doctrine, or something like it, is still current.

Croce's answer to the question of aesthetic autonomy is extremely radical. He does not simply propose some special aesthetic 'experience', and he does not simply attempt to give art a special place amongst human activities. Rather he reduces the question to its barest logical form. The notion of 'sincerity', he says, simply has a different meaning when used in aesthetics from the one it has when used in ethics. It is a thoroughly ambiguous term, its use in relation to art being only punningly related to its use in relation to people's words and actions. Sincerity as an aesthetic property is quite distinct from sincerity as a moral property.

A consistent aesthetic theory in Crocean terms would require that it is not only terms like 'sincere' which are ambiguous as between art and life, but also any other terms used to express what have been called 'aesthetic concepts'[1] – for instance, terms which refer to the emotional or expressive quality of a work of art – 'sad' 'expresses grief' and so on. I shall assume that the question is a general one about the connection between the use of certain terms to refer to people and their use to refer to works of art.

The most obvious argument in favour of Croce's view is this: if I say that a man is sincere, it could be said, I mean such things as that he does not deliberately mislead about his intentions, beliefs and feelings. He says that he intends, or wishes, to do something, for example, and he really does intend or wish to do it. Or he might express pity for someone, and he really does feel pity. But surely nothing like this applies to works of art. If a poem 'expresses' certain feelings, it does not follow that they are feelings that anyone 'has'. It certainly does not follow that the poet has or had them. We know that Milton and King had no flocks to batten, and that Milton probably did not feel the grief that is expressed in *Lycidas*.

[1] See F. Sibley, 'Aesthetic Concepts', *Philosophical Review*, 1959.

It might be held that we are nevertheless still attributing feelings of grief to *someone* in saying that the poem is an 'expression' of grief. It could be held, for example, that to say that a poem expresses certain feelings is to say that the reader is likely to have these feelings, is likely to respond in a certain way to it. But there are grave difficulties in the way of any view which proposes what we might call an 'external' relationship between the reader and the poem. Broadly speaking – and without arguing for this view here – we might want to say that although something about the response of a possible audience might be implied when we say that a poem expresses something, nevertheless any statement about what a poem expresses is categorical, and cannot be reduced to a hypothetical statement about the reactions of its readers. (Here we can see how various different theories of the autonomy of art hang together).

Therefore when we apply the notion of sincerity to the feelings expressed by, or in a poem, there seems to be something lacking – something which is essential to the term when it is used to describe feelings in a person. The point is general, and seems to apply to the whole notion of artistic expression. A work of art can be sentimental, sad, expressive and so on – and yet it is inanimate. So are we not forced to say that 'sincerity' and 'sadness' are only to be found in works of art in a metaphorical – or even, as Croce thinks – in a punning sense?

Yet this view is fundamentally improbable. The whole point of calling a work of art 'sincere' or 'sad' is to bring it into relation with the sincerity and sadness of human beings. Sincerity in art and sincerity in life seem to be parts of the same complex phenomenon. If the connection between 'sincere' for example as used of works of art and 'sincere' as used of people were merely that of a pun (or homonym) then the term would lose all its point. There are many other terms which are in the same boat – sad, sentimental, serious, gay, sprightly and so on. If their aesthetic use is only punningly related to their application to human beings, the language of aesthetics would completely collapse.

Perhaps though, we can salvage part of Croce's theory by expressing it in more moderate terms – terms which will still preserve the autonomy of art. We might say, for instance, that the use of emotion terms, and quasi-ethical terms like 'sincerity' in aesthetics, is not simply a punning use. It is metaphorically related, or related by a sort of conceptual extension, to the use of these terms to talk of persons and their mental states. It is in their application to persons that the primary meaning of these terms is exhibited; in learning to apply them to works of art, we show a more sophisticated, imaginative grasp of them.

This theory is more subtle; it retains part of the notion of autonomy, while replacing the doctrine that terms have a different meaning when applied to works of art with the milder idea that they have the same meaning, but extended, or stretched as it were. Aesthetic concepts are shown to be dependent on and secondary to ordinary (life) concepts; and the criterion for a concept's being aesthetic is that its exercise shows unusual sensitivity or imagination – the traditional notion of the aesthetic consciousness.

This view is (somewhat indirectly) supported by the following argument: If terms like sincerity are used in aesthetics in a way which is genuinely related to their use outside aesthetics, their aesthetic use must nevertheless be secondary to their use as applied to persons; for unless a man could recognise sincerity in *people*, he could not recognise it in works of art, and he could not meaningfully employ the term in talking about works of art. Or we might say, a man who does not possess the concept of sincerity in life, could not possibly come to possess it through finding it instantiated in works of art. Similarly with sadness: it is primarily persons who can be sad. If people could not be sad, we would simply have no use for the notion of a work of art's being sad. Indeed, if people were incapable of sadness, we should simply have no use for a term like 'sad' at all.

The argument can go further: When we talk about an *expression* of sadness, we ultimately rely upon the notion of people being sad. If what we now call a sad expression on a face never went with feelings of sadness, then it would not be what we now call a 'sad' expression. To call it a sad expression is not merely to give a neutral description of the disposition of the features; it is to bring it under a concept which centrally involves the notion of people being sad, of sad feelings.[1] We might say that the *expressiveness* of a sad expression – that which makes a certain disposition of the features into an expression at all – (logically) depends upon the occurrence (as a sort of general background of possibilities) of sad feelings. So to talk of 'sad' faces would be to use the term as derivatively as when we talk of 'sad' poems or pictures. It would be quite sufficient for saying that a man knew what sadness was if he were only capable of knowing that people were sad and was incapable of recognising whole areas of sad expression – for example, sad works of art, or even sad faces.

This is a plausible argument, but not, I think, plausible enough.

[1] Cf. Richard Wollheim, 'Expression', *The Human Agent, Royal Institute of Philosophy Lectures*, vol. 1.

There are certainly very many people who are sensitive to expressions of feeling in life, but who are quite unable to grasp the 'expressiveness' of works of art. Philistinism and emotional and moral sensitivity are not incompatible. (The fact that this happens has led people to think that when we talk of works of art as 'expressive' we cannot mean that they express anything; or, alternatively, if they do express feeling, then feeling as expressed in a work of art means something quite different from feeling as experienced in life.) But cases where the emotionally sensitive man does not grasp the expressiveness of works of art are usually also cases where he just does not understand them – has not grasped the conventions according to which they are written, and so on. Of course there is a sense in which to say that such a man does not understand a work of art is a tautology, because part of what it is to understand a work of art is to grasp its expression. We need to ask: could there be a case of a person who understands a work of art but only in the sense of understanding what it *says*, what it represents – its referential qualities – but fails to grasp its emotional, or 'expressive' qualities? Can we say of such a man that he makes use of certain concepts in life, but for some reason does not 'extend' them to works of art?

In fact this sort of case is very difficult to imagine. Our natural inclination, first of all, is to say that certain 'expressive' qualities are as undeniably present in a work of literature as in anything a man might *say* in actual life.

> Or ever the silver cord be loosed, or the golden bowl be broken, or the pitcher be broken at the fountain, or the wheel broken at the cistern.
> Then shall the dust return to the earth as it was: and the spirit shall return unto God who gave it.

A man who could recognise gravity and seriousness in the actual speech of other men, but who simply had no idea whether that passage from *Ecclesiastes* were weighty and grave rather than sprightly and gay is very difficult to imagine. (Or at any rate we can imagine him, just as we can imagine any sort of gross inconsistency in behaviour.) It is not a question of his making a mistake about style or conventions – as Matthew Arnold perhaps does when he discovers in his 'touchstones' a quality of stoic resignation which is certainly alien to some of them. We assume he is aware of the conventions.

Now I think a theory of artistic autonomy based upon that sort of supposition and nothing else, is just not interesting. It merely relies upon the undeniable fact that gross inconsistencies are possible in human behaviour. It is no more interesting than, for instance, a theory of morality which held that since I may usually be able to detect envy in other people, but not in myself, the term 'envy' has a different meaning when applied to others from the one it would have if applied to me.

Ultimately we must come to see that sad feelings and sad expressions are not separately identifiable. My ability to recognise someone else as sad is of a piece with my ability to recognise sad expressions. The sense in which 'sad' names a property of an expression is not subsidiary to the sense in which it names a feeling; the two senses are indistinguishable, and neither is an extension of the other. It is only because there are sad expressions that the concept of sadness has application. While it is not possible for sad feelings to exist without the possibility of sad expressions – without expressive behaviour – there are occasions on which sad expressions can exist without sadness, and hence where our judgment that something constitutes a sad expression is divorced from any inclination to attribute sad feelings to a subject. Such is the case when we read a sad poem.

It may be objected that the notion of a sad expression is still obscure. All that the familiar arguments show, it might be said, is that we cannot attribute emotion to a being except on the basis of some outward manifestation. But does it follow that the outward manifestation must be *expressive*, in the way in which poetry is said to be expressive? Might it not be sufficient, for example, if the subject merely stated that he had some emotion? If this gives us a sufficient basis for attributing emotion to a subject, why then should we need the further notion of expressiveness?

But can there be such a thing as a statement of emotion in the absence of the possibility of expressive behaviour? To imagine such a thing would be like imagining a race of people just like human beings intellectually, but with certain robot-like features. Their faces, for instance, and also their voices, are expressionless; they do not engage in expressive behaviour; they do not speak with a tone of voice; they merely state that they have certain feelings, intentions or beliefs.

There is obviously something very odd about this supposition. A man may stoically assert that he is sad – just as he may assert that he is in pain – as though he were simply conveying a piece of information. But in the absence of a general possibility of expressive behaviour it is very difficult to say how such utterances can even be taken as genuine statements or assertions. Under what circumstances, for example, could we say of an 'I speak your weight' machine that it made statements? We can imagine, perhaps, some invisible being speaking through the machine, but the being would not *be* the machine. This for two reasons: first, it makes no sense to us that a machine should make statements about its own feelings if we have no independent means of finding out whether its statements are true. For unless we can do this it will be impossible to say whether or not the machine understands the meaning of what it says, and therefore it will be impossible to know whether it is actually making a statement or not. (The idea of its making a statement just does not have application in the absence of any independent check on whether what it says is true – but if there is no expression how can there be such an independent check?) Moreover, more generally, we cannot say that a being makes statements at all (whether or not they are statements about its own supposed mental states) if it does not have beliefs. A statement is itself an expression of belief. But it can only serve as a criterion of what a creature believes if there is something more to the notion of believing than simply producing utterances: in the absence of an independent criterion the concept of belief is redundant. But we can have no independent check upon a creature's beliefs if we know nothing of its desires, expectations, etc., and we can know nothing of these if they could not be expressed in behaviour. And the expression of desires is akin to emotional expression. In other words, emotional expression is a fundamental part of the concept of mind. Without it it is difficult to make sense of the notion of communication at all. It should not be considered an objection to this view that we can easily imagine – or that there certainly exist – cases of people who are almost completely paralysed, so that their complex verbal expression is set against an extremely attenuated possibility of physical expression. The point is, surely, that we can have an idea of what sort of physical or behavioural expression would be open to them if they were not paralysed. With a paralysed human body we know how the 'unexpressed' emotion – or pain – would or could be expressed if the man were not paralysed. So we can regard paralysis as a very special kind of *impediment*. It is only in virtue of this that we can have the notion of unexpressed emotion at all. If we did not have the notion of the natural, or direct expression of emotion we could not, surely, have the notion of cases where the expression had been inhibited or frustrated.

So the idea of a sad expression may be primitive, in the sense that the possibility of attributing sadness to people may depend upon the recognition of an intrinsic quality of expression.

Any philosophy of mind must then make room for an adequate notion of expressiveness and, if this is so and if the property of being expressive has the place that we have argued that it has, then there is no reason to deny that it is a property that might as well belong to passages of literature as to the words and gestures of ordinary human behaviour.

It is here that an antinomy is likely to develop between what may seem obvious to a literary critic and what may seem obvious to a philosopher. Imagine the following case: a man suffers a bereavement, and we have evidence in his behaviour that he feels the loss deeply. However it may be that his expression of his grief is inhibited in various ways: his behaviour may give evidence of his grief without *expressing* his grief. We might be able to infer his grief from his behaviour without its being the case that anything he does is an expression of grief. (For example, a man may suffer from sleeplessness because he is grief-stricken, but his sleeplessness may not be an expression of his grief.) Now without denying the reality or strength of his grief, we might reasonably say that his expression of his grief is inadequate. Suppose now that he decides to express his grief in some more formal fashion. He places a poem in the *In Memoriam* columns of a newspaper. The poem he chooses is maudlin and sentimental – a poem which, as an expression of grief, we should wish to call both inadequate and insincere, and which as an expression of *his* grief is peculiarly false. A philosopher might well argue that we cannot deduce from this that the man's grief either was or has become insincere. Nor can we say that his feelings are inadequate, although his expression of them is. For the poem was simply a rather complex verbal expression, and as such only one criterion amongst many. The rest of the man's behaviour showed that he was sincere. Therefore the presence of one expression which we might wish on independent grounds to describe as insincere can be overruled in the light of the criteria which show this expression to be anomalous. The man was sincere. His grief was real and deeply felt, and his gesture of putting the poem in the paper, springing as it did from a feeling which we know independently to be sincere, must have been an expression of that feeling. Therefore it was an expression of sincere grief.

The philosopher might go on to argue that sincerity is essentially a moral concept. A man's expression of his feelings may be inadequate for various reasons. He may be overpowered by his feelings, and therefore unable to express them adequately. This could reflect a defect of character but need not necessarily do so. It may be that he has not sufficient strength to cope with his feelings, but it may simply be that he is verbally incompetent. He may have too limited a vocabulary, insufficient experience and so on. A man deeply in

D

love may seek to express his love in an execrable poem. The poem might be an inadequate expression of his love, and might even show that he has no very full grasp or understanding of his own feelings; but it would not be insincere.

Insincerity, it seems, is a moral deficiency. It results from such things as self-pity, self-indulgence, cowardice, selfishness and so on. The falsification of feeling involved in insincerity always has a voluntary element.

Against this a critic might argue that such an account is over-simple. Everything about the poem was maudlin and sentimental. It is just impossible that the man both understood the poem and chose it as an expression of the sincere grief that we suppose he feels. Assuming that his choice of the poem was serious – that he seriously took it as expressing his feelings – then this expression is particularly telling. It reveals perhaps a hidden quality of his feelings, and it is impossible to count it as just one criterion among many. In choosing such an expression a man may reveal an insincerity in his feelings. Alternatively, in choosing such an expression of his feelings he may *introduce an element of insincerity* into his feelings.

So for a philosopher it is true that the man is sincere; for the critic it is possibly false. Should we not say then that there are two senses of 'sincerity'? In which case we are back where we started, with Croce's concept of autonomy.

I have argued that we cannot accept Croce's view, nor any view which so radically breaks the connection between aesthetic and non-aesthetic description. It seems then that we must find a way out of this antinomy. What I wish to examine is a line of thought which does enable us to escape the antinomy while accepting both its premises. For anyone who feels an instinctive agreement with *both* lines of argument I have given, this will be the most satisfactory solution. It has, moreover, the precedent of a whole tradition of philosophical thought.

The line of thought is roughly this: we admit that the evidence adduced by the philosopher counts with what would normally be sufficient strength in favour of sincerity. But we also allow that the evidence adduced by the critic simply cannot in these circumstances be ignored. For the choice of a maudlin poem has a significance that is quite unlike that of the behavioural expression of emotion; it entirely changes our picture of the emotion in a way that I shall attempt to describe. The antinomy therefore can only give rise to a *conflict* of criteria; it is not sufficient to introduce another sense of the term 'sincere'. Our discussion will show us, in fact, that the original analysis of sincerity was extremely superficial, and that the true concept of sincerity lies somewhere between the two artificial concepts that Croce argued to be separately applicable to art and to life.

PART II

Can we say with the critic that if a man chooses a maudlin poem to express his feelings he thereby introduces an element of insincerity into his feelings? One thing that might support the critic's line of thought is that we regard poems as peculiarly lucid expressions of feeling, expressions which somehow reveal the inner nature of the feeling. So we consider poems to be expressions of grief in just those cases where they are also particularly *expressive* of grief. For example a man may find that King's *Exequy* expressed his own grief better than anything he could say himself, and better than some other poem that seemed at first to express his own feelings completely. And the superiority of the King poem may derive from its being more expressive of grief. In other words, to the extent that one values a poem as an expression of grief, one thinks of it as peculiarly *expressive* of grief.

Now the important point about the case we are considering is that finding – or for that matter, writing – a maudlin poem to express one's grief cannot be considered just an accident, a quirk of behaviour. It is an intentional act, and the choice is governed by a conception of its object.[1] Indeed, when we express our feelings in words, we very often wish to influence our feelings, to bring them into relation with some ideal. For example, in *Sons and Lovers* Mr Morel talks about his wife's death in terms which show that he does feel his loss, but also that he is unable or unwilling to accept full consciousness of it:

> He had striven (he says) all his life to do what he could for her, and he'd nothing to reproach himself with. She was gone, but he'd done his best for her. He wiped his eyes with his white handkerchief. He'd nothing to reproach himself for, he repeated. All his life he'd done his best for her.
>
> And that was how he tried to dismiss her. He never thought of her personally. Everything deep in him he denied. Paul hated his

[1] Wollheim (op. cit.) seems to suggest that all expression is essentially intentional. We can, of course, use the term 'expression' in this way, but to do so is to use it independently of the concept of expressiveness which I have tried to describe. In a sense I am trying to elucidate the difference between the intentional and the unintentional 'betraying' or 'disclosure' of an emotion. In many points I shall agree with what Wollheim says in his valuable article.

father for sitting sentimentalising over her. He knew he would do it in the public houses. *For the real tragedy went on in Morel in spite of himself.* Sometimes, later, he came down from his afternoon sleep white and cowering.

Now when Croce discusses the 'aesthetic' sense of 'sincere' he takes it to be a matter of fully achieved, adequate expression. (This is also, essentially, Leavis's and Arnold's idea of sincerity in poetry.) He thinks that this makes sincerity in art quite unlike sincerity in life. But surely we can now see that there is no such neat distinction. One way of taking Morel's behaviour is as a straightforward ('moral') case of insincerity. He cannot face his true feelings, and therefore he talks in this shallow way. He is not merely inarticulate: 'Everything deep in him he *denied*'. Morel's way of representing his feelings to himself and to others cheapens them; this is something that, in his inarticulacy, he *does*. However, to interpret this passage as a simple case of self-deception is to miss a good deal of what Lawrence intends, and a good deal of the subtlety of the passage. Morel is in fact expressing himself in a conventional way about his wife's death, saying what he takes to be the normal thing. It is this conventional way of talking that imposes insincerity upon the expression of his feelings. A language which would express his feelings adequately is not readily available to Morel. To break through these perfunctory, conventional expressions of grief in order to grasp it would require an effort of *imagination* that cannot be expected or demanded of him.

Of the other criteria of Morel's feelings – his behaviour – Lawrence says: 'Sometimes, later, he came down from his afternoon sleep white and cowering.' (I shall return to this remark.) At the same time Lawrence says that 'the real tragedy went on in Morel in spite of himself'. Now I think that Lawrence here expresses exactly the relation between feeling and expression towards which I am trying to move. At the same time this suggests a possible clash between the literary and philosophical approach. At any rate, it suggests a clash between what someone who is trying to describe human motives in all their complexity would want to say, and the sort of analysis that it is reasonable to associate with the more naïve forms of behaviourism. On that sort of analysis there seems to be no problematic 'conflict of criteria'. If a man shows one sort of feeling in a whole range of his activities, but in just one activity – what he says – he evinces a different feeling, or a corruption of the same feeling, then we have a *simple* case of 'a conflict of criteria'. One thing points one way, other things the other. Verbal and behavioural criteria do not seem to be on different levels. Indeed, behavioural criteria might well be taken to override verbal criteria. The man feels all the right things but just does not know how to express his feelings in words.

An alternative view might be expressed along lines like these: The central determining factor of how a man is feeling is how he thinks of a situation. His thought, or the description under which he sees the situation, has an importance that cannot be captured by an analysis that regards verbal behaviour as a sort of optional extra to the repertoire of emotional effects. Most – possibly all – emotions involve thought and judgment which only a language user could properly be said to possess. Whilst a dog might pine away, a man feels grief. Verbal behaviour plays an essential part in the expression of emotion. The words I use give me a picture of my feeling, and give insight into the structure of my feeling – perhaps as I would like to feel it. It is often as though I *intend*, in presenting this picture, to feel something.

This is an obscure idea, and I will try and make it a little clearer. We have the sense that the expression of a feeling in words is an attempt to match our feelings to an ideal picture of them. Often we cannot do this, or we do it in a way that is ridiculous, so that our choice of expression seems totally inappropriate to the feeling we wish to convey. This is the sort of situation that has been exploited repeatedly for its ironic potential. But there is more to the situation than simple irony. To take an example: in the scene between Bloom and Stephen in *Ulysses*, we find a conscious attempt on the part of Joyce to find an expression for Bloom's sentiments that will lie within Bloom's own capacities. An ordinary person – Bloom – at what is perhaps a significant moment in his life, expresses his feelings either indirectly, or in banal language. Yet there is as it were available an expression of his feelings which would make this moment significant in a way that Bloom is never able to make it, and as therefore the reader is never able to take it. The epic structure gives the true, or ideal valuation of the situation. It exists as a sort of ironic counterpoint, suggesting a larger, more serious context than any Bloom could have represented to himself. (Incidentally, Eliot does this sort of thing in several of his plays.)

But the description of *what* Bloom is feeling is difficult. What Joyce shows is people in situations where one might wish to attribute to them states of mind even though they cannot properly express them. The ideal form of their feeling is revealed by an ironic contrast, and in so far as one attributes a feeling to them it must be described and identified in terms of this ideal form. And their own rudimentary expressions enable us to say that, in a sense, they do feel this way. (The situation, we see, is similar to that described by Lawrence in the passage quoted.) But when we ask ourselves, do they *really* feel this way, we find ourselves unable to give a clear and decisive answer. It is not all that difficult to imagine situations in which people have been deprived of proper modes of expression, such that, at important moments of their life they are only able to produce some inadequate surrogate for the expression of the feeling that they ought to be, and in a sense are having. This equivocation about whether they are having the feelings brings out why we might want to talk about insincerity; or why some might want to talk of people being alienated from their experience. It might be impossible for such people to express themselves sincerely, and, therefore, to feel sincerely.[1]

At the end of *The Wild Duck*, after Hjalmar and Gina have carried their dead child out, we have the following dialogue:

> Gregers: Hedvig has not died in vain. Did you see how sorrow called out what was noblest in him?
> Relling: Most people are noble in the presence of death. But how long do you suppose this nobility will last in him?
> Gregers: Surely it will last and increase all his life!
> Relling: Before the year is out little Hedvig will be nothing more to him than a fine subject to declaim on.
> Gregers: And you dare to say that of Hjalmar Ekdal!
> Relling: We will talk about it again when the first grass is showing on her grave. Then you'll hear him delivering himself of fine phrases about 'the child torn untimely from her father's heart', and see him wallowing in emotion and self-pity.
> Gregers: If you are right and I am wrong, then life is not worth living.
> Relling: Oh, life would be tolerable enough, even so, if we could only be rid of these infernal duns who come to us poor people's doors with their claim of the ideal.

The point is not just that Hjalmar's grief and his memory of Hedvig will fade, but that he will help to destroy both through the words he will find to express his grief. Like Mr Morel in *Sons and Lovers* he will find ways of expressing his sorrow which will effectively shield him from the reality of it, and so trivialise and cheapen it.

---

[1] Insincerity here – whether in life or in art – is clearly a more complex phenomenon than the insincerity of an assertion.

In one sense it cannot be said that his intention will ever be to do this, but he will do it, and what is for this moment his sincere – and hence noble – grief will become insincere. And it will become so in a way that is not wholly different from the way in which an effect follows the forming of an intention.

One suggestion towards which I am moving is that we can perhaps think of the emotional life in hierarchical terms. Different expressions of emotion can have different abstract qualities; they can be more or less under my control; they may involve more or less awareness of an object; they can be more or less 'lucid'. All this can be summed up – as Hampshire has observed – in terms of a Spinozistic distinction between 'active' and 'passive' states of mind. It is at the upper end of a scale of possibilities that feelings are most 'active', most fully conscious. The true character of a feeling might be revealed in its most 'active' expression.

The behaviourist sees feelings in more straightforward terms than this. There is one category of expressions of any given feeling, and in this category some expressions are more important than others. And importance is to be explained purely in terms of a relation to a norm of natural expression – the logical connection between feeling and expression is strongest in the case of these natural expressions, and that is why they are central. But if we come to see that a feeling can meaningfully be called the same as another, while at the same time being more or less active, then there is a totally different dimension in which expressions can acquire special importance. They acquire importance not through being closely related to natural expressions, but through centrally expressing the feeling as it is valued in consciousness. Thus verbal expressions of a suitably complex kind – such as literary expressions – can be more important even when they are rather remote from natural expressions.

What is it for a feeling to be more or less 'active'? This is something which it would be difficult to discuss in detail here. But briefly, we may say the following: the 'activity' of a mental state arises through the fact that it is directed towards an object, and thus involves understanding of an object (the feature of Intentionality). And the greater one's understanding of the object of one's feeling the more active the feeling. For example, the more one's feeling involves understanding, the more able is one to control it in the light of any discovery about its object. One's discoveries will inevitably influence the development of the feeling in a rational way. (Rather in the way a man may gradually form more and more mature intentions in the light of an increasing knowledge of the circumstances in which he will have to act.) The active feeling is the feeling which has achieved a sufficient awareness of its object to be an integral part of conscious-ness.[1]

We notice again, returning to the passage from *Sons and Lovers* that Lawrence in seeking to portray Morel as incapable of doing other than falsify his grief, also gives a perfect description of a case of Spinozistic 'passivity'. In so far as Mr Morel's grief *is* expressed without distortion, it is only at the most 'passive', unconscious, behavioural level: 'Sometimes, later, he came down from his after-noon sleep, white and cowering.' For 'the real tragedy went on in Morel in spite of himself.'

Now I think we want to say – and this model allows us to – that successful expressions – such as works of art – can clarify a feeling, while at the same time leaving it as in some sense the same feeling that it was *before* it was clarified or articulated. This would, further, allow us to say what most people who take the arts seriously would want to say – that art is a form of knowledge, but knowledge of something other than fact. Works of art do not provide us with new information, but nor do they merely 'excite' feeling.

The question we have now to face is: granted that proper modes of expression enable people to have their feelings in a deeper, or more lucid way than would otherwise be possible for them, what is the relation between the lucid experiences and the more inchoate ones? What is the criterion of identity? Are they two different feelings, or two expressions of the same feeling? This of course is a fundamental question, but I do not see how it can be answered directly. There are however several points that can be made. I suggested earlier that the choice of a verbal expression is not interestingly to be compared with 'behavioural expression'. This is not only because words can be a better guide to the intentionality of the feeling, but also because the act of choosing a verbal expression is analogous to an expression of *intention*. I wish now to make a few remarks that might clarify this suggestion.

It might be objected, first of all, that one can only express oneself

[1] My account here is indebted to some remarks that Hampshire makes in *Freedom of the Individual* (p. 79): 'A spectrum of states of mind and attitudes which extends from mere feeling to belief, can be plotted; indeed it has been, at least in part, by Spinoza in his account of active and passive emotions in the *Ethics*. The spectrum would extend from sensations and those blind passions, which do not require an appropriate object, to active thinking, which is constituted as such by the requirement of appropriateness in its object. To characterise a mental process as a case of rational thought is to distinguish it as an activity that satisfies a norm of order and directedness . . .' See also Spinoza, *Ethics*, Part 5, Proposition 111, 'An emotion which is a passion ceases to be a passion as soon as we form a clear and distinct idea of it . . . In proportion . . . as we know an emotion better is it more within our control, and the less does the mind suffer from it.'

in words which are, as it were, already available to one. It cannot be the case that a man simply chooses not to express himself in the manner of Bishop King. That is true, but the important feature of the situation is this: although the words with which a man may express his grief are chosen from a limited repertoire, they are nevertheless chosen out of a sense that it is these rather than any other words that are appropriate to the thought. We might compare the situation with that of a man who is looking for a word to describe something. He hesitates, tries various possibilities, and finally comes up with one that fits. Another case would be one in which the word he finally chooses is not one that he finds himself, but one that is offered by someone else. He immediately knows that *that* is what he wanted to say. This case is analogous to a man who has been unable to find an adequate expression for his grief, and then hits on a poem which he finds completely to express what he has been feeling. It is interesting that in both these cases the question 'How do you know that *that* is what you felt (meant)?' does not arise. It is not as though one had some previous description available of what one meant or felt, so that one could compare that description with the new one and see that they express the same thing. If that were the case, one would not need the expression that is offered. The essential thing is that before this expression was available one could not say what one meant or felt. It does not follow, however, that one meant or felt something *different*. The correct description of the case seems to be this: a man feels (means) something, but cannot convey what he feels (or means) until the expression is made available to him. He can, of course, convey the fact *that* he wants to say something, or feels something, and he can express this through various approximations. But he can properly deny that these approximations convey the exact quality of his thought or feeling.

The parallel with intention seems to come at this point. To accept an expression of one's thought or feeling is analogous to *making up one's mind*. It marks the end of a period of hesitation, and gives an indication of what one will go on to say. It has, moreover, that character of direct or immediate awareness that is characteristic of intention: there is no sense to the question 'How do you know that *that* is what you meant, or felt?' Furthermore, a change in one's choice of expression can properly be described as a 'change of heart'. While it is not the case that a man can be described as having suffered a change of heart because he has ceased to weep for his dead child, he *can* be said to have suffered a change of heart if, like Hjalmar, he comes to speak of the 'child torn untimely from her father's heart' and so on.

Perhaps the parallel with intention has become clearer. If we go back, for a moment, to the discussion of intentionality (in its connection with 'activity'), we see that a feeling can be entirely determined by a conception of its object. We may completely describe the feeling in describing certain thoughts and judgments about its object. In choosing an expression, therefore, it is as though one were deciding how to see the object of one's feelings, or even as though one were making up one's mind to see it in a particular way. At the same time it is not true that before one made up one's mind one was feeling something entirely different – any more than it is true that a man means something different when he is looking for a word from what he means when he has found it. There is nothing absurd in the idea that the true character of an emotion will in some cases only be revealed in an expression which is not at present available: for we can give sense to the idea of an immediate adoption of that expression when it is finally offered. In this way we see how we can talk of the *same* feeling even where the expression of it has changed. The problem we are dealing with is brought out very clearly in some remarks Wittgenstein made about Freud. One of the things he wishes to say about Freud is that his interpretations seem compelling not because they *prove* anything, but because they have the attractiveness of a mythology:

> Many people have, at some period, serious trouble in their lives – so serious as to lead to thoughts of suicide. This is likely to appear to one as something nasty, as a situation which is too foul to be a subject of a tragedy. And it may then be an immense relief if it can be shown that one's life had the pattern rather of a tragedy – the tragic working out and repetition of a pattern. . . .[1]

Wittgenstein is talking here of Freud's use of an 'Urszene' to explain later experience, but he seems to be making a general point about the criteria of identity of the experience. He **is** pointing to the difficulties in talking of the *same* feeling, when there is, on the one hand, the inchoate and 'foul' distress which preceded the analytical interpretation, and on the other the ordered and 'tragic' suffering which may survive it. I should like to say that we *can* talk of the same feeling here, since what has changed is nothing central to our classification of the feeling as being of a certain kind. It is the intentional content, the picture of the feeling that is presented to consciousness that has changed. The patient has arrived at a new description of his experience, or a new expression of it which alters its emotional quality for him.

[1] *Lectures and Conversations on Aesthetics, Freud and Religious Belief*, ed. Cyril Barrett (Oxford, 1966) p. 51.

Perhaps this will become clearer if we take some more simple examples. Suppose I remember the feeling of contempt I had for someone on a particular occasion. On talking to a more objective friend who knows me well I may come to see that my feeling wasn't really contempt, but jealousy, which I disguised to myself as contempt. One does not need a theory of an unconscious mind or unconscious intentions here; these are cases which occur every day. Cannot the question of identity arise here also? Can I not ask 'What is the feeling which then seemed to me to be contempt and now seems to me to be jealousy?' Similarly, I can reflect upon my feelings in a particular situation – recollect them in tranquillity – and find that as a result of such reflection they emerge, take shape, become much clearer than they were before. Are the feelings in their clear form – their reflected-on and hence more conscious form – the same feelings as the ones which I began by reflecting on? If we are looking for a criterion of identity between the reflected-on feelings and the unreflective feelings, it might seem that we can do nothing more than to give a history of the development of the feelings from their first inchoate form to their final clarity. And of course in a sense one may need no stronger criterion of identity than this. But this is not all that is available to us. We can describe the original feeling in such a way that its central core of thought[1] is only made clear at a *later* time, when the subject, presented with a suitable expression, finally makes up his mind that *that* was what he had always felt. And here we have a condition of identity that reflects one of the central properties of thought: that it can pre-exist its own successful expression.

Thus we find that the maudlin expression of a feeling can cast doubt on all that has gone before in behaviour and attitude. And similarly, a feeling can be 're-assessed', and acquire a new character, through the conscious adoption of a picture of its object, while still remaining in essential points the same. This happens also with desires. On reflection I may not come to see that my desires were *other* than they seemed to me, but I may find a means to fill them out, enrich them, or understand them better. If I come to see my desires 'under a different aspect', am I necessarily abandoning my previous desires and forming new ones? Surely not.

CONCLUSION

As the choice of an expression for a feeling can clarify or articulate the feeling, so can an inadequate or insincere expression obscure or

---

[1] Cf. Wollheim, op. cit.

introduce an element of insincerity into a feeling. The final point
I wish to make is this: it is not ultimately of decisive importance in
the case either of inadequacy or insincerity of feeling that a man
choose an expression in the fullest sense of 'choose'. It may simply be
that the language available to him, or the conventions of expression,
are inadequate, debased or corrupt. It may be extremely difficult
in such circumstances for a man to experience even his most fundamental emotions in an adequate or sincere form. (This does not apply
only to verbal expression. It is worth considering what effect certain
celebrated American funerary rituals must have upon the experience
of grief.) This will seem to be a very odd thing to say if it is not accepted
that there is some intrinsic connection between the development of
expression and the development of feeling. It may be suggested that
whatever one says about adequacy of expression and its bearing upon
adequacy of feeling, *insincerity* is essentially the result of an individual
intention, of a readiness on the part of an individual to take only a
partial view of a situation, to face only certain aspects of his own
feelings. On such grounds it might be argued that the 'moral' and
'aesthetic' uses of 'sincere' are quite different. However, expression
is not simply a matter of individual choice, although philosophers,
and particularly those in the empiricist tradition are very much
inclined to treat it as though it were. A critic is likely to approach the
problem from a quite different standpoint. He is likely to stress the
necessity of a healthy tradition of expression as a condition for adequate, uncorrupt feeling. In this sense he will be inclined to see the
possibilities of expression which are inherent in the available language,
or in a prevalent artistic tradition, as to a significant degree determining the possibilities of feeling.

  I said earlier that the line of thought I have been investigating
had behind it a whole philosophical tradition. It is in fact characteristic of philosophical Idealism. At any rate in its application to Aesthetics it is characteristic of Idealist thought that it looks upon the
modes of expression of a particular period as creating, in a real
sense, the possibilities of feeling. (This is the analogue of the epistemological view that the possibilities of thought create the possibilities
of what can be perceived.) This approach has tended to be historical
rather than individualist; to the Idealist tradition is to a large extent
due the notion of Culture as a central concept, in the sense of the
'consciousness' of a particular epoch as given through the totality of
its modes of expression. One great contribution of this way of thinking is to have introduced in a much more systematic way than previously an historical dimension into Aesthetics and Criticism. Carried
to an extreme such an approach leads to an over-strict notion of the

relation between feeling and expression. In Croce and Collingwood, for example, we find the view that there is no way of talking about a feeling which does not involve a reference to its uniquely identifying expression. Such a theory makes the relation between expression and feeling as mysterious as the opposed, dualistic view which holds that there is no logical connection between what men feel and how they express themselves.

I have been trying to suggest a course between these extremes. It is necessary to try to do this if we are to see artistic expression as in some way essential rather than accidental, and if we are to account for more than a few of the phenomena of emotional expression. If one takes a simple dualistic view, or if one holds, alternatively, that in talking about a feeling one is just talking about a particular expression (so that there is no place for the concept of more or less adequate expressions of the *same* feeling) then there is, in a way, no problem. But neither of these theories even begins to give an adequate picture of the phenomena.

In his *Memorial Verses* on Wordsworth Matthew Arnold writes:

> Others will teach us how to dare,
> And against fear our breasts to steel:
> Others will strengthen us to bear –
> But who, ah who, will make us feel?

In 'making us feel' Wordsworth did not present new facts about the world, nor did he 'excite' feelings in his readers. At least part of what he did was to discover new possibilities of expression. I have suggested that it is possible to accept or adopt a form of words as expressing what one feels even though until the expression is presented one may be unable to say, or even to know what one felt. Yet when the expression becomes available one may know directly, and with certainty that *that* was what one felt, just as one may know that *that* was what one wanted to say. Now to hold, analogously, that a poet may be capable of illuminating and influencing the feelings not just of an individual but of an age, or that poetry can both express and mould the consciousness of an age, may seem paradoxical from the point of view of philosophical behaviourism. Yet it is a commonplace in Aesthetics and Criticism. We find, for instance, Goethe and Eckermann discussing whether *Werther* made the great effect it did because it appeared at a certain time, or whether 'it made an epoch because it appeared'. Goethe takes (not unnaturally) the latter view, and concludes: 'It would be bad indeed if everybody had not, once in his life, known a time when *Werther* seemed as if it had been written for him alone.'[1] We must make some place for the notion of the 'unexpressed feelings' or 'unacknowledged feelings' of an age. It is, for example, possible for the feelings of a period to outgrow (as it were) the available means of expression. As T. S. Eliot finely puts it: 'Sensibility changes from generation to generation; expression is only altered by a man of genius'. It is possible that the modes of expression available only allow a partial or even a corrupt picture of one's feelings, in which case, if one tries to express one's feelings through those forms, what results will be not only inadequacy, but something very like insincerity.

How does all this bear on the question of the autonomy of art? If we go back to Wittgenstein's remarks about Freud we notice that he seems to imply that the patient's experiences were really something less than tragic. The patient feels a sense of relief at being shown that his life has the pattern of tragedy, rather than being simply nasty – 'a situation too foul to be the subject of a tragedy'. Wittgenstein seems to imply that the patient's 'tragic' experiences are really simply painful. But is this obviously true? Might we not want to say that tragic works of literature, for instance, impose a patterning or ordering upon feelings which would be felt in ordinary life as simply painful? A work of literature may – if only momentarily – enable someone to discover a pattern in his own life of feeling, and so to feel differently – as Goethe thought was the case with the reception of *Werther*. Without such an imposed patterning the feelings might be very different; but it does not follow that new feelings have been created rather than old ones illuminated. Lawrence quite correctly says of Morel that the real tragedy went on in him despite himself. If the man who reads *Werther* feels that it has been written for him alone, he is neither deceiving himself nor being deceived by the author. Again Eliot puts the point very well when he talks of the 'ultimate function' of art as being

> . . . by imposing an order upon reality, to elicit an order in reality, bringing us to a condition of peace, stillness and reconciliation . . .

If a poet can create new possibilities of feeling, and if he can do so while neither presenting new facts about the world nor 'exciting' emotions then perhaps one thing he may be doing is altering the picture people have of their own feelings. Or rather (to return to the model of the movement from 'passivity' to 'activity') he may alter feelings as they are valued in consciousness, and hence as they are experienced. If in doing this he replaces inadequate, or corrupt or insincere modes of expression with more adequate ones, then his

[1] *Conversations with Eckermann.*

achievement is not primarily a moral one. It is, rather, a triumph of *imagination*. To attain, in certain periods, to sincerity and adequacy of feeling about all sorts of matters may require an effort both of mind and imagination that is not possible for everyone. Art has traditionally been regarded as one vehicle for such efforts, one way of escaping from 'the general mess of imprecision of feeling'[1]; but it is not the only one. The same may be said for efforts of the historical, moral and even philosophical imagination. Such efforts of the imagination are part of the normal processes of mind, rather than specialised activities. Art, which has always been associated with the exercise of the imagination, is one possible way of clarifying feeling, one possible way of 'expressing' feelings so that they take on a clearer, more conscious, more 'active' character. It is, however, only one way of doing so. In one sense then art is not autonomous since, like imagination, it is a natural stage in the development of mind. Yet it is autonomous in another sense in that, in common with all efforts of reflection and imagination, it gives to the original experience a character that it demands, but which it would not otherwise have had.

[1] T. S. Eliot, *East Coker*, v.

5

IMAGINATION IN THE EXPERIENCE OF ART

R. K. Elliott

IN this paper I shall not be concerned with the imagination as insight, but only with certain aspects of 'magical' imagination, that division of the concept which centres upon the notion of an image. In the *Philosophical Investigations* (II xi) Wittgenstein makes the extremely interesting remark that when a printed triangle is seen, for instance, as a mountain, it is as if an image came into contact, and for a time remained in contact, with the visual impression (i.e. with the object as seen by me). He goes on to say that in a picture a triangular figure may have some such aspect permanently – in the pictorial context we would read the figure at once as a mountain – but that we can make a distinction between 'regarding' and 'seeing' the figure as the thing meant. I take him to be contrasting those common experiences in which we see a figure in a picture as depicting a person, or as a 'picture-person', with those rarer experiences, referred to by art-critics when they talk of 'presence', in which it seems as if the person depicted in the picture is there before us 'in the flesh', and I assume that, like Sartre, Wittgenstein would suppose that imagination plays a part in experiences of this latter kind. In this paper I shall be concerned not with this sense of the presence of the object depicted, but chiefly with types of imaginal experience in which the image which seems to come into contact with what is perceived is an image of something which is *not* depicted or described in the work, but which nevertheless achieves a certain strength of presence. I shall consider, also, some types of imaginal experience which we would not naturally describe as an image's coming into contact with what is perceived. Though I shall relate some of the examples I discuss to my starting-point in Wittgenstein, I do not claim to be elaborating Wittgenstein's remark in a manner which would have been acceptable to him. My aims are to give some indication of the nature and scope of the imaginal experience of art,[1] to defend the aesthetic relevance of this type of experience, and to suggest why the imaginal experience of art has been, and still is, valued.

When contemplating Chagall's picture *The Falling Angel*, the observer places himself in the time of the represented world at the moment depicted, retaining in memory some part of the angel's descent and anticipating its immediate future. In this mode of imaginal attention he relates himself to the depicted angel very much as he would to a bird or aeroplane which he saw falling in real life. As the event absorbs his attention it may seem to him that there is movement in the picture itself. An image of movement comes momentarily into contact with the depicted angel, but he cannot hold it there long enough to be quite sure that it was ever present at all. Imaginal attention has involved him in the ecstasies of the represented time, but he is still bound by perception to a static object. A sort of struggle ensues between the real and the imaginal for possession of the visual impression. Since Imagination cannot create the impression of a movement in the pictorial image, then whenever the spectator relates himself imaginally to a narrative picture, he will never be able to live imaginal time through to a consummation, but will always be dragged summarily back into the real present of the static work.

The only solution is for Imagination to set the percipient free from his role as spectator, and enable him to experience the depicted movement in his own person, while at the same time preserving him in his spectatorial role in order that perception of the stimulating work shall be continuous. This is accomplished by the emergence of an imaginal self or ego which enters into the world of the work, most commonly by identifying itself with some depicted person. Grunewald's *Buffeting*, for example, induces the spectator to identify with the only powerfully active character in the picture, a soldier whose fist is raised in the act of striking Christ. Imaginally the spectator-participant has already gathered up his physical force and is ahead of himself at the moment of impact. Now there is nothing to stop the blow from descending, since in so far as he is experiencing the movement from within it is no longer something which he can be aware of only through sight. Thus the fact that the soldier's arm does not descend does not prevent the spectator from living the movement of striking through to its consummation in imaginal time.

[1] For a more complete account see also R. Meager, 'Aesthetic Concepts', *British Journal of Aesthetics*, October 1970; and my 'Aesthetic Theory and the Experience of Art', *Proc. Arist. Soc.* 1966–7.

The experience is a momentary one. In it I do not merely imagine myself striking at nobody in particular, nor do I seem to aim a blow from where I am standing in front of the picture. It is as if I were in the world of the picture, in the place of the striking soldier, delivering a blow at the Christ, whom I see from my ordinary spectatorial standpoint. But although in the place of the soldier, I am not performing the action on his behalf. The satisfaction I feel is not his but my own. From within, it is as if I had been substituted for him, and am behaving like him; but from without I still see the soldier with his fist upraised. Imagination has no difficulty in accomplishing a powerful synthesis of these two aspects of the experience: the inner one in which I am the striker and go through with the blow; the outer one in which the striker is a soldier and the movement is frozen in the instant. In some sense an image of a blow came into contact with what was seen, but it was achieved by adding to it an imaginal dimension of inwardness, thus circumventing the need to get a change into the visual impression.

Imagining oneself in the world of the work is nothing very remarkable in itself, since it can be accomplished by voluntary imagination, albeit rather sluggishly and with some shoring up of detail. I think that in the end, in this limited respect, voluntary imagination is rather more successful than involuntary imagination. Involuntary imagining is a spontaneity, but the spectator has no sense of having been thrown or jerked into the picture. He seems to have entered it freely, and the movement has a quality of achievement. From this point of view the experience is an exhilarating one – far more so than the efforts of voluntary imagination. But the most striking aspect of the spontaneous imaginal experience is the synthesis of inner and outer which it accomplishes, and which is quite beyond the power of voluntary imagination. It is as if spontaneous imagination had great energy, of the sort which enables one to comprehend a multifarious and difficult subject matter at one synoptic stroke. Most remarkable of all, in the experience the spectator seems to have been fully involved in imagining and fully involved in perceiving at one and the same time. The experience is a *tour de force*. It seems a pity that it should result in uncomfortable self-knowledge, and a sort of implication in the Crucifixion.

It is possible for the spectator to become involved in the world of the work without identifying with any character in it. According to Kuo Hsi certain Chinese pictures are specifically for wandering in,[1] and this might well be said of many of Corot's works, his *Homer and the Shepherds*, for example, or his *Bridge at Narni*. While con-

---

[1] *An Essay on Landscape Painting* (John Murray, 1959) p. 34.

templating these delectable pictures the spectator may suddenly find himself enjoying imaginal aesthetic experiences of parts of the landscape which are seductively indicated but not actually shown in the works, and seems to remember having crossed the intervening distance in order to reach them. In experiences of this kind no difficult synthesis with any contradictory perception is required, but it hardly seems correct to regard them as instances of an image coming into contact with the visual impression. What happens is more like a spiriting away of the self. This is one of the things for which Imagination is famous. It makes the absent present, puts spirits into inanimate objects, and carries us away.

At some point we are bound to ask about the aesthetic relevance of these imaginal experiences. *Prima facie* there seems to be a good case for them, if they can be thought to be invited by the picture and if, as Harold Osborne says, 'In making contact with particular art-works no single rule is more important than that of flexibility and complete adaptability to the demands of each work'.[1] It may be that persons of unready imagination simply do not get to the heart of the work, no matter how skilled they may be in perceptual discrimination. Corot's pictures are as if designed to trap Imagination, and, so far as Grunewald's picture is concerned, might not the imagining contribute precisely what is necessary if the painter is to communicate his meaning? Grunewald would probably not have identified himself with an innocent bystander at the Crucifixion. An account by David Sylvester of his experience of a picture by Soutine suggests that for some works an imaginal response is virtually essential.

Soutine's picture *Landscape at Céret* depicts a house on a precipitous hill. David Sylvester says that we read the picture in terms of forces, a downward rushing and an upward striving movement, but that the picture evokes further experiences

> . . . of a kind that engage our whole bodies: swinging, diving, falling, staggering, skating, climbing, gliding, riding downhill, teetering on a cliff edge. It evokes them as if they were dissociated from any firm contact with external objects. We enact them as we act in a nightmare, in the void of a nightmare. They arouse panic: only this panic is resolved, for the opposing forces are all somehow held in balance by the overriding rhythm of the picture as a whole . . . which resolves confusion and conflict into an unexpected serenity.[2]

[1] *The Art of Appreciation* (Oxford University Press, 1970) p. 186.
[2] Quoted in A. Forge, *Soutine* (Spring Books, 1965) pp. 38–9.

This strange experience does not seem to have involved any definite entry into the world of the work. It seems that the work induced a series of sensations, and that the spectator, possibly influenced by the representational content of the work, imagined himself to be undergoing movements and adventures of a kind appropriate to them, or of a kind which they would bear, and did so so unreservedly that the whole experience became like a nightmare and induced panic. In this case it cannot be said that images came into contact with the visual impression of the picture, or that images came into contact with the sensations the picture evoked. Rather the spectator involuntarily surrounded the sensations with appropriate fictions, and so made himself a nightmare out of what otherwise would have been, at most, a touch of giddiness. Yet surely this was a right way of experiencing the work. Soutine's pictures do not call for a lighthearted and shallow response, and they do tend to give rise to experiences of the kind described.

Mr Sylvester discovers a tragic quality in Soutine's *Landscape at Céret*, but the serenity induced by the overriding rhythm of the picture could not eventually have resolved confusion, conflict and panic unless these had first come into being through the spectator's imagination. If the work did not tend to engage imagination as it does, it could not have tragic quality but only a sort of formal balance. It seems that in this case an important aesthetic quality of the work is available only to those who are able to respond imaginally to it.

Fancy, the power by which the mind associates things which are in some respect alike, in some obvious respects unlike, is commonly active in the experience of Architecture. Most often it operates by putting us in mind of some object which bears an analogy to some part of the work, but I shall be concerned chiefly with experiences in which it seems that the work is inspired or invaded by the nature of the object to which it bears an analogy. These experiences are akin to those which Virgil Aldrich calls 'visual metaphors'.[1] They are also akin to those invasions of the Present by the Past which Proust describes in *Remembrance of Things Past*.

The kind of Fancy sometimes called 'Animistic Imagination' is active when St Alban's Cathedral, for example, gives an observer the impression of a living animal. The cathedral seems to acquire a bodily posture, life, and intelligence of some sort, august and brooding. The content of the visual impression is not reorganised however, and the cathedral is still seen as a cathedral, its stone as stone, its tower as a tower. An experience of this kind is possible because

[1] See Form in the Visual Arts', *British Journal of Aesthetics*, summer 1971, pp. 215–26.

imagination is already deeply committed in perception. We do not actually *see* the life and organic unity of a recumbent lion or a tree, but project these 'inner' qualities into what is seen. We see a cathedral as a living being by involuntarily directing to it imaginal intentions which are appropriate in the perception of its analogue, in this case a lion. Yet, in the animistic experience, the cathedral acquires *its own* spirit, one appropriate to its look and our feeling towards it. It may be that at first we see the cathedral, on the basis of the analogy, as presenting the idea of a crouching lion, but imagination sensitively adjusts itself to the object of response. Here we very much want to say that an image has come into contact with the visual impression, but there are few cases of imaginal experience in which we are more certain that the visual impression has not changed. Since the cathedral seems to have received a self or life, it could be said paradoxically that an image of something invisible has come into contact with the visual impression.

In his book *Cathedrals of France* Rodin tells us that he commonly saw the forest as a cathedral, and that in the cathedral the image of a forest imposed itself upon him. If we see a cathedral nave as a forest, it is because, although the content of our visual impression scarcely changes, the noetic aspects of our perceiving approximate to those of our perception of the forest. By the operation of animistic imagination we see the columns of the nave as having a sort of organic life which we perceive (or imagine) in trees; and our awareness of the walls of the nave recedes to the fringe of consciousness, so that our sense of them as limits falls into abeyance. Similarly, we cease to be conscious of the roof as an enclosure, and become peripherally aware of the sky as up there beyond the tangle of ribs or branches. Some associations of the forest may then be evoked, and of a sudden the enclosed cathedral world seems to be invaded by the open world of the forest. We experience a rush of associations, astonishment, a sense of privilege and freedom, and, since the world of the forest is a remembered world, perhaps a feeling of nostalgia. It is as if the spectator suddenly experienced the meaning of some joyous idea which had been gathering force in his unconscious. In this experience there is some sort of reorganisation of the visual impression, since some parts of the visual field are allowed to recede to the fringes of attention, but it would be going too far to say that an image of the forest came into contact with the visual impression. But one might say that the *world* of the forest enters into that of the cathedral – if the sense of a world is conveyed not so much by visual sense as by imaginal intentions in perception. Although we do not actually see the stone columns as trees or the floor of the nave as the ground of the forest, nevertheless we may spontaneously intend what is seen in totality as a forest, and it is able to return to us a sense of the world of the forest, even though our visual impression is still an impression of the cathedral.

Both these kinds of experience are obviously operations of analogical imagination, or Fancy, but there are others which are less easily classifiable. The West Front of Wells Cathedral sometimes seems not to be resting on the Earth but floating or, rather, as if suspended like the iron curtain in a theatre. The whole cathedral may seem to be weightless. This experience is not based on any analogy, but I assume that it comes into being through the falling away of our every-day perceptual-imaginal habit of seeing large masses of stone as pressing down, the habit weakened perhaps by our prolonged aesthetic attention to the work. Even more strange is the sense of a spirit *within* the cathedral. It cannot be located in any particular place, but is felt to be there in some place, sometimes as if it were on the point of manifesting itself. The correlate of an empty intention acquires a sense of presence, rather as something represented in a picture does, but nothing is actually seen except the cathedral, and the spirit itself cannot even be visualised. An intense experience of this sort is as striking and evocative as any analogical perception. It is fantastic, of course, but also marvellous. At one stroke it makes the percipient intimate with the place.

The sounds of music are much more responsive to analogical imagination than is the stone of a cathedral. When our attention is absorbed in a symphony sometimes a melody will appear as a single being floating or gliding or making a tender gesture; the music of the symphony itself may appear as a single being making some sort of journey, turning this way and that in search of something, and we may identify with it, as we identify with a character in a play or picture; a horn call may be heard as if it were a voice, which some other instrument seems to answer; the sounds of the various instruments of the orchestra as a multitude of voices restlessly discussing or expressing something, or as a crowd of beings moving restlessly about; or the sounds may suddenly seem to fly up, like a flock of birds; or they become again one thing and assume the momentum of an immensely powerful force or machine. The list could be extended indefinitely. Perhaps the most surprising feature of the imaginal experience of music is the instantaneity of the analogical perception: we do not cast around for an analogy, but hear the music immediately as moving, etc. The syntheses themselves are extremely various. The sounds are animated sometimes individually, sometimes collectively, and receive images of natures which we think of primarily in visual rather than in auditory terms. If I hear a *tutti* on the brass as 'aggressive', I may be aware of the sound as out-thrusting, and as if it were an armed host. It is as if the *visual* image of an armed host had come into contact with the auditory impression. Very often we hear 'the music' not as a succession of sounds but as that which is passing successively through the sounds, as something moving passes through a series of points. Thus an image of an analogue of motion comes into contact with the auditory impression; we hear the music as moving, but the perception is metaphorical in a double sense. If 'imitative' music seems somehow redundant, it is because no composer could possibly match the common achievements of his listeners' spontaneous imagination; and the Protean character of the auditory impression helps to explain why a great romantic symphony gives us the sense that we are experiencing a world.

It is not always recognised that poetic evocativeness is often reciprocally related not only to expressive but to aesthetic formal qualities. At a first cold reading a line of poetry may exhibit only a certain frigid elegance or honest straightforwardness, but it may have the power to stimulate imagination, and if it does, imagination will in its turn inspire the line. For many readers the second line of Yeats's *Byzantium*, 'The Emperor's drunken soldiery are abed', evokes ideas of imperial grandeur, brutality and banal humanity. These attain fulfilment in mental images, and at the same time the reader experiences feelings of qualified admiration, alarm and, finally, relief. This is no doubt an acceptable way of describing what happens, but it is far from adequate. The reader is imaginally there in Byzantium, and – especially if in his time he has been a drunken soldier and alarmed by drunken soldiery – he will be both with the revellers in the thoroughfares of the city and somewhat vaguely on the fringes of the hubbub hoping for the tumult to subside or pass on. The poetic line seems to respond to the heightened activity of his mental power. Each word develops an auditory mass, and other images come into contact with it. The word 'Emperor' becomes so inflated that imagination can scarcely pronounce it; 'drunken' becomes two sharp items which draw apart from one another and have to be pulled together by an act of the reader's will; 'soldiery', a company of sounds of various sizes, rings with the image of a clash of arms, and even seems to reflect the flashing of light on armour; 'abed' becomes dense, lumpish and only moderately soft. Critics frequently describe formal and expressive qualities of a line of poetry in some such manner, and are doubtless aware of the creative contribution made by their own imagination. The imaginal syntheses are extremely complex, partly because the poetic word is visible as well as audible.

Examination of the text of Yeats's poem shows that there is no mention of anything done by the 'drunken soldiery', but the poem can be said to have *suggested* their typical behaviour and provided an environment for it. The imaginal experience of the poem was rather like 'entering into' a picture of Corot's and 'seeing' what is not actually shown in it. Yet if we have an imaginal experience of this sort, how much more effective is the later sense of a silence descending, and how much more significant is the later mention of 'the fury and the mire of human veins', when the reader has just experienced in imagination both recklessness and fear.

By defining Beauty as the expression of Aesthetic Ideas, Kant makes poetic evocativeness a condition of aesthetic value in Nature as well as Art.[1] Kant thought that the perception of Beauty induces in the spectator 'a multitude of partial representations', a great wealth of undeveloped thoughts and images.[2] This is the state of aesthetic rapture, much valued in the eighteenth century and attributed usually to Fancy, though it is an activation of general associative rather than analogical imagination. At some stage in the contemplation of a work, suddenly it evokes a whole world of thoughts and images. Many attain a degree of realisation, but the rapid and transient play of Imagination does not allow attention to become fixed on any of them. We seem to be aware of indefinitely many further ideas and images which are on the point of coming into being. It is a state of intense psychic vitality, the sort of ecstasy which a great work for which we feel a special affinity sometimes produces in us when we experience it in exceptionally favourable circumstances. All the imaginal experiences I have described tend to be thrilling, but aesthetic rapture is indeed an end in itself, the supreme experience which Art in conjunction with Imagination can provide. As I have described it, aesthetic rapture is a rare condition, but Kant writes as if every experience of beauty is rapturous. This is not a gross exaggeration, for we can think of the state of rapture as having degrees, in which case Kant's opinion that all beauty is poetically evocative seems to be correct. In aesthetic contemplation we frequently experience at least the beginnings of rapture. When in reading poetry we have 'associations', these are not inert images present to a disenchanted consciousness. Often 'having associations' means being startled and carried away by the work, perhaps to worlds as remote – and close at hand – as Yeats's *Byzantium*. Imaginal displacement of the self easily passes over into a state of rapture.

---

[1] *Critique of Judgement*, ed. J. C. Meredith, bk II, § 51, p. 183.
[2] Op. cit., § 49, pp. 175–80.

At this point I cannot help remembering a surprising remark of Rodin's. He has just described enthusiastically how he had heard the bells of Rheims Cathedral as the soul of the life of the city, and as a prophet turning this way and that to proclaim the festival. Then in a paragraph containing only the one sentence he writes: 'Suddenly I hear, "What a heap of rubbish!"'[1] This, I am afraid, is what anyone who takes up the cause of Imagination is fated to hear, if not from others then certainly from within himself. Imaginal experience *may* be of the highest aesthetic importance; but perhaps it is all superstition, and describing it an elaborate exercise in self-deception.

* * * * *

In most cases imaginal experiences of the kinds I have described soon cease to be available for voluntary recall. We can remember having had them, but within a very short time – say by next morning – it is no longer possible to re-live them in imagination. Often we can reproduce neither the objective aspect of the experience, nor the energy of the spontaneity which held it in being. Our memory reduces to an ability to reconstruct a ponderous and lifeless model, often deficient in important detail, its various aspects held together by mere thought. Descriptions made immediately after an imaginal experience are scarcely less defective, and are beginning to lose their authority even before we have written them down. What exactly *did* the cathedral look like when it was as if floating? Did the world of the forest invade the cathedral, or did I merely have a vivid mental image of the forest? Did I have even that? Did I really enter imaginally into Grunewald's picture, or Corot's, and if I did, what exactly was the experience like? Remembered contents of a state of rapture always seem very scanty and disappointing. I can read Yeats's poem again, of course, but I cannot now experience it as I did when it made its decisive impact upon me. Every subsequent reading seems to have been to some extent a reconstruction of that original one. Jalaluddin Rūmī well understood this aspect of imaginal experience. In one of the poems of his *Diwan Shams Tabriz* he writes, concerning his own poetry[2]:

> My verse resembles the bread of Egypt –
> night passes over it and you cannot eat it any more.

[1] *Cathedrals of France*, trans. E. C. Geissbuhler (Beacon Press, 1965) p. 162.
[2] In A. J. Arberry, *Mystical Poems of Rūmī* (University of Chicago Press, 1968) p. 107. I interpret the last line of the poem to mean: 'What you drink is really your own *new* imagination . . .'. See Arberry, p. 191.

Devour it the moment it is fresh, before the dust
  settles on it.
Its place is in the warm climate of the heart;
  in this world it dies of cold.
Like a fish it quivered for an instant on dry land,
  another moment and you see it is cold.
Even if you eat it imagining it is fresh, it is
  necessary to conjure up many images.
What you drink is really your own imagination; it is
  no old tale, my good man.

All this is true – or at least tends to be true – of imaginal experience
generally.[1]

This evanescence of the imaginal means that claims made on
behalf of Imagination are extremely vulnerable to the sceptical
intellect. Since to a cold eye the imaginal has no more reality
than a dream, we are strongly disposed, when in a critical mood,
to see it as mental rubbish, to tip it out of the aesthetic, and to put
our entire trust in stable 'objective' aesthetic qualities, available
at any time to any aesthetically educated person. But this tendency
can be resisted, for even if we cannot re-live our imaginal experiences
of Art, still it is possible to have a qualified faith in our memory of
them, and we are constantly having new experiences which again
suggest both that imaginal experience is necessary for the full understanding of certain works, and that it is one of the most valuable
gifts which Art has to offer. We can go along with this suggestion,
rather than with the other one, that the imaginal is a heap of rubbish,
and learn to live with the sceptic within ourselves; just as, if we chose
scepticism, we should have to suffer the constant re-awakenings of
belief.

Many philosophers of Art subscribe to or are deeply influenced
by a basic objectivist Aesthetic which is unsympathetic to the operations of Imagination which I have tried to describe in this paper. I
call this Aesthetic 'objectivist' because it interprets aesthetic experience rather strictly on the model of inspecting and coming to
know an object. In its most extreme form this Aesthetic presupposes
that the sole aim of aesthetic contemplation is the perception or other
cognitive grasping of intrinsic qualities of the objective work, without
any use of Imagination. According to this view the aesthetic spectator is not called upon to imagine anything but simply to apprehend
what is there to be seen. No one would deny that perception is an

───────────

[1] Philosophers sometimes write as if the work was never fresh, and will never
become stale no matter how often we experience it.

important end of aesthetic contemplation, but the presupposition that the only consummatory experiences of Art are strictly perceptual ones is challengeable. A part of the task of Philosophy of Art is to understand the structures of the kinds of experiences which are appropriate ends of our communion with a work of art as such. It remains an open question whether imaginal experiences are included among these aesthetic ends.

In its less extreme form the objectivist aesthetic does not maintain that Imagination has no place whatever in aesthetic contemplation, but it presupposes that the work is phenomenally objective: that is, whenever the work appears to us it appears as something 'given' at the objective pole of consciousness, separated from the perceiving subject by an intentional space. This allows Imagination to help create 'aspects' (e.g. turbulence) which when they dawn on us appear as perceptible or *quasi*-perceptible qualities of the object. I do not wish to question the idea that the work is an object, but the objectivists presuppose not merely that the work is an object but that every 'aesthetic' or 'consummatory' experience of the work has a certain noetic-noematic character: it is, *for the experiencing subject*, entirely an experience of the work as an object within his world, entirely separate from him. But an experience can be an experience of an object without having a structure of this type, and an experience which does *not* have such a structure may yet be peculiarly appropriate to the object experienced. In so far as the spectator is emphatically involved in the work, or 'spirited away' by it, his consciousness is not related to the work as to a thing in his world; it is related to the work *as to* a world, a world to which in some sense he belongs. Though there is no suggestion that at any stage in his experience of Soutine's *Landscape at Céret* David Sylvester ceased to perceive the picture, he was also the protagonist of a sort of dream, existing in an inner world; yet this also was an experience of the work. In such cases the important thing is the quality and significance of the experience as a whole, not qualities of the work as a separate phenomenal object. The notion of 'the aesthetic object', or the work with all its aesthetic qualities shining forth from it, incorporates the presupposition that every aesthetically relevant property of the work can be discerned upon its surface. To make this notion acceptable we would have to allow that the aesthetic object may in a certain manner contain the experiencing subject.

Critics describe a work at various stages and levels of realisation. All goes well so long as the critic is merely describing or pointing out objective features and qualities of the work, but if, as David Sylvester did, he gets beyond the stage in which he is related to the work simply as a phenomenal object, there is nothing he can do but begin to 'describe his experience'. As soon as he does this he is liable to be castigated by the objectivist philosopher, on the ground that he is talking about himself rather than about the object. This part of his criticism will be called 'impressionistic', and deemed not to be criticism at all. It will be said that, necessarily, all *true* criticism is in accord with the objectivist presupposition, but that because they frequently relapse into naïveté critics often fail to live up to the proper standards for their craft. This philosophical procedure has been effective in moulding opinion but, logically speaking, it begs the question of the aesthetic validity of some kinds of imaginal experience.

So far as I know, the only argument brought against imaginal experience is that it necessarily involves a lapse of concentration, yet concentration is at its most intense when the work is experienced imaginally. When I see a cathedral as if weightless, or find myself inside the world of Corot's picture, or stand in rapture before a picture by El Greco, it does not seem to me that my concentration has lapsed, as it has done on occasions when I have fallen into a daydream at a concert and then begun to worry about the next day's business. On the contrary, if I had not been concentrating so keenly it would have seemed to me that I was concentrating rather well.

Perhaps the real objection is not that concentration lapses but that attention becomes impure, by being directed not only towards the work but towards other things also. The spectator is concerned not only with the cathedral but with the forest; not only with Soutine's picture but with his own imaginal adventures while contemplating it. This is no more than an assertion of the presupposition that aesthetic contemplation aims at nothing beyond the perception of the phenomenally objective work. It has a certain plausibility because we do sometimes think of irrelevant matters when listening to music, for example; but it does not follow from this that *any* experience which involves a reference to something beyond what is given to nonimaginal sense, or which involves the spectator in some experience which is not simply a perception or quasi-perception of the objective work, is aesthetically illegitimate. It is said that in such cases attention must be to some extent 'turned away from the work', but the question to be asked is whether these imaginal experiences may be appropriate responses to the work. If they are, then in making them we enter into a right relation to the work, and they cannot be in any bad sense a 'turning away' from it. Again the question of the aesthetic validity of imaginal experience has not been answered by the objectivist Aesthetic, but evaded. So far as fancy is concerned, why should we suppose that it is never appropriate to relate what is perceived to anything else, not even when the work powerfully or seductively invites us to do so? The objectivist Aesthetic asks us both to suppress Imagination and to remain completely flexible to the demands of each individual work, yet even free fancy, of the sort which sees faces in the fire, may be appropriate for a particular work.[1]

I cannot see that any sound reason has been provided why imaginal experiences of the kinds I have discussed do not constitute proper aesthetic responses to particular works. We could conceivably accept imaginal experiences of Art as aesthetic experiences, but not consider them to be relevant to the aesthetic evaluation of the works. That would be a matter of convention. But no such convention exists at present. Many excellent critics – Andrew Forge, for example – report experiences which are more strange than any I have described,[2] and value the relevant works partly because they provide such experiences, and because of what is communicated through them.

There is no need to think that if we admit Imagination into aesthetic experience we shall be opening the way to chaos and confusion. Kant suggests, albeit rather unemphatically, that the various mental contents of the state of aesthetic rapture are related to the central idea of the work by a rule of relevance.[3] The point could have been put more strongly, for the state of rapture is not a progressive drifting of the mind away from the work. It seems to have a double movement: an expansive moving out from the work along lines of relevance, and a turning back upon the work which concentrates the additional ideas and images around it like a nimbus. One might add that Imagination obeys not only a rule of relevance but a rule of decorum, for the rapt state would be at an end if a thought or image which was felt to belittle the work obtruded into it. Normally the non-ecstatic operation of fancy is orderly also. For the most part it keeps in harmony with our attitude of respect, seeming to be aware that its task is to enhance the work, not to diminish it. When it does blunder, we suppress the offending analogy.

How we assess the appropriateness of particular imaginal experiences is a complicated matter which I cannot consider adequately here. Perhaps it is safe to say that they must have a sufficient basis in

[1] See, for example, Thomas B. Hess's account of his response to Soutine's *Hill at Céret*, quoted in A. Forge, p. 39.

[2] See, for example, his account of his response to Soutine's *Page Boy at Maxim's*, in A. Forge, pp. 30–1.

[3] Op. cit., § 49, p. 177, l. 15.

the work and be consonant with its general character or spirit, but
there is an element of circularity in these criteria. What constitutes
a sufficient basis for a particular imaginal experience has to be
interpreted out of an understanding of what Imagination can and
commonly does accomplish. It would be absurd to demand that
in the experience of art Imagination should confine itself to what
would be considered reasonable in, say, the reading of a philosophical text. Imaginal experience of art often has a poetic character:
much is achieved on the basis of mere hints and suggestions. Similarly,
the spirit of a work is revealed partly through imaginal experience.
This is why it is sometimes impossible to demonstrate the appropriateness of an imaginal response to someone who has not
experienced it. To him there may seem to be an immense gap – almost
a difference in kind – between the work as he perceives it and the
work as the imaginally susceptible person claims to have experienced
it. But once he has himself experienced it imaginally he knows
how easily this gap can be bridged, his understanding of the character
of the work changes, and he comes to see the work as he imaginally
experienced it latent or prefigured in the work when he perceives it
non-imaginally.

I have acknowledged that if we trust Imagination we run the risk
of self-deception, but we run a similar risk if we choose to distrust it.
It is easy for a philosopher to suppose that whatever makes a work
good or great is open to the observation of any and every sufficiently
sensitive person, without any need for the intervention of 'subjective'
imagination, and yet to accept the consensus of critical opinion
concerning which works are good or great, presupposing that at least
some critics will have experienced the works in the restrictively
'objective' manner, and that that is enough to justify the admiration
in which these works are commonly held. Might not self-deception
be operative here? It is likely also that qualities which in fact depend
upon imaginal response will be treated as if they were simply
perceptible or intelligible qualities of the object – the 'vividness' and
'profundity' of Yeats's *Byzantium*, for example. Even if we notice a
discrepancy between the objectivist aesthetic and our own experience of art, still we may assume that it is our practice that is faulty,
that we are not good aesthetic percipients. Such a failure of nerve
would amount to a complete victory for self-deception. What we
are concerned with here is not the meaning of a word, to which
variations of individual experience would be quite irrelevant, but
what constitutes a proper response to a work of art, and it may be
that a work of art is precisely the kind of thing which calls for imaginal and personal response. One might say that that is its essence

and its life, and that the objectivist aesthetic extols not the work itself
but its husk or corpse.

* * * * *

From a standpoint in faith it is possible to suggest, by seeking the
ground of wonder in imaginal experience, why people value experiences of the kinds I have so imperfectly described. The first
import of imaginal experience is one of freedom. Imagination breaks
the domination of our ordinary habits of conception and perception
– including aesthetic perception – which seem to bind us absolutely
to the given world. When we hear the music as floating, for example,
the work does not do us a favour by presenting us with a strange
perceptual quality; rather our imagination, in its freedom, con-
summates and glorifies the work. At the same time it refers us to our
freedom, for in imaginal experience we are at least implicitly aware
that what we are perceiving we are also spontaneously creating and
maintaining in being. Particular experiences may have further
special significances: the experience of the floating cathedral
challenges habitual imagination as much as habitual perception;
that of the forest cathedral the separation we habitually make between Art and Nature; that of the imminent presence of a spirit in the
cathedral our conception of a wholly mundane world, and so on.

If we find ourselves wandering in a picture of Corot's, for example,
then it is as if the self has suddenly been set free from its imprison-
ment in the body, and in our naïve depth we do not fail to take the
hint that the given world of ordinary perception may not be the
only one in which we can live and move and have our being. Thus
the second import of imaginal experience is of the existence of the
separate soul, and not far beyond that is an intimation of immortality.
Marvell expresses the developed idea in his poetic account of his
experience of The Garden:

> Here at the fountain's sliding foot,
> Or at some fruit-tree's mossy root,
> Casting the body's vest aside,
> My soul into the boughs does glide:
> There, like a bird, it sits and sings,
> Then whets and combs its silver wings,
> And, till prepared for longer flight,
> Waves in its plumes the various light.

Marcel Proust indicates why the state of aesthetic rapture is
highly valued. In his account of Swann's experience of the 'little

phrase' in Vinteuil's sonata – a work I would dearly love to hear –
he maintains that: '. . . great artists . . . do us the service, when they
awaken in us the emotion corresponding to the theme which they
have found, of showing us what richness, what variety lies hidden
unknown to us, in that great black impenetrable night, discouraging
exploration, of our soul, which we have been content to regard as
valueless and waste and void.'[1] In the state of rapture we become, as
it were, superabundantly generous, able to lavish upon the work a
wealth of images and ideas which are not normally at our disposal
or which, though available at will, have a character of fixity and
inertness, sharing what seems to us the flat and hopeless poverty of
our psychic life. In the state of rapture the spectator 'comes into
his own'. It is as if his spirit had risen from the dead, and had risen
transfigured, for – if we can believe Kant – there is no other experience which provides so keen a sense of the vitality and harmonious
functioning of the mental powers. No doubt all that our experience
of rapture has the right to suggest is that so long as we live there is
always a hope of a rejuvenation of the sort it provides; but our naïve
being (i.e. our Imagination) seizes upon its absolute without waiting
for the permission of the critical intellect, and without the critical
intellect's even being aware of what is happening. In imitation of
Kant and Proust, I suggest that a hint of spiritual resurrection or
rebirth, without qualification as to place or time, helps to make the
experience of aesthetic rapture seem so strangely important to us.

Thus imaginal experience of Art refers us obliquely to three
metaphysical Ideas to which it is hard for us to be indifferent:
freedom, the existence of the soul, and spiritual renewal. No doubt
these ideas are themselves products of Imagination, they are all
exceedingly vague and ambiguous, and the experiences which evoke
them cannot strictly be said to *present* them. But their appearance on
the horizon of consciousness would explain why many people regard
imaginal experience of art as something very much more than an
illusionist entertainment.

*   *   *   *   *

Harold Osborne maintains that '. . . art demands the strict sub-
ordination of all that is personal and fanciful, and a willingness to be
subjected to the art work.'[2] It is not necessary to adopt an excessively

---

[1] *Swann's Way*, Part II, trans. C. K. Scott Moncrieff (Chatto and Windus, 1960)
p. 183. This passage is discussed by M. Merleau-Ponty, in *The Visible and the Invisible*,
trans. A. Lingis (Northwestern University Press) pp. 149-51.
[2] *The Art of Appreciation* (Oxford University Press, 1970) p. 186.

1 Marc Chagall, *The Falling Angel*

2   Grünewald, *The Buffeting* (or *The Mocking of Christ*)

3 J.-B.-C. Corot, *The Bridge at Narni*

4 Pablo Picasso, *Weeping Woman*

5   Samuel Palmer, *Study of a Garden at Tintern*

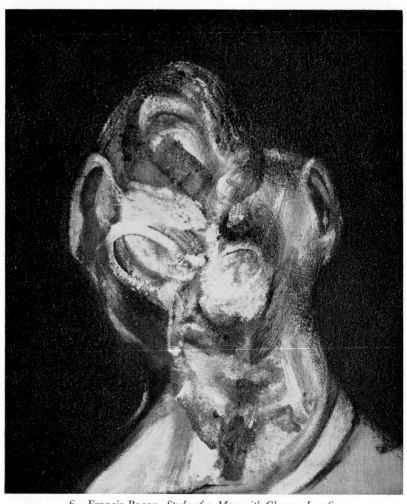

6 Francis Bacon, *Study of a Man with Glasses, I, 1963*

7 Pavel Tchelitchew, *Hide and Seek*

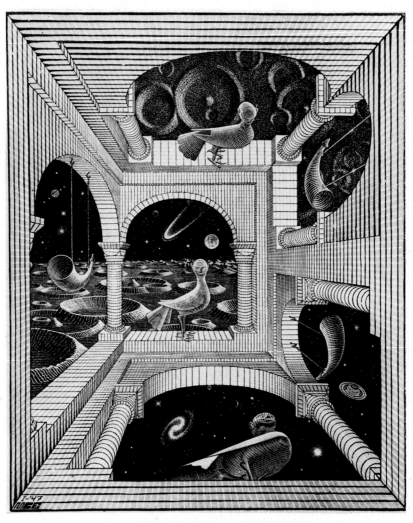

8   M. C. Escher, *Another World* (woodcut)

reverential attitude towards a work in order to respond to it un-selfishly, however; and the spontaneity with which the self contri-butes to and celebrates the work need not be depreciated in favour of the self-control which 'lets the work be itself', since these two are not incompatible. Because the degree of self-control which is aes-thetically requisite falls a good deal short of self-suppression, aesthetic asceticism is possible and those who practise it whole-heartedly may compel a certain moral admiration. But it should not be represented as obligatory upon those who are not temperament-ally inclined to it, or as the only attitude to art which can justly claim to be a kind of love. Against the more austere ideal, Rodin may be cited as the type of an aesthetic spectator who combines acute sensitivity and formidable technical understanding with warm and generous imaginal susceptibility. His example should make us wonder whether our reverence for the work as a perceptual object has remained on this side of idolatry, or whether, by inducing us to suppress imagination unduly, it has led us to deny the ancient magic of art.

E

6

REPRESENTATION AND
CONCEPTUAL CHANGE

Andrew Harrison

I. INTRODUCTION

THIS paper[1] suffers from a disconcerting generality. I need an
excuse for wandering from Wittgenstein's *Tractatus* to Picasso's
drawing of a Weeping Woman, via the philosophy of science and
the theory of sense data. The thesis of the paper is that I have such
an excuse. These are all areas where the concept of representation
either exists in its own right, or has been found to be illuminating
by philosophers. An important question is whether it could be the
same concept in all these cases. I wish to claim that there *is* an
illuminating common concept, even though to find it may require
some fairly drastic modifications of some of the philosophical theses
that are involved.

The second thing I wish to claim is that there are important and
discoverable ways in which what we customarily think of as scientific
thinking can be identified with ways of thinking normally associated
with the arts, namely those concerned with recognising that something is a representation of something else. Put very shortly, my
thesis is that representational change involves conceptual change,
but does not involve, though it may be the groundwork for, theoretical change.

In his lecture *On Drawing an Object*,[2] Professor Wollheim takes up
what he refers to as Wittgenstein's 'stray thought' in the *Investigations*
concerning the 'representation of "what is seen"'. There he
suggested that to follow its light might be to 'find that areas of

---

[1] I should like to thank my colleague Mr David Hirschmann for his help in
reading and criticising earlier versions of this paper.
[2] Inaugural lecture at University College London, 1 December 1964.

thought that we had believed disparate prove contiguous'. Though the similar sounding thoughts that I propose to follow are slightly different ones, and though I propose to follow them in a somewhat different direction, the result is in this respect the same. Right in the background of my enquiry stands another assumption, namely that that group of problems we recognise as having to do with Aesthetics may have this sort of discovery of the need for a philosophical regrouping as its characteristic virtue. This is not, I hope, the same thing as the wrong sort of generality, though it may mean that some of the things that have to be said must be said more sketchily than one would like.

2. LEARNING TO SEE

It is a truism among those who have to do with the art of drawing that to learn to draw is to learn to see: most ordinary people in this sense never learn to see. What is this sense of 'see' in which it may be something that one can fail to have learnt to do? A partial and quite natural answer is that it is a matter of learning to notice and pay attention to the detailed visual aspects of what one has to learn to draw: in this sense one must learn to 'really see', really to pay attention to what one is looking at, if one is to be able accurately to represent it by reproducing its visual aspects as they are. In the spirit of this answer are such 'naturalistic' slogans and instructions as 'paint what you see and not what you think you see', the claim that there is no such thing as 'local colour', as supported by the challenge to look closely at what one would normally claim to be an object of a certain colour (say a red-brick wall) and notice that it is 'really' a whole mass of different and unexpected colours, and the claim that people never really notice the planes and surfaces that are before their very eyes all the time and which they would have to pay attention to were they to attempt a drawing. What this shows is that however unsophisticated the matter of noticing and failing to notice may seem, such answers are not so simple. Such answers are positively philosophical, and are moreover part of the traditional philosophical topics of appearance and reality. Such answers at least raise the preliminary philosophical question whether it makes any very clear sense to talk of the visual aspect an object 'really has' that may lie unnoticed to the untrained eye. Do we have clear criteria of what is 'really before one' in these cases, and what are such criteria derived from?

These sorts of answers presuppose a simple, though not necessarily naive, Naïve Realism about what it is for a drawing to be a successful and accurate visual representation of something, namely that it visually reproduces a visual aspect of an object, or collection of objects. Two assumptions are involved in this. The first is that visual reproduction is how visual representation works, more idiomatically, that an accurate drawing must look like what it represents, and the second is the assumption that it not only makes sense to say that such and so is how an object really looks, but that if we clear our minds of cant, that is to say, learn to pay attention to what we really see as opposed to what we think we see, we shall in so far as we are normal human beings equipped with normal vision all come to notice the same thing. These are highly unfashionable beliefs, both among sophisticated students of drawing and painting and among philosophers, and they have gone out of fashion as the twentieth century has become older for a number of closely connected reasons. At the turn of the century, and for some time after, they were fashionable, even obvious things to say. The two claims underlie the theory and practice of, as well as the propaganda for, realistic Impressionism, and the second could amount to a sketch for that form of philosophical Realism which attempted to establish a foundation of radical Empiricism on a theory of Impressions (or sense data). One might parody the connection between the reasons for the change in fashion among sophisticates of drawing and among sophisticates of philosophy by saying that in each case the theory of realistic impressionism foundered on the rocks of subjectivism, and that efforts to refloat the vessel have had to result in almost total reconstruction. What is of some importance is that the connection between the philosophical and the artistic theory was not fortuitous.

In a somewhat less Realistic manner the connection between learning to draw and learning to see might be expressed in a way derived from Professor Gombrich's thesis in *Art and Illusion*. Very roughly indeed, what Gombrich has argued is that, contrary to the Realistic thesis, there can be no case of 'just recognising' that something is a drawing or painting of something else by seeing that the visual appearance of the one is the same as a visual aspect of the other; to 'read' a drawing as a drawing of something presupposes an elaborate background of mental habits, assumptions, and mental sets that have to be learnt, even if they have been in some cases learnt so readily that we are not aware of having done so. In a very generous sense of 'theory', the judgment that *a* is a picture of *b* (let alone an accurate picture) is a theoretical judgment, not a simple recognition. Accordingly, in the spirit of this sort of view, we could say that the sense of 'see' involved in the claim that to learn to

draw is to learn to see is that in learning to draw one learns to
develop that number of mental sets, assumptions etc., that are presupposed in producing the drawing. The analogy here between a
drawing and a statement in a language is explicitly drawn. For
Gombrich there is an important sense in which one learns to 'read'
a drawing as a drawing of something. Accordingly, in learning to
draw there is presumably an analogous sense in which one learns to
'write' it. Accordingly, there is something 'conceptual' about the
sense of 'see' in which to learn to draw is to learn to see, or perhaps
it is that the sense of learning to see that is involved occupies an
uneasy borderline between a perceptual skill and a conceptual skill.
However these expressions are still labels for analogies and they will
remain so until it is clearer in what sense it is illuminating to talk of
'reading' a picture.

In the first place, whatever may be unclear or not quite right in
Gombrich's account there are a number of very good reasons why it
must rather obviously be preferred to what I have called the realistic
impressionistic thesis. The most obvious of the considerations is that
there are a number of drawings and paintings which we can quite
easily recognise as successful and accurate representations of their
subjects but which do not reproduce their visual aspects. I am not
thinking of twentieth-century 'semi-abstract' painting, but the sort
of drawing that might well have been supposed to have provided
examples for the realist thesis: a standard Renaissance drawing
of an egg or a face will present the viewer with a mass of lines and
hatching that certainly represent, but do not at all resemble, the
surface of an egg or the appearance of skin. Moreover it is perfectly
clear that we can make drawings of things which have no visual
aspects for the drawing to resemble, not because they do not exist,
but because they are invisible: for example, I might make an accurate
drawing of the lines of force round a bar magnet. In these cases it is
quite pointless to look for a confirmation of the accuracy of the
drawings by attempting to compare the impressions received from
them with the impressions received from their subjects 'in real life'.
Moreover, it is quite clear that in some way I have to know, even
to be instructed in, the mode or syntax of representation in many
cases before I can sensibly ask whether the drawing is accurate or
not. This is obviously true of blueprints and engineers' drawings;
why should it not be true, though less obviously so, in the case of
traditional line engravings? (There seems to be no good reason why
we should rule out such examples as blueprints as not relevant to
the question of how it is that learning to draw may teach one to see,
simply on the grounds that they are not 'Art', since the arts can

provide parallel examples; such things do in an apparent, if not
very clear, sense, help one to see, and in any case the problem
concerns learning to draw, not learning to make works of art.)

In the second case, it is by no means a peculiarity of Gombrich's
thesis alone that an analogy should be drawn between the way in
which drawings, and pictures in general, work and the way in
which language refers to the world. Wittgenstein's 'picture theory
of meaning' in the *Tractatus* maintained that picturing was a
paradigm of language itself. It is often held by philosophers that
since Wittgenstein apparently abandoned the thesis of the *Tractatus*
the picture theory of meaning must be at best a museum piece.
This is absurd. In the first place, the so-called picture theory was
not one theory but a number of claims and conjectures rather
specifically related. Without embarking on an exposition of the
Tractatus, it would be folly to attempt to list and disentangle the
conjectures involved in any detail, but it should at least be clear
that any theory that makes linguistic meaning explicable in terms of
the way pictures work must itself presuppose an account of the way
in which pictures do work – a 'meaning theory of pictures', a thesis
that is, concerning the nature of representation. Secondly, while it
may well be the case that the specific thesis that pictures are
paradigms of units of language, or units of sense, has to be severely
modified, the original conjecture that the nature of picturing
may be of central significance for understanding the nature of
thinking need not be mistaken. Indeed, it seems to me to be quite
obviously right. Finally, the mere fact that Wittgenstein came to
be critical of the Tractarian doctrine is no reason why we should
take his word for dismissing it altogether – a first rate philosopher
may even be his own worst critic. It is, however, evident that
Wittgenstein himself continued to be concerned with the philosophical importance of the parallel, particularly with the question
of learning to see while learning to draw, and with its suggestion of
an uneasy border between a change in a perceptual skill and a
change in a conceptual skill. In *Zettel* 255, for example, he says
'How can one learn the truth by thinking? As one learns to see a
face better if one draws it.' But what is the analogy here?

Two rather large and amorphous philosophical problems seem to
underlie these questions: there are changes that we can make in
ways of picturing, or more generally, in ways of representing; what
effect do they have on changes in our ways of thinking, and can these
changes be sensibly distinguished from changes in ways of seeing? A
preliminary and equally general question would be accordingly,
what representation is, whether it is or could be one sort of thing.

3. THE MEANING OF 'REPRESENT'

Common sense, that is to say common beliefs and prejudices of people, suggests that representation could not be just one thing, that the supposition that it might be is absurd. We can talk of a portrait representing its sitter, X representing the spot where the treasure is buried, of a Viceroy representing the Queen, and of a member of Parliament representing his constituents, or of a certain action representing just about the lowest form of treachery we can imagine, and it is hard to see how any relationship could be so general as to be able to account for such a variety of cases without doing so trivially, or at all events, boringly and uninformatively. In this, it would seem that English common sense is at odds with English usage. My thesis concerning what it is for one thing to represent another is, however, that the word 'represent' is broadly speaking univocal. One *can* do no more than speak broadly on such matters. For *a* to represent *b is* a very general relationship, though it need not be uninformative to say so.

4. THE NATURE OF REPRESENTATION

Paul Ziff, in *On What a Painting Represents*[1] asks what makes a painting a representation of *a* and the first candidate for a definition which he rejects is that 'P is a representation of *a* if and only if there is a certain correspondence between P and *a*. Thus, if P is a representation of a horse, elements of P correspond to elements of a horse and certain relations between the relevant elements of P correspond to certain relations between the relevant elements of a horse'. He rejects this account on the grounds that it fails to make a distinction between how a painting represents an object which, in the sense in which he is concerned with the problem has to do with a pictorial representation of certain visual aspects of an object, and the way in which a blueprint represents an object, which need pay no such specific attention to visual aspects. So for him this *is* how a blueprint represents an object. This is over-charitable to the rejected account, since a much greater difficulty with it is that as it stands it makes no distinction between how a blueprint or a map can come to represent an object and how a bucket might represent any other bucket whatsoever – which is no way at all. In other words, since if any object which can be conceived as having parts will also be conceived as having relations between the parts, any two remotely similar

[1] *Journal of Philosophy*, LVII (1960), reprinted in *Philosophical Turnings*, 1966.

objects can be conceived as having their parts similarly, and thus in every general sense correspondingly, related. What is the nature of the correspondence, if it is to be non-trivial?

The thought behind the account Ziff rightly rejects is however clear, though, as we shall see, still fraught with difficulties. It is that the relationship between a model and what it models is essentially that the model reproduces the structure of what it represents, and in so doing enables us to say precisely what bit of the model 'belongs to' what bit of what it represents. To know that a model represents something, and to know what it represents, is to know what structure the model exhibits in its subject and thus to know which bit of the one corresponds with which bit of the other. To know one is to know the other, and to understand the nature of being able to make a model of something is to understand what it is to recognise it as having a structure. What I have called the 'meaning theory of pictures' in the *Tractatus* is simply the application of this account to pictures. After that it is extended to significance in general, but a first question is what follows if we apply it to pictures. The source of the account in the *Tractatus* is 2.12 and the entries immediately after:[1]

2.12   A picture is a model of reality.

2.13   In a picture objects have the elements of the picture corresponding to them.

2.131 In a picture the elements of the picture are the representatives of objects.

2.14   What constitutes a picture is that its elements are related to one another in a determinate way.

2.15   The fact that the elements of a picture are related to one another in a determinate way represents that things are related to one another in the same way.

Let us call this connection of its elements the structure of the picture, and let us call the possibility of this structure the pictorial form of the picture.

2.16/2.17 [What a picture has in common with what it depicts is its pictorial form.]

This familiar highly formal thesis is expressed in a highly formal manner, and in common with all philosophical theses so expressed may seem more artificial than it is. It is in fact highly general and more general than it may seem at first sight, since it will apply, if it applies to anything at all, to far more than pictures and models. It

---

[1] In the translation by D. F. Pears and B. F. McGuiness, London, 1961.

applies as others have pointed out, to all or most of those cases where we can talk of one thing representing another. To see why, it is necessary first to suspend judgment on the matter of *how* we are acquainted with the relevant structures.

What the claim boils down to if we suspend judgment in this way, is that one thing represents another either if the two can be relevantly held to be similarly structured so that in accordance with this structure it is possible to pair the units of the one with the units of the other, or else they are themselves such units. A negative consequence of this is that one simple object which is regarded as neither having a structure nor as being part of one cannot represent. As Professor Anscombe points out,[1] Wittgenstein's account here involves a metaphorical extension of a mathematical sense of one figure's being a 'projection' of another. As she does not point out, but as we shall see, the difficulty with the Tractarian account was that it did not sufficiently detach the metaphor from its origin. Thus for example a Viceroy represents a Queen when he occupies a position in a political procedure that corresponds to the position that the Queen occupies in her 'constitutional slot'. How far he represents the Queen in general, or on any occasion, will depend on the size and scope of the 'slot', i.e. on the structure of the Imperial constitution. A member of Parliament represents his constituents in the sense that, and to the extent that, his rights and powers (to speak and decide) correspond to the rights and powers of the constituency he represents (which is why he has a lot more power in practice than his constituents). He represents his constituency via a 'slot' of rights. A portrait represents its sitter similarly in that the patches of paint on the canvas correspond, in so far as they are in the context of their structure on the canvas (and only so far) to similarly organised distinguishable units in a visual aspect of the sitter's face. It is a matter of proxies in structures. One thing may go proxy for another in the context of their each belonging to corresponding structures. This account of representation has received closest attention in the context of discussions of the *Tractatus* which has to a certain extent tended to obscure its general interest and importance for Philosophy as a whole, and Aesthetics in particular, partly because it has been seen as being too specifically bound up with the 'positivistic' doctrines of the early Wittgenstein. For this reason I make no apology for repeating what is in many ways a familiar account.

The kernel of the account is that it is not possible for a simple to represent a simple, or what comes to the same thing, that the

[1] *An Introduction to Wittgenstein's Tractatus* (1967) p. 69 n.

understanding that a unit in one structure 'goes with' a unit in another structure comes about *pari passu* with an understanding of their being relevantly corresponding structures. This is a conceptual matter (for the *Tractatus* it is of course the paradigm of all conceptual matters, since an account of the understanding involved amounts to an understanding of what it is for something to have a sense, to be a symbol for something else: I am not concerned here with that wider thesis). There is a way of illustrating this thesis which largely follows the account Professor Anscombe[1] gives that is both pedagogic- ally successful and suggestive enough to bear repeating, since it raises important further questions. It also has the value of being in more than one sense highly informal. In a pedagogic context it is usually convenient to choose an example that has emotional as- sociations for an audience and is conceptually oversimplified to the point of insolence – these factors are my own contribution.

The demonstration consists of a game of 'christening within a pattern'. The moves are, I place a blackboard eraser on a desk and say, 'That's the Pope!' (or 'that's the Prime Minister!') The only possible response that an audience can have at this stage is 'So what?'. I then take the waste paper basket and invert it over the eraser, and call that 'The Curia!' (or 'the Cabinet!') and the light in the ceiling above I christen 'Divine Illumination!' (or 'Political Wisdom!'). At this point with any luck the audience gets the point. Getting the point is equivalent to understanding a proposition to the effect that the immediate organisation surrounding a leader isolates him from the source of his wisdom to lead. But what does this demonstration really show about the game we have played?

If the account quoted above from the *Tractatus* is correct what this example illustrates is that the *sense* of the representative structure that we have constructed (the 'model') derives simply from the parallel ordering of the representation with what is represented, that while a piece of simple naming can be quite insignificant on its own, within such a structure it may contribute enough significance for the result to be regarded as amounting to the sense of a proposi- tion. It both raises, and at the same time answers the question how a proposition (even an elementary one) can be in the words of the *Tractatus*, 'a concatenation of names', since it shows how such a structure or 'nexus' can be enough to give the 'mere names' in it a sense, simply by their being 'mere names' marking the points of correspondence of the elements of one structured state of affairs with those of another actual or possible one. Moreover, as a consequence

---

[1] Op. cit., p. 66.

of this, it makes the Tractarian distinction between what can be said and what can be shown as absolute as the absolute impossibility of being able to draw a picture of the fact that it is possible to draw a picture of a bicycle[1] – and also as harmless. What I am presumably hankering after if I wish to prove to myself that a bicycle can be pictured, I can quite easily find by simply picturing it. (If the picture-paradigm of description is accepted this amounts to saying that the only way to discover, or to show that, something is describable or possible, is to attempt to describe it: there can be no proof of picturability that is transcendental to picturing.) However, though the example helps to illustrate these claims, it does not prove them and moreover suggests some disturbing questions about them. The most important of these arises from the very informality of the example, and it concerns what might be called the 'boundaries of the "mode" of representation'. What happens if I turn off the light? Do I then represent the Devil (or the Revolution)?

It is an essential part of this account of representation that there should be a perception of a common structure between the representation (Wittgenstein's 'picture') and what it represents, but what is absent from the account is what the conceptual preconditions are for this to occur. It is clear that there must *be* such preconditions, and moreover, if the account is in any way correct, that these will also be conditions for recognising what is to count as possible unit objects within the structure. Very generally, these preconditions establish the 'grammar' of the representational projection. What is by no means clear is that we can simply 'read off' the 'grammar' from our ability to 'read' the picture. It would seem to be an assumption of the *Tractatus* that we can, or that, what might well come to the same thing, the 'grammar' of all representational projections is in some sense 'ultimately' the same. This would not have been an assumption that would have been made had the later Wittgenstein retained anything corresponding to the picture paradigm of meaning. In its philosophical context such an assumption has much in common with a Kantian assumption of the uniqueness of our conceptual categories, since it makes a corresponding claim concerning the homogeneity of what makes sense as a possible

[1] The distinction between saying and showing does not on this account rule out self-referring expressions. A picture may depict itself, e.g. the Model Village in Bourton-on-the-Water in Gloucestershire depicts the village in which it stands, and so depicts itself (up to a limit of 1/64 of the actual size of the model). 'Theoretically', it could do so indefinitely without absurdity. The advantage of the distinction between saying and showing is that it makes it very clear that not being able to state that P is significant, and not being able to refer to P are, for P, two very different things.

projection of a state of affairs (which in this case, turns out to be equivalent to what makes sense as a projection of a possible state of affairs). It should be clear from the very informal example that we have considered that this is a very rash assumption indeed, since what our example does not make clear is whether our religious or political cartoon with everyday objects shows the possibility of talking about the Devil and of the possibility showing a further possible analogue between the Devil and a Revolution, or not. On that point the 'picture' simply hangs fire. To parody a well-known remark of the later Wittgenstein, it is not that concepts may turn out to be like blurred pictures, but that the mode of picturing itself, its 'grammar', may become blurred. This seems to me to be a *good* reason however, for *retaining* the general account of representation, though for rejecting its Tractarian consequences.

If we do so we shall be faced with two sorts of unanswered questions. One set of questions will be concerned with what kinds of judgments are involved in the required 'structural preconceptions', and the other sort concerned with their relation to each other, and to other sorts of judgments. I shall try to illustrate these questions by applying the general account of representation I am considering to what might be supposed to have more to do with Aesthetics, namely pictures produced by artists. First, however, it may be convenient to summarise what has been discussed from a slightly different point of view.

5. 'TRANSDUCTION' AND PARADIGM

Ordinary common sense, though it tends to assume, I believe mistakenly, that there is not one single concept of representation, does tend to assume, and I believe rightly, that a picture is in the normal way of things very closely related to a model, as for instance a picture of a railway engine is a two-dimensional version of what railway model makers make in three dimensions. In the context of the philosophy of science however the notion of a model has a much wider application than this. Roughly speaking, this wider sense of model does seem to parallel the wider sense that philosophers such as Wittgenstein have given to the notion of a picture, since it corresponds to the idea of one thing being seen in a specific way as structurally analogous to another. In this section I wish to assume and test this parallel in order to see what consequences it may have for the philosophy of science and what consequences for a serious extension of the Tractarian view of picturing as a paradigm of sense. Just as to take the Tractarian view seriously ought to involve us, though it regrettably rarely does, in examining the serious possibility of a 'meaning theory of pictures' for quite ordinary pictures such as photographs and oil paintings, so equally I wish to claim it is essential to a serious investigation of the idea of a model in science that however we extend the concept we should not detach it from its roots in the world of dolls' houses and train sets as well as the physical models that may be made in laboratory workshops.

This is not made easier to do by the tendency of some scientists and even some philosophers of science to talk as if a scientific model were very little different from a theory or else, more usually among philosophers of science, to suppose that a scientific model must always be the outcome of a previous theoretical enquiry. To claim that one comparatively complex thing may be interpreted as having a structure that corresponds to another comparatively complex thing (can be seen as a model of it) *is* to make a theoretical claim, but one which follows the perception of a structural analogy and not the other way about. The relation between a model and what it models is not that the model has to be supported by some sort of inductive inference from what is observed to an unobserved reality, it is rather that the model is very much more simply an *expression* of an observation of a structure in its topic, i.e. what the model models, which may be, but need not be, the result of a previously formulated theory. However to say this is to re-locate many of the problems which have commonly been seen as having to do with the formulation of theories as problems concerning the expression of structural observations. Picturing, even in this sophisticated sense, may precede theory-making.

I am inclined to think that a term introduced by J. E. McGuire in a recent paper[1] is worth borrowing in this connection. There, he used the expression 'transduction' to refer to that tendency in Newton and other seventeenth-century scientists to draw an 'analogy of nature' from the data which had to be explained to a simpler conceptual model (e.g. in terms of corpuscles). He is not of course responsible for any misunderstandings of the concept that are the result of my stealing his terminology, but he is right I think in finding it useful to introduce an expression in this context that suggests the drawing of an analogy that 'leads across' from what is observed in experience to something not observed but which does *not*, as he stresses, designate a special kind of *inference* from the one to the other. He locates the term as having to do with problems specifically involved in seventeenth-century natural philosophy

[1] J. E. McGuire, 'Atoms and "The Analogy of Nature"', *Studies in the History and Philosophy of Science*, vol. 1, no. 1, 1970.

but it is generally valuable I think, to have a term which refers to the expression of the perception of a structure in the imaginative or practical construction of a model (here a causal one) which does not imply, though it may precede, a further theoretical justification for a claim that the model itself represents an independent reality. Seen in this way 'transduction' may turn out to include a process in the development of the scientific 'explanatory investigation' that belongs with a bundle of slightly problematic intellectual activities that are engaged in by both scientists and artists (and thus doubtless the rest of us) which includes the construction of conceptual models in wood or wire as well as the construction of pictures. Making the bundle thus is a way of partly backing the Tractarian hunch.

At all events in most central contexts the concept of modelling can be applied to representation. However there is an important difficulty with the Tractarian account of representation as it stands. Not only does it make no allowances for the fact that any 'picture' is dependent on background assumptions for its being able to make sense, and so consequently 'hangs fire' where those assumptions become blurred or where their application does, but it suffers from the further difficulty that the relation between what is pictured and the picture is, on the face of it at least, symmetrical – which is not so in the case of the analogies and models considered above. A further problem is how are we to distinguish trivial structural analogies from non-trivial ones. Any complex object may trivially be said to have a structure in so far as it is possible to distinguish parts within it; therefore these parts will be related in some ways so that in a very trivial sense any similarly complex object may be said to have an analogous structure. I could very trivially and un-informatively find a structural analogy between virtually any two things. It is necessary to find a way of describing structural analogies in general that makes them not trivial in this sense. This turns out to be somewhat difficult since while we must be careful to exclude enough, it is equally important that we allow as non-trivial analogies those which have a certain possibility of 'looseness' about them, otherwise we will be in danger of excluding too much. Fortunately I do not have to perform this difficult task, but there is one characteristic that non-trivial pictures and models all have, namely the capacity to be used heuristically or interpretively.

An illustration of this might be the claim on the part of seven-teenth-century scientists that the structure of the invisible, micro-scopic, world can be understood in terms of a model that takes account of the inter-relations of the observable, macroscopic world considered solely from the point of view of elementary Galilean dynamics: this is the thought behind Locke's claim that properties that are necessary and sufficient for a merely dynamic description of interaction in the macroscopic world were 'representative' of those in the microscopic world, a claim which has to be distinguished from the much stronger claim that as such they were also the primary qualities, that is to say that such a model gave a picture of 'material reality', though it is not altogether clear that Locke saw these two claims as distinct. The last claim depends on the 'metaphysical' thesis that 'all causation is by impulse and by nothing else'[1] together with a tacit assumption that a microscopic account of reality always explains a macroscopic one and not vice versa. A similar account with corresponding distinctions can be given for a very large number, perhaps the majority of, interpretive models in the sciences. Not all interpretive models however, have to be reductionist: the highly simplified maps that are printed for the guidance of passengers on the London Underground do not require us to suppose that the relations that they select are in any sense 'more real' than the ones that they do not. Reductionist claims are not entailed by claims that a map or model is true of, or successfully explanatory of, their subject matter in a sophisticated or unsophisticated sense, though they may always be made independently.

This has an important metaphysical consequence for a philosopher who would account for all descriptions in terms of modelling or picturing. Ordinarily where reductionist claims are not made for a model it will tend to be the case that the model will be simpler than the reality that it represents, its topic. Even where reductionist claims are made the 'true nature' of reality as shown by the model tends to be simpler than we hitherto supposed it to be, if for no other reason than that it is thus easier to understand than its topic. Given that the account of picturing as suggested by the quotations from Wittgenstein and Ziff seem to make the relation between a model and its topic a symmetrical one, this may seem to be simply a matter of our ability to comprehend simple patterns more easily than complex ones. But if the relation between a model and its topic is logically symmetrical then it would seem also to follow that a model could be more complex than its topic as easily as that it could be more simple. However if a model is to be capable of being adopted as an interpretation of its topic this is impossible, since as such it may be interpreted as being true or false of what it depicts. There are two ways in which a model so interpreted can be true or false of what it depicts. It may show, truly or falsely, that such and

---

[1] Locke, *Essay*, bk II, chap. viii.

such is the structure, or a simplified form of the structure, of its topic, or it may show truly or falsely that such and such is how the units of the topic are arranged in terms of such a structure. In either case a more complex model than reality would show something false. For example, a diagram of a railway system may show, truly or falsely, that the track always runs from station to station, which is a true, if simplified, claim, or it may depict that there are stations in a certain relative position on the line. It would always show something false were it to show a pattern of relations in the railway system to be more complex than in reality. A model can be true or false while being less complex or no more complex than its topic. It will always be false if it is more complex. Were the relationship between a model and its topic to be logically symmetrical, or were the asymmetry to be merely a consequence of our capacity to grasp something more easily than another this would not be so. The picture of picturing in the *Tractatus* might lead us to suppose just this sort of symmetry.[1] This would be like supposing that God might create the world to stand as a picture of the language that we use to describe it. But if a picture can be used to show something that is true or false, this would be tantamount to God, being omniscient, constructing a model of the simple picture we have of His creation. Under such conditions, God would always be mistaken in His picture of our language, so long as we were of more limited understanding than Him!

Another way of putting this is that if we are to take a paradigm of picturing seriously for the relation that language (or even a part of language) may have to the world, we have to account for models being capable of being structurally false. This makes them have an interpretive relation to what they model. The mere claim that the structure of one thing corresponds to the structure of another so that the units of the one correspond to the units of the other is not equivalent to this, and as such will not serve as an account of modelling or picturing as it stands. If models or pictures are capable of being interpreted truly or falsely they will be structural analogues,

---

[1] Cf. Anscombe, op. cit., p. 67 'What I have called the externality of the correlations between the elements of a picture and actual objects is an important feature of Wittgenstein's account. Giancarlo Colombo, S.J. . . . commented on Wittgenstein's theory of the "isomorphism", as it is called, between language and the world, that it was difficult to see why a described fact should not be regarded as itself a description of the proposition that would normally be said to describe it, rather than the other way round.' It is just these sorts of consequences of the 'externalist isomorphism' of Wittgenstein's Tractarian account which show why we have to modify it severely, at least if it is to be capable of illuminating development.

merely. Normally they will be selective analogues of their topics. As a result two models may be equally accurate of the same reality and not correspond with any degree of precision to each other. Accordingly, no model is capable of showing that it is the only possible correct model of the reality it depicts, and its failure to correspond with a rival will not itself go to show that the rival is inferior to it from the point of view of truth. This does not in itself imply relativism, but what it does show is that a non-relativistic interpretation of an analogy of Nature, or even of a part of Nature, requires some further reductionist premiss. Radical reductionism of the kind that seems to lie under the surface of the *Tractatus* is inconsistent with the Tractarian thesis that 'picturing' or modelling gives a paradigm of significance, at least so long as it presumes a notion of a reality that is independent of whatever may be pictures of it.

If, on the other hand, picturing is in this sense a matter of the production of what may be interpreted as a 'transductive' analogy of reality, to picture something is in any case to lay the ground for interpreting it, and to picture something differently is to lay the ground for interpreting it differently. Pictorial change will involve conceptual change, change in how we understand things. This applies equally to paintings and drawings, to pictures in the more familiar sense. What I am arguing is that we can carry much of the account of models and analogies in the sciences, of transductions, over into the area of pictures that are made by artists. Learning to 'read' paintings involves learning to recognise those objects in the world to which the unit objects and relationships between them in the picture correspond if the picture is to be a successful representation. This is, as Gombrich has pointed out, a conceptual matter. It involves the same sort of development of skills and habits of recognition that is involved in the development and learning of new concepts. Representational ambiguities in a picture, whether present as a result of confusion on the part of the maker of the picture or as a result of confusion on the part of the observer of the picture, require for their resolution not only a shift in our awareness of what is going on in the picture but may also require a reappraisal of what is going on in the world, real or imaginary, which the picture purports to represent. It is this which makes it possible for a picture, model or transductive analogy to be used in the development of new understandings and different theories of the world.

At this point however it is important to take care that we do not slide from seeing a picture as a conceptual matter to taking the 'reading' of a pictorial projection simply as a theoretical matter.

The essential point about pictures is that while they may be conceptual artifacts, they are not in themselves propositional artifacts, but are rather pre-propositional. What this means is simply that while we may *use* pictures to enable us to develop theories and hypotheses, they are not themselves such things, neither do they have to embody them. This point has been made for the more general and abstract 'picture theory of meaning' account of pictures by such commentators on the *Tractatus* as Stenius who have insisted that the account of the sense of an expression in terms of picturing should only apply to what he calls the 'sentence radical', i.e. that part of a sentence which may be said to be true or false, but which does not itself make that assertion. A picture cannot assert or deny its own truth. The same point is made more simply by Gombrich when he says, 'If all art is conceptual the issue [of "truth" in art] is rather simple. For concepts, like pictures, cannot be true or false. They can only be more or less useful for the formation of descriptions.'[1] Elsewhere in his account, however, Gombrich says a number of things that seem to conflict with this. *Art and Illusion* is a Popperian book, embodying Popperian styles of argument. These employ a central, perhaps an over-central, use of the notion of the employment of a hypothesis both in making observations[2] and in the interpretation and understanding of pictures. Certainly Gombrich is right in his insistence on the conceptual nature of such things, on the role of thought in the matter, but for the very reason he gives there is something wrong with talk of hypotheses here. What is involved can be used in the formation of hypotheses which may be either true or false, but conceptualisation and picturing as well as the development of perceptual skills are pre-propositional matters, they do not in themselves embody theories that may be either true or false.

A closely related notion to that of a pictorial analogue is, as far as the sciences go, the notion of a 'paradigm' introduced by Kuhn[3] in his account of the nature of revolutionary change in scientific thinking. This concept has perhaps received its due of attention in recent discussions, and what seems to be fairly clear is that, as Margaret Masterman has pointed out,[4] it refers to a number of fairly distinct things. At least one of these is fairly close to a familiar

[1] E. H. Gombrich, *Art and Illusion*, p. 89.

[2] *Art and Illusion*, p. 321, 'Every observation, as Karl Popper has stressed, is a result of a question we ask of nature, and every question implies a tentative hypothesis'. Professor Richard Gregory in his *Eye and Brain* makes very much the same use of the notion of the brain employing unconscious hypotheses.

[3] T. S. Kuhn, *The Structure of Scientific Revolutions*.

[4] I. Lakatos and A. Musgrave, *Criticism and the Growth of Knowledge*, pp. 59–79.

sense of picture and overlaps with the more general concept we are seeking here. 'Kuhn's paradigm's "way of seeing" ', she says,[1] 'really is different from a scientific hypothetico-deductive theory not only because his paradigms already exist when the theory is not there. It is different because his paradigm is a concrete "picture" of something.' What she is insisting on here is, among other things, that the *central* notion of picture, that of an artifact made of pigment, wire and so on should be preserved in the context of the wider concept. It is central to this 'paradigm of a pictorial analogy' that it is, as we have seen in the case of our picture 'hanging fire', 'finite in extensibility', also as we have seen above, that two pictures may be equally good of the same thing, but not similarly correspond to each other, and that the use of such pictorial analogues should lead to further conceptual developments. These are very much Margaret Masterman's conditions. For her 'The heart of the problem is that of envisaging a crude analogy that uses ambiguous words as an artifact; pictures and wire models can be fitted in with comparative ease, after this central problem has been faced.'[2] We have enough evidence of the continuity of the problem of the inter-relation of pictorial and conceptual change in the sciences with the same topic in the arts to make it more than likely that a study of the one can illuminate the other. Accordingly, I shall give two very different examples of this sort of relationship as it may be seen in the history of painting. I cannot hope that the examples that I shall give will solve any problems, but I can hope that they may raise the right sort of questions. We tend to suppose that the ways of thinking in the arts and in the sciences are exceedingly different. This is a prejudice that we must overcome if we are to make headway in this area.

6. 'REALISTIC' PAINTING

But if picturing is a conceptual matter is it not also a perceptual one too? Whether all concept formation can be accounted for in terms of representation, it is I think clear that a great deal can be. To the historian of representational art it may be of more importance to show the effect of changes in peoples' classification of the world and changes in their beliefs about it on their schema of representation, but if there is a connection at all it will run both ways. Possibly the clearest example of this inter-relation is, as I have suggested earlier, that between the representational schema of Impressionism and the impressionist theories of Philosophical Realism. To learn to

---

[1] Ibid., p. 77.
[2] Ibid., p. 81.

'read' or to 'write' Impressionism as a style of painting is to learn to see sense data.

In view of the role of the concept of sense data in philosophy it may be seen in itself paradoxical that sense data could be the sort of thing that one could learn to see, but the very idea of sense data is not in itself inconsistent with this. What is inconsistent with the view that one can learn to see sense data is the view that awareness of sense data is something that is from all points of view conceptually primitive and this thesis makes far wider claims than are made by the mere use of the concept of sense data by philosophers. Sense data theories are by now virtually completely outmoded in philosophy and it is not part of my argument to give them support or to attack them as such. On the other hand a superficial historical glance at philosophy in this century might well warrant some surprise at their rapid demise. The expression 'sense data' in itself seems to be not only innocuous, but natural and obvious, since it suggests merely that the senses receive certain information which is given to them and it is hard to see how this could fail to be true in a very obvious sense. This is not, however, anything like so obvious if the expression is taken in the singular when, that is, it is taken as suggesting that we can individually and selectively 'just recognise' a single item of sensory information, a sense datum, the red patches or particular looks of things out of which, according to what was a common theory, we are (or, perhaps are not) able to 'construct' more complex perceptual claims. What seems so odd about sense data theories is not the very idea of there being data of sense nor the idea that such information may as a matter of physiological fact come in packets, but the idea that the information that we receive of the world via our senses should come, as it were, ready-individuated. It takes a great deal of concentration and skill to become aware of the table before one as a series of brown, brownish and other coloured patches. No philosophical theory of sense data ever denied this (though it was at times conveniently forgotten) but what the philosophical theories did instead was to reinterpret the process of concentration and skill as something that was, if not a matter of clearing the mind of cant, at least a matter of learning to ignore interpretation and inference in order to concentrate on what was 'really (and merely) before one', what, in other words, was known by acquaintance alone.

It is necessary to distinguish phenomenalist versions of this thesis, which holds in effect that reality can be equated with units of experience, from realist versions of it which hold merely that our experience of reality can be accounted for in these terms. The best exponent of the latter thesis was undoubtedly Moore, a character-istic of whose position was that he was nagged by speculation that sense data might be equated with parts of the surfaces of things.[1] Though the word 'impression' in philosophy is most often associated with the former position, it can be illuminating to compare the kind of thing that Moore wanted to say about sense data with the theory and practice of that method of 'realist' painting in European Art that culminated in Impressionism. A way of doing so is to consider the heuristic claim made by painters and teachers of painting within that tradition that 'there is no such thing as local colour'.

As it stands this claim is not a deep philosophical denial but a practical reminder concerned with the development of a complex skill. What the reminder amounts to is that there is simply no answer to the question what colour a particular object before one really is. This is not the same point, though it is related to it, that there is no answer to the question what colour (cf. Austin) a deep sea fish really is.[2] The main reason why there are no answers to questions concerning the 'real' colours of deep sea fish and the like is that it is impossible to give a dogmatic and at the same time sensible answer to a question concerning the normal standard conditions for per-ceiving such things: the colour of deep sea fish is in fact brilliant in the depths and a dirty grey on the deck of a ship. (Unlike red roses which look dull brown in green light or white paper which is red in red light, we have not, in the case of deep sea fish, such standard situations from which to describe their variations from a norm, for the philosophically uninteresting reason that we are not ourselves at home in the depths of the sea – what is, of course philosophically interesting is that this should be a philosophically uninteresting reason.) In contrast to this the denial of local colour does not depend on any problem concerning 'standard conditions' for seeing, but rather on what we see in very ordinary circumstances, but normally do not pay attention to. Neither of the two arguments is a sceptical argument.

If I place a polished black vase on a coloured tablecloth in a normally-lit and normally-furnished room, what I shall see if I attend to it closely will certainly not be an even black filling the outline made by the horizon of the vase. I may even see very little black at all but rather darker, though less saturated, versions of the surrounding colours. That a face is not an even skin colour, that a plain blue dress is not an even blue if we pay attention to it, are true claims about what things look like under normal conditions of

[1] Cf. Moore, *Commonplace Book*, e.g. pp. 73–5, 117, 138, 156, 326.
[2] Cf. *Sense and Sensabilia*, p. 65.

seeing. What is not clear in this case is what is meant by normal conditions of paying attention. It is certainly true that if I pay sufficiently close attention to what is before me, to what I am looking at, I will be able to distinguish these sorts of details, but the matter of paying attention will be very much a matter of what I am paying attention for. Even if I attend to very fine perceptual details I shall be able, given certain assumptions, to reconstruct the coarser grained claims (in this case that the vase is black, that the face is pale or dark, that the dress is a particular even blue) from the finer grained observations, but it does not follow from this that the finer grained observations are for that reason epistemologically superior to the others: certainly they are not more innocent of reflection. These ways of paying attention correspond to ways of isolating visual units that for a painter within a certain familiar 'realist' tradition of painting go to make up a pictorial projection. In accordance with the account of representation we have discussed above, the construction of a pictorial structure, if successful, will go along with a recognition of the possibility of a corresponding structure in the actual or possible world it is a picture of. Accordingly the construction of such pictures entails that if they are successful representations of the world we see, we shall be led by them to recognise a structure in our visual experience. This involves recognising units of experience that correspond to the units within the structure of the picture. We need however to recognise an important further distinction here. In the first place, any picture may be said to have a certain 'pictorial mesh'. That is to say, if we mask off areas of a picture into smaller and smaller units there will come a point where the area is too small for the pattern we see in it to be pictorially significant. This area will vary from picture to picture and from point to point in the picture, and it is very simply empirically discoverable. Anybody who has done a jigsaw puzzle will know what it means in this sense for a piece to be smaller than the pictorial mesh. Secondly, a particular painted surface will have smeared on it a pattern of marks that tend to a certain average unit size. This is one of the more obvious factors that go to make for a particular style of paint handling. Finally, it is a familiar experience of visual perception that some perceptual experiences may be 'below a threshold' of complexity to the extent that they do not amount to enough perceptual information for us to be able to recognise them as sights of identifiable objects.

The practice of the tradition of painting (not drawing) that culminates in Impressionism tends to bring the first two sorts of units together so that they act as visual relata within the relationships of the painted surface, and thus correspond to a recognition of relata within the perspectives of visual experience. Thus there is a tendency for each unit brush stroke or patch of pigment to come to correspond to a unit of visual experience. The theory of sense data may be compared to the mistaken view that this atomicity in a form of picturing reflects a fundamental atomicity in experience itself. It is significant how much of the vocabulary of this sort of picturing finds its way into the philosophical exposition of the theory. It is a compelling and misleading picture that we 'construct' objects out of perspectives of sense data in much the same way that a painter constructs images of them out of patches of paint. I am not maintaining that the philosophical theory is a direct consequence of the practice of painters – if only because philosophers have not been sufficiently knowledgeable about that practice. Nor am I maintaining that there is a direct causal link the other way about. What I am maintaining is that the philosophical theory derives its plausibility from the fact that we can learn to see sense data and that we can learn to do this just as easily as we can learn to see a painting whose surface is made up of patches of paint as a picture of something. The philosophical theory and the painterly practice are parallel forms of a certain kind of visual literalism. The very technical and aesthetic validity of this form of painting should however show what is invalid in the philosophical theory.

One of the most important factors in a painting which contributes to its aesthetic interest is the fact that we may see the painting both as a picture and as a paint surface. A way of doing this which is invited by the pictorial style of much Western European 'painterly' painting is to concentrate one's attention below the representational mesh of the painting. If one pays attention to a unit area of the paint surface that is smaller than the mesh one is bound to pay attention to it as a brush stroke rather than the detail of, say, the end of a nose. The coarser the mesh of the painting the easier it may be to do this. This is far more important a factor in the style of the painting than the size of the brush strokes. It is perfectly possible for a brush stroke to be larger than the mesh of the painting – that is to say, one may, for example, paint a perfectly recognisable object in one continuous brush stroke. On the other hand, as in the case of much so-called primitive painting, the representational mesh may be far larger than the unit size of the marks on the picture surface. What is sometimes called semi-abstract painting in this century may be described in the same way. We sometimes tend tacitly to suppose that in a 'naturalistic' style the pictorial mesh size and the average brush stroke size should more or less correspond.

This is a bare possibility in the case of that kind of painting that represents by placing patches of paint against each other, but is not even a plausible speculation in the case of line drawing. Equally, while it may be just barely plausible to suppose that 'painterly' painting represents by arranging units of paint so that they correspond to visual impressions – a more sophisticated claim than that a painting represents a visual aspect of some real or supposed object by resembling it – it is not even plausible to suppose this for line drawings.[1]

In fact it is misleading to suppose that a visual representation of an object of which we might, or could suppose that we might, be visually aware represents by presenting to us a pattern of visible objects (e.g. marks on paper) that correspond to a pattern of visible units in its actual or supposed topic. We do not see anything in the real world that corresponds to the outlines and hatchings in a line drawing except in the importantly special sense that we may become visually aware of horizons, planes and surfaces that correspond to the outlines and hatchings in the drawing. A horizon is the division between two visible objects; to 'see' the planes in the surface of an apple is to note certain relationships between different parts of the apple's visible surface. Accordingly it would seem more natural to suppose that in the case of a line drawing what the marks on the paper correspond to is relationships in the topic, not relata.

This sort of consideration might seem to be fatal to even the most modified version of the doctrine of representation discussed in the first part of this paper. Moreover if it applies to line drawings it must surely also apply in some large measure to 'painterly' painting, since the manner of representing the visible world with the former technique can be continuous with the manner of representing with the latter. If I draw with a brush with coarse bristles I can produce an effect that in many cases it would be quite artificial to contrast with that produced by drawing a series of hatching lines across the surface of the drawn object that represent a plane in the object drawn. However this is not fatal to the general account if it is borne in mind that what is required for representation to be effective is the presentation of a structural analogue that can be held to correspond to its topic as a model corresponds to what it models. A seesaw is a legitimate model for a political system of checks and

[1] In this respect William Blake was justified when he opposed 'dear Mother Outline' to 'brushing and daubing' as part of his attack on what he saw as the evils of Empiricism. Cf. *The Complete Writings of William Blake*, ed. Geoffrey Keynes (Nonesuch Press, 1957) p. 553.

balances even though the beam of the seesaw (an object in the model) corresponds to a relationship in the topic. (This is, incidentally, why Mrs Daitz's[1] attack on Wittgenstein's pictorial account of language, which holds in effect that since a sentence in a language may be of the form aRb and thus in containing a sign for a relation will always contain one sign too many, misfires against the *Tractatus'* claim that aRb may be regarded as having the same form as a simple spatial relationship between a and b; for the Tractarian claim to be true it is necessary only for there to be an unambiguous distinction between the sign for a relation and the sign for the relata, and that condition could very well be fulfilled by having the sign for a relation a visible mark and the sign for the relata a distinctly indicated absence of such marks.) There seems to be no reason why we should not hold that this is the case with a simple line drawing. The representational coherence of such pictures depends on there being clear clues about what are to count as signs for units and what as signs for relations. We can see this to be so if we recall those pictures which fail to work because of this type of ambiguity, where for example it may be unclear whether lines of shading represent the direction of a plane (a relation) or stand for an object such as a shadow. They may also do both, unambiguously to the extent that the ambiguity is resolved in the pictorial context. Not only may unit 'pictorial mesh' size not necessarily correspond to the unit object represented, or to the unit size of the marks within the picture; the marks within the picture need not correspond to 'unit percepts' (or possible unit percepts) for the picture to be capable of representing a reality. Learning to see sense data as part of the process of learning to read certain kinds of pictures corresponds to the trick of attempting to co-identify these different types of units. It is an almost possible trick, and a useful one, to attempt for certain circumstances, but it is certainly not essential for 'reading' even a majority of types of pictorial representation.

However, even if it were essential it could not warrant a *theory* of sense data. At most it would warrant a reliance on an exclusive paradigm (in something like the Kuhnian sense) of, or for, perceptual experience. And paradigms are neither theories nor hypotheses, though they may be the conceptual background for such things. The mistake of sense data theories is simply that they are taken to be theories of the nature of perception rather than accounts of the conceptual sets that may be invoked by certain rather specific kinds

[1] Edna Daitz, 'The Picture Theory of Meaning', *Mind*, 62 (1953) pp. 184–201, repr. Flew (ed.), *Essays in Conceptual Analysis*, and Copi and Beard, *Essays on Wittgenstein's Tractatus.*

of perceptual situations, in particular those typified by making sense of certain specific kinds of pictures.

It would however be a mistake, and a fairly important one, to assume that the conceptual influence of a style of pictorial projection is always as general as that indicated by the relation between Impressionist painting and the theory of impressions. It is in fact a characteristic of the kind of 'pre-propositional' conceptual shifts associated with picturing that they may lack generality. Generality of the kind involved in a theory of sense data, or even the readiness to subscribe to one, is inclined to be the result of a pre-propositional stance stepping off in the direction of a theory which is capable of being true or false. In fact it is largely because this is rather rarely the case that the borderline between perceptual skills of recognition and their corresponding conceptual assumptions is an area of such lively change and variety. Conversely, a reason why the very idea of conceptual change can give trouble may be the tendency for those who consider it to be over-impressed by the case of the alteration and abandonment of whole theories, possibly on the assumption that concepts only exist in theories and that theories must be wholesale or else unserious. Certainly totality is what the self-conscious and self-respecting philosopher seeks for his system of beliefs, but it would be a rather gross mistake for him on that account to read such an ideal back into the non-self-conscious reality of our (and his) ordinary beliefs and attitudes, still less into our non-propositional picture-assumptions.

Accordingly, it might be well to conclude with some indication of how the conceptual influence of a picture may operate quite specifically and non-generally. A perhaps over-dramatic example of this is, I suggest, given by Picasso's 1937 etching of a *Weeping Woman*[1] which is part of the series of works connected with *Guernica*. Its effect is to shift our conception of weeping, of outraged female grief, and the outrage of such grief, by the method of representation employed. John Berger says of *Guernica* 'What has happened to the bodies *in being painted* is the imaginative equivalent of what has happened to them in sensation in the flesh.[2] The same may be said of the smaller work. One way of seeing the picture is to see it as an at best ambiguous, at worst inaccurate line drawing of a weeping woman. It is important that this *is* the reaction of those whose expectations of what a picture represents is conditioned by the idea that it must represent a visual aspect of its topic visually. This is only partly the case with the etching in question: the very shifting

[1] John Berger, *The Success and Failure of Picasso*, p. 169.
[2] See Plate 4.

of the expected positions of the parts of the face of the woman, the fact that the shapes point to the corner of the woman's right eye may represent either the line of tears running down from the eye or nails driving into it, that the shape above the nose of the woman may be either the line of a hand clutching the head or a forehead bursting with pain are in this case best described, not as ambiguities in the representation, but as non-ambiguous representation via an expected ambiguity, of the very disintegration of grief. That is how grief feels. The picture shows us that that is how we may recognise a particular variety of weeping. The picture is a structural analogue, not merely of an appearance, but of an experience. As with all such structural analogues, it presents us with a paradigmatic possibility. It shows us the form of a possible experience, something we may not have attended to in this form hitherto. This is a genuine shift in, or addition to, our concept of grief, but it is not an addition to any theory of grief.

7

REPRESENTATION IN MUSIC

J. O. Urmson

A SATISFACTORY discussion in depth of all the philosophical problems that could be raised concerning musical representation would require much more space as well as more ability than I have at my disposal. Nobody should believe, or believe that I believe, that what follows is more than a rather sketchy examination of a few central issues.

Music has frequently been declared to be the most abstract of the arts. What that means is not wholly clear, but probably most of us would agree that there is much music of which it would be inappropriate to ask what it represents, depicts or portrays. No doubt much of this music, perhaps all that has any merit and also some that has not, could be naturally and idiomatically characterised as grave, gay, stately, sad, lively, majestic, or in some similar way. Some, less economically, less idiomatically and more tendentiously, will say that the music expresses sadness or joy rather than that it is sad or joyful. But to characterise music in either of these fashions is very far from ascribing to it any representational function. Beethoven directed that the slow movement of the Piano Sonata Op. 10, No. 3 should be *largo e mesto*; but if, properly performed, the music is indeed sad, it by no means follows that it represents, portrays or depicts anything. So far as I know, it does not.

On the other hand, it is quite clear that some music is representational, or at least contains representational elements. It may, as Tovey urgently insisted, be unimportant, but it is true that the songs of the cuckoo, quail and nightingale, as well as other natural phenomena, are represented in Beethoven's *Pastoral Symphony*. It is equally obvious that in Haydn's *Creation* and *Seasons* we find representations of lions roaring, tigers leaping, stags running, horses galloping, frogs croaking, crickets chirping, whales swimming and elephants stamping, to mention but a small selection. No doubt all these examples are of representational elements confined to a few notes or bars. But Haydn, who should know, informs us that the Introduction to the *Creation* is a representation of chaos and that in the *Seasons* the introduction to *Spring* depicts (*vorstellt*) the passage from winter to spring, the introduction to *Summer* depicts dawn, the introduction to *Autumn* has as its object (*Gegenstand*) the husbandman's satisfaction at the abundant harvest and the introduction to *Winter* portrays (*schildert*) the thick fogs at the beginning of winter. So Haydn at least attempted to represent quite abstract matter in reasonably extended movements.

In fact, however infrequent representational music may be as a proportion of all music, it is easy to find a host of examples, long and short, in music of all periods, by composers great and small, that are clearly intended by the composer and recognised by the hearer to be representational. It is so easy that I shall not waste time on producing more examples.

I take it then as being beyond argument that some music is representational and some is not, and that some representation is very obviously so. There are also cases, no doubt, in which it is not clear whether the music is representational or not. Some of these cases are without theoretical interest, though perhaps relevant to the correct understanding of some particular piece of music. Whether, as Schindler asserted, Beethoven represented the yellow-hammer as well as the nightingale, cuckoo and quail in the *Pastoral Symphony* is not of theoretical interest. If he did, he did it unconvincingly, and probably he did not. Other types of case are more worthy of attention. It may for example be hard to decide whether the music to a dramatic ballet is merely an appropriate accompaniment to a dramatic representation on the stage, or is an integral part of a single representational whole, or is a musical representation of what is at the same time visually and dramatically represented on the stage. But let us now concentrate on the cases in which the music is clearly representational, and forget the more difficult and the marginal cases.

Let us indeed start with what at any rate seems to be the least problematic case of all, that of the representation of sounds. This might at least seem to be an easy case, for the most obvious explanation of representation to offer is in terms of resemblance or likeness. In saying that this explanation is the most obvious I do not mean that it is obviously true but that it is the most likely to occur to us, as it has most frequently occurred to our predecessors. If representation is a matter of likeness, it seems easier to see how musical sounds could be like other sounds than how they could be like such other things as thick fogs at the beginning of winter.

Yet, even if we restrict ourselves to the simplest, most tractable case of musical representation, that of sounds, resemblance or likeness cannot at any rate be a full account of the nature of representation. Even here we cannot say simply that for A to be a representation of B all that is requisite is that A should resemble B.

In the first place, resemblance is a symmetrical relation; that is to say, if A resembles B then B resembles A. But it is certainly not the case that if A is a representation of B, then B is a representation of A. No song of any cuckoo is a representation of anything in the *Pastoral Symphony*, for example. Representation is at least a non-symmetrical relation, and is even asymmetrical, unless I have failed to spot some very atypical exceptions. I can think of no case where two things are mutual representations.

Moreover resemblance cannot be a sufficient condition of representation because A can resemble B without either being a representation of the other. This is in general obvious. Peas and identical twins are not representations of each other. But it is also true if we maintain our restriction to the case of sounds. One hoot of an owl is not a representation of any other; one occurrence of a musical cliché is not a representation of any other occurrence of the same cliché; and there are many descending thirds in music which are not a representation of any cuckoo-call.

These difficulties, as so far developed, can be readily met by a small but important addition. For A to be a representation of B, we may say, it has not only to resemble B, but must be produced with the intention that it should resemble B. Or it may be yet more plausible to say that for A to be a representation of B it need only be intended by its producer to resemble B; for a representation need not be a good one, and it will be a good one if the resemblance actually is achieved. Thus if the maker of A intends it to resemble B, but in fact it resembles C more closely than it resembles B, that is a reason for saying that it could be a better representation of B than it is, not for saying that it is in fact a representation of C. Or perhaps it would be still more accurate to say that while it is necessary that A should be intended to resemble B for it to be a representation of B, it is also necessary that some minimum degree of resemblance should be achieved. All sorts of mildly improbable sounds could pass as (bad) representations of a dog's bark, say; but a high-pitched squeak would go beyond the most generous bounds. With some such modification as this the most obvious forms of our objections can be avoided. Thus resemblance, unlike representation, may be a symmetrical relation, but intended resemblance is not; the difficulty about cuckoo-calls representing bits of the *Pastoral Symphony* has gone. Similarly no problem will arise from shared musical clichés, or from those many descending thirds that resemble cuckoo-calls but are not intended to.

But though I believe that the introduction of intention into the analysis of musical representation is a proper move and must survive, perhaps in a more subtle form than any I have suggested, in any adequate theory of musical representation, we are by no means out of the wood yet. It would certainly be false to claim that any sound intentionally produced to resemble another sound will be a representation of it; thus if you sing an A and I follow suit with a note at the same pitch, what I sing will be a copy, or imitation or replica of what you sang, not a representation of it; nor is a variation on a theme even an approximate representation of the theme. In the specific case of musical representation it would seem that the representation must be music and what is represented must not be music.

I raise these problems of detail not to pursue them now, but because they make us think immediately of another far greater one. In the way in which a copy or imitation, perhaps a tape-recording, resembles its original, perhaps a live performance, it is clear that musical representations do not very closely resemble the thing represented, usually. Perhaps a representation of a cuckoo-call on a clarinet may achieve extreme fidelity; perhaps if we wanted to imitate a cuckoo-call we could not do better than to use a clarinet in exactly the way it is used in some piece of musical representation. But is this life-like fidelity what is important in musical representation? I think that we can see that it is not, even if we restrict ourselves to this most plausible, but quite untypical, case of the cuckoo-call.

If a composer using the conventional orchestra were to put his cuckoo-call on the trumpet we might possibly want to criticise this from the restricted viewpoint of adequacy of representation, on the ground that the timbre was not right. But nobody would criticise the representation of a cuckoo in a piano piece because the timbre was wrong, and nobody would say that you cannot adequately represent a cuckoo on the piano. Unlike the orchestral composer, the composer for the piano has no choice of timbre; for this very reason we do not take the timbre into account when assessing the adequacy of the representation on the piano, as we should in the case of an orchestral representation. When you have no choice of timbre the timbre is irrelevant to the merits of the representation. But while you may choose to represent a cuckoo on the piano, the piano could produce only a most imperfect copy, replica or imitation of a cuckoo-call.

Maybe a composer with the technical skill of Richard Strauss could compose a score for orchestra such that its sounds would be indistinguishable from the sounds of a rural garden. But the better the copy or imitation was the less likely it would be that it would be recognisable as a piece of music. The orchestra would have become an exotic effects department. Since the sounds of the world around us are in general readily distinguishable from anything that could be called music in the conventional sense, it follows that musical representation will be in general rather unlike what is represented.

So even in the case of pitched sounds we must not say merely that representation is a matter of producing intended resemblances to them. For representations are not in general faithful copies. But we should not on these grounds withdraw our hypothesis but rather say that such departures from strict fidelity as are dictated by the nature and conventions of the medium do not count as impairing the resemblance. The resemblance that is relevant is only such as is compatible with the representation being music and the represented being a natural sound. Nobody acquainted with music needs deliberately to discount the infidelity of timbre when the piano plays a cuckoo-call; it would no more occur to us to think that the timbre was wrong than it would occur to us to think that the colours were wrong in a pen-and-ink drawing.

If the argument so far is satisfactory, there can be no serious difficulty raised by the representation of sounds of indeterminate pitch in music. If we take a thunderstorm as an example of a set of sounds indeterminate in both pitch and rhythm, such a phenomenon has often been represented by composers; Rossini never missed an opportunity. It seems clear that in listening to musical representations of such phenomena we disregard the determinate pitch and relatively regular rhythm as being inherent features of the medium, in a way exactly analogous to our disregard of the timbre of the piano when used to represent a cuckoo-call. No doubt this requires education and conditioning; perhaps someone entirely new to Western music would no more recognise a Rossini thunderstorm than a cat apparently recognises a photograph of a cat. But when we have learnt the nature and conventions of Rossini's art, when we know what is relevant and what is not, the resemblance is there for all to hear.

So the hypothesis we have before us about the nature of musical representation (which we have made no attempt to extend to other types of representation) goes somewhat as follows. There is such a thing as natural likeness or resemblance between sounds, which can be recognised without any knowledge of any artistic medium or its conventions. Such a likeness, as it increases, approaches indistinguishability as a limit; as in the case of two A's on two good tuning-forks. Though it is possible for there to be such a likeness between a musical representation of a sound and the sound represented, as in the case of a cuckoo-call on an appropriate instrument, this sort of likeness is unusual in and not essential to musical representation. A musical representation preserves only such features of the sound represented as is compatible with the nature of the medium and its conventions, as is compatible with its being music, or piano music or tonal music. Some other features it modifies in accordance with the exigencies of the medium and its conventions; others it ignores in accordance with the same exigencies. Such modifications and omissions do not present themselves as infidelities to a hearer who is aware of the nature of the medium and its conventions. This hypothesis we have so far tested only with reference to the representation of sounds, and it appears to have survived this very limited ordeal.

Before we go on to consider more ambitious forms of musical representation than that of sounds the point must now be made that, even in the relatively simple case of the representation of sounds, some extra-musical evidence is normally necessary to make it clear what exactly is being represented. This evidence is, typically, a title annexed to the piece or, in the case of vocal music, the meaning of the words. The reason why this evidence is necessary even in the case of the representation of sounds is obvious: many sounds are very similar to others of a quite different nature, and such differences as there are have often to be neglected in music because of its own nature. Thus, given that a static orchestra is playing before a static audience, there is no musical way of distinguishing a crescendo which represents the approach of a sounding object from one which represents an increasing sound from a static object. It is not imaginable by me how a musical representation could distinguish between the sound of the fall of a philistine temple and that of the fall of Westminster Abbey; we hear Handel's symphony in *Samson* as the former because we have the extra-musical evidence. The representation of the fall of the temple is none the worse, given the extra-musical evidence, because without that evidence we should not have known it to be such. Given the nature of Handel's orchestra, the conventions of musical composition of his time, and the fact that musical considerations would outweigh the claims of realism, the sound that we hear is as like the fall of a philistine temple as one could want. Once we are told that the representation is of the fall of

F

such a temple, any accidental likeness to anything else, however great, becomes irrelevant.

If we now consider the adequacy of the hypothesis that we have before us in the light of examples other than those of the representation of sounds, certain types of case do not seem to present any theoretically important difficulties. It is obvious that any passage of music has, as well as pitch and timbre, that are characteristics only of sounds, other features that can be quite literally shared with things other than sounds. Tempo and rhythm, or absolute and relative speed, are obvious examples. That composers constantly represent natural events with a characteristic rhythm by music with a rhythm as similar as the conventions permit is so obvious as not to need extended discussion or explanation. Thus there are innumerable rhythmic representations of horses galloping. Perhaps you need extra-musical evidence to make it quite certain that it is a horse and not a zebra, or that the horse belongs to this or that Valkyrie. But the fact that the music has no colour, as the horse has, being inevitable, is therefore irrelevant to the representation. There is an obvious resemblance of a quite clear type, and it seems hard to deny that this is the essence of the representation.

Again, at a more abstract level, the number of voices or parts in the music can be the same as the number of participants in a scene represented, and thus represent them. This again is so obvious, and examples are so easily brought to mind, that detailed discussion would be out of place. An example involving velocity, rhythm and number would be the two doggedly plodding parts at a constant interval of a third, representing Joseph and Mary plodding along together, that we hear in the accompaniment of Wolf's *Nun Wandre Maria*.

Now the examples of musical representation that we have been considering have not only been comparatively simple but also, in a way, unproblematic. For while the hypothesis that musical representation is to be analysed in terms of resemblance is clearly open to doubt, it could scarcely be denied that a piece of music may resemble some non-musical phenomenon in the respects so far noted. It would be very paradoxical to deny that pitch, timbre, rhythm, tempo and degree of loudness are features some or all of which may be common to a portion of a musical composition and some non-musical phenomenon, whether this fact is relevant to the explanation of musical representation or not.

But we must now turn to more difficult matters. I have already deliberately smuggled in one case of what I called resemblance which is by no means so clearly legitimate. I suggested that the parallel movement of the thirds in the accompaniment to *Nun Wandre Maria* represented the parallel movement of Mary and Joseph as they walked together to Bethlehem, clearly implying that this could be counted as a case of resemblance. But it may well be doubted whether this is, in a straightforward sense, a case of resemblance, for the expression 'parallel movement' is by no means clearly univocal. Can a musical part move in the same sense as a person moves, and can two musical parts move in parallel as two persons can move in the same direction side by side?

We have here just one example of a general problem that may be stated as follows. There is a wide range of characteristics, beyond those so far considered, that we unhesitatingly ascribe both to passages of music and to other things, of which parallel movement is but one. It would seem natural to claim, if we are to follow consistently the hypothesis about the nature of representation developed in this paper, that representation of things having these features is achieved by writing music that has these features. But if parallel motion, and the other features in this class, are not genuine cases of resemblance, or are cases of resemblance only in some extended and philosophically puzzling sense, then our hypothesis is either refuted, or is shown to be philosophically void.

It would be impossible to give an exhaustive list of characteristics, such as parallel motion, that we ascribe both to music and to non-musical phenomena, but raise the sort of problem that we have noted in the case of parallel motion; nor would it be wise to assume that the class would be homogeneous. But it will be useful to give some examples. A musical sound may be high or low, as may a place or a number. A musical sound may be sweet, as may a taste or smell. Composers frequently direct that their music should be *mesto, gaio, giocoso, maestoso, piacevole, energico, dolce, dolente, morendo, amoroso, grazioso*, and these terms, or their English equivalents, are also commonly used in other quite disparate situations, totally unconnected with music. Again, musical sounds may be called sombre or bright, terms which also have a visual use. Clearly the list could be endlessly extended. Music may be said to have any of these characteristics without there being any suggestion that it is representational. But equally music having these characteristics may be used to represent other situations that have the same characteristics. But are they the same characteristics? That is our problem. I am far from thinking that I can now treat it adequately, but something must be said about it.

The first thing to note is that we are not faced with a problem which is exclusively, or even primarily, one of aesthetics. We started from the fact that we can call the motion of Mary and Joseph, walking side by side at about the same distance from each other, parallel motion and that we can call the series of thirds in the accompaniment, sounds that remain at a constant interval from each other, a case of parallel motion. Thus we apply the terms 'interval' and 'distance' both to a spatial relationship of bodies and a pitch relationship of sounds. But is this in principle any different from the fact that we apply the terms 'interval' and 'distance' to both temporal and spatial relationships? Both a spatial interval and a temporal interval may be called long or short. But it seems scarcely possible to claim that the adjectives 'long' and 'short' are used univocally here. If precisely the same feature were attributed to space and time when we speak of them being long there would surely be an indisputable answer to such questions as whether fifty miles or six months was longer, or what distance was exactly the same length as six months. Again, the weather, a conversation, a person, a colour, a knife-blade and a pain may all be called dull. They could scarcely all share exactly the same feature, nor is there anything especially aesthetic in this way of speaking. If by 'metaphorical' we mean only something historical, that a term was used first in one context and only later in another, then presumably both 'long' and 'dull' must be metaphorical in some of the usages noticed; but which are metaphorical in this historical sense I do not know, and few, if any, seem to be metaphorical in any other than this jejune sense that the terms must have been used in one sort of context first. If 'dull pain' is metaphorical, what is the literal equivalent?

So it seems that many terms, a few of which we have noticed, occur frequently, in both aesthetic and also quite utilitarian contexts, with application to series of sounds and also to colours, smells, tastes and many more complex phenomena. It is clear also that some musical representation is achieved by the composition of music to which the term in question may be applied to represent other phenomena to which the same term may be applied. But it is not easy to find any clearly true and illuminating account of such a use of terms.

Certain special cases of this general problem have received a great deal of attention in writings on aesthetics; pre-eminently the case of the ascription of sadness to both persons and pieces of music. I should like briefly to consider two very obvious hypotheses which have, in some form, been widely held. One of these hypotheses is that to call a piece of music sad is to say that it expresses the sadness of its composer; the other is that to call a piece of music sad is to say that it causes sadness in the hearer. In other words, one theory holds that *sad*, when applied to music, means 'expressive of sadness', in the sense of 'sadness' applicable to people; the other holds that it means 'causing sadness' in the sense applicable to people.

The first point about these theories that I should like to make is that, even if one is true, they touch only the fringe of our problem. They will explain only a handful of cases of the application of emotional terms to both music and persons. They leave untouched the problem of the application of the term 'interval' both to pitch differences and to spatial differences and to temporal differences, and countless similar cases. But they will not even apply to the use of such musical terms as *maestoso*. Both a person and a piece of music may be called majestic, but it could scarcely be maintained that a piece of music that is properly marked *maestoso* by the composer is thereby claimed to express his majesty or to cause majesty in others. So *maestoso* and *mesto* will be terms of different type.

But is either theory true? That some composers have from time to time expressed their sadness in their music, and that music from time to time makes its hearers sad is something that nobody would presumably wish to deny, but the question is whether when we say that a piece of music is sad we wish to say that the composer was expressing his sadness or that it tends to make us sad. That the expressive theory is false seems to me clear from more than one consideration. In the first place, even a quite bad piece of music may be none the less recognisably sad; by making use of the recipes so admirably given by, for example, Mr Cooke in his *The Language of Music*, I believe that I could write a short piece of music that would be recognisably sad without thereby expressing sadness or indeed anything else. Nor is it plausible to suppose that the composer of Baroque opera, writing a series of arias which could be said to be successively angry, sad, gay and the like, feels and expresses a series of such emotions. Faced with this undeniable fact, the proponents of such a theory have sometimes claimed that the composer is expressing the universal emotion, not what he feels at the time. But, first, this answer does nothing to dispose of the problem of bad sad music, which clearly does nothing so exalted; secondly, any talk of the expression of emotion by a person who does not even purport to feel the emotion at the time of expression involves a novel and unclear use of the term 'expression'. Now 'expressive of the emotion in general' will be an expression itself needing explanation, not a clarification. Finally it seems worth adding that sad music does not much resemble the sounds that people make to express their sadness, which are typically disagreeable and even raucous.

As for the causal hypothesis, some considerations against it are parallel to those against the expressive theory. Thus sad music of

low quality, if it causes any reaction in us at all, is likely to cause
boredom rather than sadness. But such considerations are of minor
importance. It is much more important to observe that 'sad', when
applied to music, does not have a sense similar to that which it has
when applied to news. I am willing to allow that 'sad', when applied
to news, has a meaning somewhat like 'causing sadness'. In the first
place, sad news is normally unwelcome and unpleasant; if it is
welcomed it is a sign of a neurotic condition. But sad music is
pleasant to listen to, if it is otherwise worth listening to; much great
music that is sad makes us happy when we listen to it. In the second
place, if one wants to write music that will cause people to be agonised
one will not write music like Mozart's G minor Symphony, which
Mr Cooke reasonably calls agonised. A far more certain way of
causing agony in his audience would be for the composer to direct
that a piece of music, otherwise similar to a Johann Strauss Waltz,
should be played by an orchestra with brass pitched at A = 435,
woodwind at A = 440 and strings at A = 445. One is far more likely
to feel what could genuinely be called agony under such conditions
than when listening to any Mozart.

I have, of course, no desire to deny that there are terms applicable
to music that can be properly regarded as standing for causal properties. One may call a piece of music exhausting, tiring, deafening,
ear-splitting, boring, demanding, puzzling, and the like. These are
spectators' terms for describing the effect of music, or the appropriate
effect of music, upon the hearer. As such they differ markedly in
character from those of the type we are considering. There is a world
of difference between calling a piece of music exciting and calling it
excited, for example.

So theories such as those just considered are in themselves without
plausibility, as well as having only a narrow range within which they
could be even claimed to apply. We must therefore find another
account of the use of terms to apply both to pieces of music or
elements of pieces of music and also to other quite disparate phenomena. I am far from thinking that I can give an adequate treatment of this very large problem; certainly it cannot be disposed of
at the tail-end of a more general paper. But something must be said
about it.

The first point to which I wish to draw attention is that a very
large number of terms used to assign sensible characteristics are used
within the sphere of two or more senses. We have noted already that
tastes, smells and sounds may all be called sweet and that pains and
sounds, as well as colours, may be dull. Colours as well as felt bodies
may be warm or cold. The sound of a brass instrument may be sour,

like the taste of a lemon. Colours as well as sounds may be loud. Examples of this sort may be multiplied indefinitely; 'mellow', 'bitter', 'acid', 'smooth', 'rough', 'sombre', 'sharp' and 'strong' are all used normally and unpoetically to describe the objects of more than one sense. It is, perhaps, harder to find terms of sensory description that are confined to one sense than ones that are not. We all employ these terms in this way without hesitation, poetic licence or misunderstanding. Some individuals have indeed gone further than most of us are prepared to go. Beethoven and some others have applied colour-words to musical keys, and there is the famous story of the blind man who when given sight said that red was like the sound of a trumpet. Psychologists tell us of strange people who apparently use terms across the boundaries of the sense-modalities with a quite wild profusion, a phenomenon that the psychologists call synaesthesia. It seems that what these strange people do is not something in principle different from what we all do; rather they find it natural to carry to much greater lengths something that we all constantly do. We are all prepared to call a sound as well as a taste mellow; we may not follow Beethoven when he ascribes a colour to a key, but need we find it an odd type of phenomenon?

But, though shared between the sense-modalities in quite a promiscuous fashion, our store of words that appear to be devoted primarily to the description of the sensible features of the world by no means suffices us when we need to describe more subtle and more complex sensible phenomena. If asked to describe the visual appearance of a woman, I may say that her hair is brown, her eyes are blue, her skin fair and freckled, and the like, but still be conscious that some of the most important things remain unsaid. I may then add such a comment as that she has a fragile look. Now *fragile* is not primarily a term of sensible description, but a term for a tendency or disposition to break easily. But when I say that a woman has a fragile look I do not mean anything so ridiculous as that she will break easily, or that I judge from her appearance that she will break easily, or that people of that appearance statistically break easily. I am describing her appearance, while knowing full well that though some people may have fragile bones it is in general absurd to talk of people physically breaking at all, though they may break down in physical or mental health. When I say that a woman has a fragile look I am quite simply describing her visual appearance, how she looks. There is a certain look that things may have that is appropriately called fragile, even when the question of their actually breaking could scarcely arise. No doubt this use can be explained by the fact that many things with such a look do break easily, but a genetic account of how a word comes to have a use is not to be confused with an account of its use. We constantly employ adjectives that are not primarily used for visual description in this way, adding 'look' to show that the term is being used purely for visual description. Thus I may say that a mountain has a majestic look without raising the absurd question whether it is really majestic, or say that a man has an opulent look without suggesting that he is rich or committing myself to the view that most rich men look like that. Sometimes we may omit the word 'look' when it is in any case sufficiently obvious that we are concerned only with visual appearances; thus I might simply say that a mountain was majestic, since nobody would suppose that I was attributing to it a character-trait.

Thus words that primarily have other uses may be commandeered to serve for purely sensible description. One may add that we also sometimes employ words that seem to be primarily ascriptive of sensible characteristics to stand for characteristics that are not purely sensible. Thus I may speak of a sweet girl, a bitter quarrel, a colourful personality, a dark deed and a bright pupil. I am, incidentally, informed that the same Hebrew word may be used to translate 'sweet', whether we speak of a taste, a sound, a smell, or a girl.

Now it would be ridiculous to claim that there must be some one account that must hold universally to explain every single term that is used to describe music and its elements when the term is not uniquely dedicated to the characterisation of sounds. But in general it seems to me that those terms that we set out to consider – *high, low, sad, gay, majestic, peaceful, energetic* and the like – are used with reference to music as terms of purely sensible description. To describe a passage of music as sad seems to me very like describing a mountain as majestic, or describing a woman as having a fragile look. Similarly, when we call a sound high, we seem to be doing something very similar to what we do when we call a colour bright.

When we thus use terms that have other, non-auditory uses as descriptive of sound, it is at least often possible to find certain scientific analogies between the varying situations to which we apply the same term. No doubt the frequency of vibration is given by a higher number when we have a high sound and by a low number when we have a low sound; no doubt energetic music requires a higher output of physical energy by the performer, as does energetic physical activity of all types; no doubt the oscillograph-pattern of a smooth melody more resembles the shape of smooth things than the shape of jagged things. I am not only willing to concede, but positively expect, that there will be frequent analogues in the scientific explanation of things and phenomena to which we apply the same epithets. But this sort of explanation, even when possible, does not serve as an account of the meaning of the terms in question. In general, it is not the scientific analogue that links the meaning of the terms, and most of us are ignorant of it, even when the scientific analogue makes it intelligible why we use the terms as we do.

So I think that it is most plausible to regard the ascription of such characteristics as we have been considering to music as a special case of the very pervasive ascription of characteristics across the boundaries of the sense-modalities (e.g., sweet sounds, smells and tastes) and across the boundaries between sensible and non-sensible characteristics (e.g., fragile chair, fragile look; harsh sound, harsh decision). It is, in my opinion, a mere special case of our general way of characterising the world in non-aesthetic as well as in aesthetic contexts, and it is unplausible to hypothesise any special aesthetic explanation. Further, I think it plausible to regard most of the adjectives that are primarily under consideration as ascribing sensible features, often of a complex variety, to the music.

According to me, then, these terms present themselves to us as appropriately used both to ascribe a sensible feature to music and for other purposes, and the appropriateness is intrinsic, rather than depending on some extrinsic causal relation or other associative principle. If we ask why this seems appropriate to us I cannot think of anything very revealing to say. I have argued that it is not something that requires a very special explanation, that it is a case of the same phenomenon that we have when we call both a time and a spatial interval long, a smell and a taste sweet, a mountain and a king majestic. But a basic philosophical account of the general phenomenon is hard to find. One may say that we are aware of some analogy, that the sweetness of sounds is to sounds as the sweetness of tastes is to tastes and that length of time is to time as length of space is to space. But this is to say little.

If we are determined to maintain an unadulterated resemblance theory of musical representation, we shall have to try to speak in some other way than in terms of analogy. We shall have to claim that here too we have to deal with cases of resemblance. We shall then claim that the resemblance between the height of a place and the height of a sound, in virtue of which we call both high, between the sadness of a situation and the sadness of a musical passage, and so on, can be used in order to represent the high place or the sad situation that we wish to represent. This no doubt will often be done in conjunction with the utilisation of resemblances of a simpler sort. We may represent a horse galloping to a higher place by an ascending passage with the characteristic rhythm, for example. If we insist on claiming that we have here cases of resemblance, there is clearly no problem how we are to utilise them in a resemblance-theory of representation in music.

Clearly, if we are to limit the concept of resemblance to cases of the sharing of features, generic or specific, if pure univocality is required, we are not dealing with cases of resemblance when we consider the relation between high places and high sounds, sad situations and sad sounds. If it is not clear that the term *resemblance* must be so limited, we may perhaps mark these cases as being cases of transmodal or transcategorical resemblance. If we are to deal seriously and fully with this issue we shall have to start by a far more careful and fundamental analysis of the concept of resemblance than I have attempted. Such an enquiry would not lack interest, but for our present purposes it is not very important. For it does not matter very much whether the explanation of representation given in this paper can be called an unadulterated resemblance-theory. What matters is that the explanation should be true and reasonably clear. My explanation needs to be made a lot clearer, but I hope that it has been made clear enough to be understood, discussed, rejected, or accepted as a basis to work from.

One final remark is perhaps wise. If we wish to explain any case of representation, the most obvious explanatory concept from which to start is that of resemblance. The ancient Greek theories in terms of *mimesis* took this for granted. But in recent years some very excellent work, most notably Gombrich's *Art and Illusion*, has thrown great doubt on the possibility of explaining representation in general, and in particular in the visual arts, in terms of resemblance. In the case of the visual arts I am much impressed by the negative arguments of Gombrich, Wollheim and others. For my own part I am quite certain that dramatic representation should not be explained in terms of resemblance, though I do not think that the positive views of either Gombrich or Wollheim could be easily applied to dramatic representation. Nor can I see how an account of dramatic representation could be applied to the visual arts without gross changes. So in claiming that at least part of the explanation of representation in music is to be given in terms of resemblance I am doing something unfashionable. But the reader should be clear that in so doing I am in no way committing myself to the view that all representation is to be explained in terms of resemblance, a view that I believe to be false. Representation in general has many forms and may be achieved in many different ways.

8

PRESENTATIONAL OBJECTS
AND THEIR INTERPRETATION

David Pole

THE work of artists is to make works of art, and of theorists theoretical works. In our ordinary dealings with such things, elusive as ontologists may find them, we seem to know well enough in either instance how we should regard and handle them. Ontological questions are none the less raised: what species of entity may they be? It is a question, I confess, to which I could never respond with much enthusiasm. My own interest in art is more ordinary; I care about paintings and poems, about what serves to make them good or bad, about how we should look at or read them. Yet it may prove after all that the two issues are not wholly unrelated.

'Grammar', says Wittgenstein, in one of those dark teasing dicta of his, 'tells us what kind of object anything is.'[1] Where an air of obscurely charged potency clings to philosophical utterances it seems to affect different readers differently; but perhaps we can ignore that, and seek simply to get at the issue. At least this present saying seems to me to reward the labour it demands.

First, presumably, there may be objects of all sorts: people, pebbles, propositions, works of art. The parenthesis 'Theology as grammar' suggests that Wittgenstein himself would have added the Deity. These are things which we speak of in different ways; which for example we grasp or avoid as we do material things, at least those of appropriate dimensions; or which we blame or expostulate or fall in love with, these of course being attitudes proper to people; which again, in the case of propositions, we affirm, doubt or write on blackboard; which we pray to or worship or blaspheme against, in the case of God. Here, I recall a saying of Professor Wisdom which,

[1] *Philosophical Investigations*, I, § 373.

I think, proves helpful and relevant; namely that ontological and epistemological questions prove ultimately to be one and the same. Philosophers of the past used to ask what was, say, a table in itself – behind 'the veil of appearance', the real thing. The veil in question however proves to be a kind of net. We have the criss-crossing of forms of speech and forms of conduct and talk of appearances among them. Together they define our different concepts. And the whole complex, it would seem, can hardly sensibly be thought of as interposing between us and objects; for it itself serves to establish the latter and marks out their logical contours. In general it defines for us our different notions – notions which would otherwise be vacuous. Perhaps however I need not labour the point; all this by now, I assume, is tolerably familiar. There are, I said, objects of all sorts; yet a twofold distinction exists too.

We may use the word first to accord 'ontological status' to favoured candidates (I use jargon deliberately to leave open the issues it obfuscates). But there are, secondly, intensional objects, for instance objects of concern, or thought, perception and the like. Now as to the 'furniture of the universe', in Russell's phrase, there will presumably be diverse items of furniture. And footstools, ontological footstools, will differ from ontological armchairs; which, where 'object' is used intensionally, no longer holds. For what I merely think of, you may see; what I worship, perhaps the brute image of Dagon, you in your righteousness may abominate. Here we have objects that differ as objects of intensional attitudes, but which are, ontologically, the same. Yet this difference at a certain level grows less clear. Ontological objects, I suggested, are defined by appropriate attitudes; by the ways in which they are known or may be known, and perhaps others too. Chairs and tables may be seen as well as thought of; they cannot be affirmed or denied. Propositions, precisely conversely, are things that can be doubted or believed, which lies in their nature; but they cannot be seen, smelt or tasted. The upshot is this: when we are speaking not of actual but only possible attitudes, and again not of individuals who see or think of things, but of people quite generally, the pattern changes. Here kinds of ontological object are kinds of object for cognitive and similar attitudes too.

I am of course by devious tackings, and through waters not wholly untroubled, approaching my own objective, works of art. A work of art is a thing *sui generis*; so much can be said tolerably tamely. As a convenient formula to summarise these platitudes – namely that these things are known, viewed and valued precisely thus, as we all very familiarly understand them to be known, viewed and valued – I shall speak of them as presentational objects; though it will appear that I use the phrase rather differently from Professor Wollheim, from whom I have stolen it. (In philosophy, perhaps, one may innocently play at Robin Hood; in other words, theft becomes excusable when it is taken as serving the general interest.)

Wollheim opposes this theory to another that he himself advocates; works of art, with certain qualifications, are to be identified with physical things. What should one say? I find the whole notion a perplexing one; what sort of identity can be in question? Certainly I can imagine possible contexts for it. 'That statue,' one may say, or even perhaps 'that piece of marble is – is identical with – Bernini's St Longinus.' I dare say with ingenuity one might even imagine some odd context for 'The physical object is Bernini's St Longinus.' But in fact he asserts it wholly generally. And of course the trouble is that it looks at face value patently false; I mean that it looks like the false assertion that what Wittgenstein calls the 'grammar' of the two concepts – the sorts of discourse and 'forms of life' that sustain them – are not in fact different but the same.

Wittgenstein appears later in Wollheim's book; at this stage he is little in evidence. 'It is plausible', he writes, 'to assume that things are physical objects unless they very obviously aren't.'[1] Again I am puzzled. It is an assertion that has to me an odd air of willing itself to its conclusion by a kind of autosuggestion, by treating it as already arrived at. We are offered two phrases; Wollheim refers to 'what it is plausible to assume' and again to what things 'obviously are'. Certainly assumptions may be plausible and views obvious; except that the latter adjective is perhaps somewhat stronger, they might, I think, be taken as virtually synonymous. Wollheim's manoeuvre, it seems, is first to prise apart the two sides of the tautology, and next, having done so, as it were, to use the leverage of the one to hoist up the other. For myself, I might add incidentally, I fail to find the assumption plausible at all. Why should material objects, chairs, trees and pieces of marble, have some privileged ontological status? Platitudinously, they are what they are, and are known in appropriate ways. They may indeed, as Professor Strawson argues, have a primacy of a different sort; without these things we could never conceive of others. But that is a different sort of difference, providing no passage to reductionism.

But perhaps my criticisms pass Wollheim by. He seems to advance from the ontological options offered in the first part of his book to some sort of Wittgensteinian view at the end; the transition in question is what eludes me. I expect that I may have failed clearly to

[1] R. Wollheim, *Art and Its Objects*, p. 3.

have followed it. I shall not pursue the issue however; as I indicated, my interest in what I call the presentational theory is, I think, rather different from his.

My concern is with the integrity of art, with the integrity of particular works as well as that of the concept itself. The point of presentational theory is, as I understand it, precisely this: it asserts, platitudinously, that works of art are what they are. But it serves, too, to compare them with other things; to register, on the one hand, their likeness to physical objects, say, stones or tables; on the other to propositions or theories. They are also of course unlike both; our concern is with both likenesses and differences. The quasi-propositional character of much art is to Wollheim a main objection to the theory; for me, at least for my version of it, I take it to be a paramount advantage. Theories have a kind of autonomy and a kind of publicity too; when you and I discuss, say, the Quantum Theory, we are, it seems, considering the same object, in some sense a public object, then, and one that is unique of its kind. The same is true, I believe, of works of art. Theories, too, are irreducible to material things, even to types of material thing; classes of inscription, for instance. Of works of art, I suggest, the same holds. And further and more important, a point I shall have to return to, they belong to history. The history of thought is a mosaic where each piece is wedged in its place. The same holds for history of art. Theories too are called good or bad; they are intrinsically objects of assessment. And these merits or demerits are their own, and not alterable with their creator's intentions. In some sense, at least, the same is pretty obviously true of works of art. Yet another likeness: they invite interpretation, which can succeed or fail. It follows then that they are vulnerable to misinterpretation too – especially at the hands of those who ignore history. Some theorists use history, the history of thought or of art and some again political history, as a kind of Rorschach test, upon which to project their own preoccupations or fads. Each is malleable material to be manipulated; one can rebuild it, if not nearer the heart's desire, at least nearer one's own interests, or nearer those of one's own clique or culture. Old works are brought up to date. *Hamlet* to some Freudians is a study in the oedipus complex; the sculpture in the Medici Chapel was sometimes taken by Italian patriots of the period of the *Risorgimento* as having to do with the political dismemberment of fifteenth-century Italy.

Now the past is still of course a living past. It would be superfluous to illustrate the fact that artists use the work of their predecessors, which sometimes might have looked pretty remote, and is strangely transformed in the process. But that remains honest and open; it is plainly neither interpretation nor misinterpretation, but merely part of the normal creative process. Interpreters such as I have been speaking of, I mean those who give themselves leave to ignore history, are, one may suspect, often at bottom perhaps artists *manqués*, producing variations on a theme – a thing harmless in itself. Francis Bacon and other artists have done it explicitly and overtly. A philosopher similarly may use Kant or Aristotle, though translating what he uses into a different philosophical idiom. Cézanne set out to re-do Poussin 'd'après la nature'; one might similarly perhaps, concerning oneself with the conditions of any possible language, seek to re-do Kant after Wittgenstein. No sensible person would object, at least not in principle. All that would be obviously vicious would be to confuse the historical Kant, the philosopher of the eighteenth century, whose background was Leibniz and Wolff, with what later analytic thinkers educe from him. That confusion, however, would be gratuitous. Pater's *Mona Lisa* by contrast or Jones's oedipal Hamlet form, as it were, an indeterminate mode, neither fish nor fowl; though indeed, forgetting their professed status as criticism, one may still enjoy in the former the elegiac elegance of its laboured prose – though the cadences are a little weary – and even a kind of ingenuity in the other.

Let me briefly enlarge on the last point, adding a more specific example. There is a moment in *Henry IV, Part I* where the Prince has got rid of the Sheriff; 'certain men', the latter says, having been traced to the house after the robbery. And he adds:

> 'One of them is well known, my gracious lord,
> A gross fat man.'

To which the Carrier briefly subjoins, 'As fat as butter'. Falstaff must have been easy to identify. And the Prince afterwards, having extricated himself with 'a true face and good conscience', observes – with that odd mixture of contempt and amusement, perhaps a kind of affection that characterises his attitude – 'this oily rascal is known as well as Paul's'. Now Shakespeare in general, seeking appropriate epithets for Falstaff and his enormous bulk, seems positively to glory in hyperboles, in the extreme and gross preposterousness of his comparisons. For myself, with the reference to St Paul's, I could never help thinking of the great drum and dome that Wren was to build a hundred years later; perhaps a still happier image than the Early English Gothic of the contemporary building. The point is worth pausing on, I think. My dominant concern, I repeat, is simply the integrity of works of art. And I answer with Johnson that the old reading may not be better; it suffices that it is Shakespeare's. Johnson, it is true, was speaking of licentious emendation; but the questions raised by licentious interpretation would seem to be essentially the same. 'If phraseology is to be changed', he writes, 'as words grow uncouth by disuse, or gross by vulgarity, the history of language will be lost; we shall no longer have the words of any author; and, as these alterations will often be unskillfully made, we shall in time have very little of his meaning'.[1] On behalf of interpreters it may be said that they at least leave the object intact; and subsequent generations may still dig it up again, extricate the ancient forms from among the rubble. Why they should on their own principles is obscure; at least where, like Wollheim, they positively acclaim the grand liberty they allow themselves. If so, I find no difference between them and those eighteenth-century editors who rewrote Shakespeare to accord with their own superior taste – even if, by comparison, modern interpreters lacked the courage of their convictions, or perhaps only opportunity to implement them. For a few small changes would surely make *Hamlet* fit Jones's reading far more convincingly than the quarto or folio text fits it.

A work of art, I have said, belongs to history. Wollheim himself says the same, at least at one point in his argument. To appreciate particular works we need some understanding of their background, for the history of art raises problems – once again like the history of thought – which these works may precisely seek to solve. Now with that I would certainly agree; though as to the example that Wollheim uses to illustrate the point I have some doubts; namely of the steeple of St Martin-in-the-Fields. The façade is to be seen, Wollheim writes, 'as a solution to a problem which for fifty years exercised English architects; how to combine a temple façade or portico with the traditional English demand for a west tower'.[2] I see no trace of such a tradition.[3] But the general thesis remains unaffected.

So far my conclusion is this: works of art invite comparison, a rewarding comparison in many ways, with works of philosophy or

[1] Samuel Johnson, *Plays of William Shakespeare*, Note on *Hamlet*, IV, v, 84.
[2] Op. cit., p. 62.
[3] A portico is very different from a temple front. The former presents no special problem. Gibbs himself had handled it wholly comfortably in his little chapel of St Peter's, Vere Street. The attempt to combine a steeple with a temple front is quite another matter, a temptation that was understandably strong. That can help to make Gibbs's failure intelligible; it could not possibly transform it into success. And, it seems, the pediment was anyway a feature Gibbs was never happy with. With no temple front, instead a semi-circular portico, in the west façade, it is the one inept feature marring the otherwise exquisite church of St Mary-le-Strand. And the podium-like ground floor of the Radcliffe Camera hardly does better.

science, which is one thing the presentational theory – if any such
theory indeed exists – can be usefully seen as insisting on. Each can
be spoken of as objects. We apprehend each in its own way, and each
must be thought of accordingly. For such apprehension defines the
concept. But the comparison it more obviously insists on is with
objects of ordinary perception: trees, tables, teaspoons and the like.
There is some sort of immediacy, we feel, in our awareness of so-
called aesthetic qualities, say, the serenity of an early Renaissance
façade or the dynamism and power of its Baroque counterpart;
an immediacy that is naturally comparable, as I said, to our ordinary
perception of shapes or colours. The point is a familiar one, and for
present purposes can be taken for granted, though doubtless much
more might be said. It is more relevant to note that this immediacy,
however we regard it, need do nothing to block further enquiry.
We can still seek to explain or understand it. Now perception,
naturally enough, has a physiological and psychological basis; an
unremarkable fact, long supposed – by a familiar fallacy – to cast
doubt on the status of its objects. I see a red apple in front of me;
but the redness could not really be 'in' the apple, for the fact that
I see it depends on the state of my eyes and my brain. Nor, I suppose,
could two and two really equal four – at least I have no reason to
think so – for without a brain I would certainly never apprehend
it. We do of course see things like apples, and their qualities are
real qualities of those objects; the explicability of the fact does
nothing to render it problematic. How could the discovery of an
explanation be grounds for doubting the fact that it explains? The
same holds of so-called aesthetic qualities, or again of those 'presentational objects' that theorists are supposed to believe in. In literary
theory at least something like the latter notion does certainly occur.
Now those who uphold the view, as far as I know, are in fact content
to leave it there. As for such qualities, it is as though their mere
'perception' sufficed and no further explanation is called for; which
may have helped to bring the theory into disrepute. One can in fact
explain them, I believe; though the enterprise is one I shall not
remark on at present. (I have elsewhere attempted to throw light on
our quasi-immediate apprehension of what I call aesthetic form.)[1]

Those, of course, are *qualities*, not objects; and, we may observe,
Wollheim himself believes in such qualities. He speaks explicitly for
instance of representational and expressive qualities; which are
presumably not to be 'perceived' quite as colours and shapes are
perceived. And Professor Beardsley and Professor Sibley talk of

[1] In my paper 'The excellence of Form in Works of Art', *Proceedings of the Aristotelian Society*, LXXI, 1971–2, pp. 13–29.

qualities, so-called aesthetic or regional qualities, apprehended in their own special way. Yet neither, I believe, talks of objects; only *objects* are what Wollheim seems to quarrel with. I find the point a somewhat puzzling one; it can hardly be that the whole hot dispute is over the use of an adjective or a noun.

For another powerful exponent of the presentational theory, at least as I myself understand it, I mean to invoke the name of Collingwood. Wollheim of course puts him in the opposite camp; but, I find, the issue invites further scrutiny. It is complicated, for one thing, by Collingwood's metaphysic. Material things, as he sees it, are 'constructs', they are somehow put together out of sensa. And these sensa he thinks of as private. The passage from such private sensa say to public chairs and tables may be one that presents logical difficulties; but those are not our present concern. But allow it to be possible, and for public works of art the same holds. It is of course true that to perceive any qualities belonging to them we must bring to bear appropriate faculties. 'But', Collingwood writes, 'this applies equally to colours.'[1] Let me put the point in a more realist terminology: works of art may be thought of as physical things apprehended imaginatively. I would not say that Collingwood never confuses the two relevant adjectives, namely 'imaginary' and 'imaginative'; he does so in fact in the very passage I have quoted from. He sometimes indeed makes it look as if what he is speaking of were a species of private or imaginary object that could only exist 'in our heads'. But he certainly conceives of the artist as starting work, so to speak, with the senses, with what he calls sensa; and hence with a particular medium. And one great advantage of his view is precisely the stress it enables him to lay on the medium. The artist's gift is to see it imaginatively, in other words, grasping its inherent potentialities.

But that does not affect his basic thesis: art is the expression of emotion. Such is Collingwood's theory, which connects it with dreaming and daydreaming. The same connection had been noticed by psychoanalysts. Collingwood's contribution however, which he makes in the section called 'Imagination and Make-believe'[2] – a minor landmark in the history of aesthetics – is to see not only the likeness but the difference, which is broadly this: it is the difference between a disciplined and a self-indulgent use of imagination. Wollheim too stresses the distinction, but I cannot but think that he mishandles it. The difference for him is the difference between the privacy of day-dreaming and the public institution of art. But

[1] *The Principles of Art*, p. 150.
[2] Op. cit., vii, iv.

Collingwood had anticipated the point; day-dreaming can be publicly institutionalised too – a process, as he says, that has proved vastly profitable to those who exploit it.

I have sought so far to champion the so-called presentational theory; I have gone along with it as far as I can. But there remains another critic to be met, if not precisely of that theory – anyway, as we found, a somewhat elusive object – at least of a similar approach which sees the appreciation of art in terms of the perception of aesthetic qualities. Miss Meager in an excellent article[1] – only marred by what seemed to me compulsive and distracting genuflections to the sage of Königsberg – put her finger on the relevant difference, aesthetically relevant, not merely metaphysically. I mean the difference between physical objects and works of art. The former we merely perceive, and perceive better with keener discrimination; the latter we inwardly respond to. Let me take an example: I do not know whether the antechamber of the Laurentian Library brings my faculties into harmonious interplay. It hardly seems to. I find no liberation, no free play, and certainly no reaching towards infinity. Yet it strangely troubles, oppresses and fascinates me. Here Michelangelo indeed makes me see, but also feel; and the two things are hardly to be distinguished.

It may seem then that the theory breaks down. Yet we find in fact critical discourse circumvents the difficulty remarkably painlessly. Critics both of literature and visual art are much concerned, doubtless rightly concerned, with the responses of either readers or viewers; with the difference, more especially, between right responses and wrong ones. In other words they implicitly distinguish between a response and its object; the latter is of course the work itself. It is at least a style of discourse that seems to work, to accommodate whatever we need. We can side-step ontological issues, which might possibly or profitably be pursued further. But I shall not attempt the enterprise. My own interest in the presentational theory is, as I indicated, more limited; it is confined to its usefulness in illuminating questions that belong more properly or essentially to art, to its appreciation and understanding *qua* art.

Now for such understanding and appreciation another issue is certainly central, one that I have already touched on. I mean that of right interpretation which, I think, stills calls for fuller treatment. Two people who 'read' a work differently are likely to evaluate it differently; and – the normal view, I think, and perhaps naïve one, which I none the less mean to maintain – if one reading is right, the other, we assume, must be wrong. Interpretations, we find in point

[1] 'Aesthetic Concepts', *British Journal of Aesthetics*, x, iv, 1970, pp. 303–22.

of fact, spawn freely in the writings of critics; they cover the true face of art, as it were, with some distorting, translucent jelly. Understandable efforts have been made to bring some sort of order into this chaos; to define clear rules for right interpretation. But no general rules are to be found; the enterprise, however tempting or promising, seems to me a mistaken one. Works of theory, I have argued, like works of art, may be seen as presentational objects. Now it seems that for the right interpretation of, say, Aristotle or Newton there exist no rules. Nor I believe has anyone sought to formulate rules. At most there is the vacuous rule that the best interpretation makes the best sense of them – always bearing in mind the simple but crucial qualification that I have insisted on. These works are historical entities; interpretation must not violate history. For the rest, they will vary indefinitely, and make sense in ways that differ indefinitely. We can state no finite list of aesthetic requirements. One may stress the requirement of unity; it is one feature that is very generally valued. Accordingly in Mr Savile's account of interpretation it figures prominently.[1] That doubtless is eminently plausible; yet it remains one feature only, one among others. Artists, I think, left to themselves, rather than perfecting unitary works, might be happier to tinker indefinitely; such is my own limited impression at least of painters' studios cluttered with bits and pieces, or poets' papers with fragments and odd lines. Yet such fragments surely may already possess aesthetic qualities, nor wholly defy interpretation. As to those 'whole objects' that Wollheim has also spoken of, unitary objects, I suppose, we owe them, I suspect, as much to the pressure of dealers and publishers as to any deep psychic needs explored by Mrs Klein. Not that I would discount other and more intimately relevant considerations; the connected concepts of unity and aesthetic form I mentioned that I myself have spoken of elsewhere.

There exists, I said, one right interpretation; ideally only one, I shall argue. The capacity to produce in every age some new unpredictable response has sometimes been ascribed to works of art; and in a way rightly, as we shall see. It has even been made their defining property; it is equated with the greatness of great art. Now if so, it is a mysterious property. Let me take an analogy: dexadrin produces excitement, alcohol intoxication and barbiturate sleep. Imagine the following properties as belonging to one and the same drug: in the eighteenth century it served to rouse excitement, in the nineteenth intoxication and in the twentieth it induces sleep. In

[1] Cf. Anthony Savile, 'The Place of Intention in the Concept of Art', *Proceedings of the Aristotelian Society*, LXIX, 1968–9, p. 116.

some sense, at least, works of art are widely allowed to be mysterious. I cannot see that we illuminate one mystery by invoking another. And, pretty obviously, to get any further what we should need would be, first, to isolate this singular property, and then, if we could, go on to explain it and its curiously various manifestations. I find besides that the theory breaks down; it has already been falsified by the facts. Art is mysterious, certainly, and our powerful response to it is mysterious. It is natural enough then that critics should seek to explain it, and hardly less natural that they should often fail. They respond strongly, and seek to explain the fact. Their explanations – interpretations – often differ. But we must add this: we find in fact that it is not only masterpieces that invite an indefinite variety of interpretations; the same holds of minor works, too. 'This was sometime a paradox, but now the time gives it proof.' The academic industry has taken over. There exist nowadays not only emotional factors at work, leading people to explore what underlies acknowledged masterpieces or to project on them their own *idées fixes*. We find institutional pressures as well. And, as I say, minor works prove no less patient of the process in question than those of great masters.

I may perhaps seem to be hinting that the activity itself is illegitimate. I mean only that it is widely abused. But the term itself must not pass unexamined; it can be used to mean widely different things. Let me illustrate: I recall a lecture in which a distinguished English scholar set out explicitly to discuss the topic. He placed side by side, first, different interpretations of a novel of Conrad's (namely *Under Western Eyes*), and secondly different interpretations – the same word was used – of certain primitive fables or myths. Now for most of us, I take it, Conrad's novel already makes sense; in one way then interpretation is superfluous. The latter case was radically different. I cannot recapitulate the fables in question; but precisely that sense was what one lacked. The narrated events, to people of our culture at least, seemed wholly pointless. In other words they cried out for interpretation; just that point was what one wanted to know. There are in brief at least two different ways in which art may admit of interpretation. A work that needs no interpretation in one sense, that achieves effect without interpretation, may invite it in another. We may ask how those effects are achieved. For instance, Professor Empson taught critics long ago to tease out ambiguities from poetry, and thereby helped to explain the ordinary readers' response. The process, clearly enough, also presupposed that response. Otherwise, using such methods, we would be interpreting nothing, and that requires very nice instruments.

Not that I doubt that experts exist by whom appropriate instruments have been perfected. For the rest, old works, for obvious reasons, can call for interpretation in a different and more radical sense. The same goes for obscure works; and the vogue of obscurity currently provides much employment for academics. Nor would I deny, even in explanatory criticism, that occasionally the two processes merge, that to highlight a given response, or rather to highlight what underlies it, can also be to vivify or reinforce it. And yet in a sense it remains true that successful works should need no interpretation, that that need is a measure of failure. Otherwise one must imagine the following: that a serious artist will consciously rely on critics to help him out; that he will be content to let the effect at which he aims turn on the lucky chance of finding a critic who gets it right. Now such works have of course been produced. But the practice, I believe, carried beyond a certain point would undermine the very conditions in which art as a meaningful institution can exist.

And here I must return to Professor Wollheim. His rejection of the presentational theory goes along with a view of art as something in this way distinctive; it is and must be indefinitely re-interpretable. He denies – using examples from literature – that any line can be drawn between what he calls 'fact' and interpretation. Yet he himself needs the distinction. For he favours the innovations of interpreters; later ages, he argues, will always reveal to us old masterpieces in new ways. But then, one must ask, what is it that they are supposed to re-interpret? There must be something for such interpretation to work on, something contra-distinguished from interpretation if we are to speak at all of 'the same work' as re-interpreted. Besides it is as plainly a fact in Shakespeare's play that Othello is a Venetian general, or at least a general in service of the Venetian State, as that, in the University of London, Professor Wollheim is Grote Professor of Mind and Logic. Considerations of essentially the same sort, *mutatis mutandis*, will serve in either case.

I have already mentioned Jones's oedipal Hamlet, as indeed Wollheim does, too. He himself further favours a homosexual Iago; and I myself finally have suggested the possibility – I take it a pretty fanciful one – of reading a phrase in *Henry IV* as referring to the cathedral built by Wren. Now in each case, as I myself see it, the same simple objection is decisive; each reading is grossly ahistorical. Certainly, as regards Hamlet or Iago, an alternative view remains possible, if not very plausible, perhaps. Shakespeare himself, let us imagine, obscurely felt, merely felt, what he wrote was somehow right, and relied on his audience to feel the same – yet without either being able to say why. That was left to Freud, centuries later. This is however a possibility that I am happy enough to disregard; and I do so on Wollheim's own authority. For as to the interpretation he favours, it was, he supposes, 'not open to earlier generations to perceive'.[1] The phrase, perhaps, is not wholly unambiguous. It might be the very thing that I referred to, the unknown explanation underlying an actual response that was, as we are told, 'not open' to contemporaries. But the reading is an unnatural one; and besides Wollheim's other examples, and an epigram that he quotes from Valéry – the French love to philosophise in epigrams, this one being that 'A creator is one who makes others create' – would seem to leave the point in no doubt.

Now none of these interpretations is merely arbitrary. For each, it may be argued, not only fits but positively enhances the work; at least the passage in question. The rights and wrongs of these arguments do not concern me. (In fact I think it false in the cases of Hamlet and Iago, but true of the reference to St Paul's.) And each age brings we are told, new ideas, a new outlook, to alter the features of old masterpieces. It seems now however that we are back with our magic drug; for, we must ask, why only masterpieces? It would seem to be a mystery past fathoming. Why in that period should one man, namely Shakespeare, have produced so many works which repay this interesting process – undergoing, let us recall, transformations that he himself could never possibly have foreseen – while so many others, a sizeable body of anonymous hack dramatists, produced, as far as I know, none at all? We saw, indeed, that they are equally subject to re-interpretation. But here re-interpretation, it seems – and this is what I call arbitrary and mysterious – never serves to transform them into masterpieces.

Perhaps it is attributable to chance. Of the mystic of chance glorified by Arp (in a passage quoted by Mr Forge in one of the lectures of the present series), I shall say nothing – influential as it has proved amongst artists. I have no space to argue the issue, even if I thought it deserved it. But to remain with Wollheim: suppose a Freudian reading does indeed fit and enhance one character in the play, or one passage. What of others? We ought, it seems to me, to take account of what diligent research might be reasonably expected to reveal. There must be passages or features that would benefit no less say, by a Jungian reading, a Lévi-Straussian reading, a neo-Marxist reading and so on. Should we switch our reading from line to line? As to that possibility, I think Wollheim himself, with his

---

[1] Op. cit., p. 76.

interest in whole objects, will hardly welcome it. But then any pre-
ference will be arbitrary. Besides, countless further possibilities will
always remain to be explored. Works of art prove creative indeed,
and make other people create; Valéry is vindicated with a vengeance.
One can go further; Wollheim is not, I hope, merely denying the
possibility of history. Yet we not only interpret works of art – I
previously mentioned the sculpture in the Medici Chapel – but also
thinkers, say, Machiavelli, and again political figures, say Savonarola.
Machiavelli and Savonarola have in fact both been seen as prophets
of Italian unity. Now here, I presume, we have views that admit of
historical assessment. But if so, there ought also to be the possibility
of a historical approach to works of art. Wollheim then, even on his
own terms, should surely distinguish between two equally possible
viewpoints, two ways of regarding such works, either on the face of it
being legitimate – or if not, the point emphatically calls for argument. And these are the historical and the ahistorical. But in fact, as
we see, with the latter any work will break up, not only from age to
age, which Wollheim welcomes, but even at any given moment, into
an indefinite multiplicity. The argument argues art out of existence.

Now the concept of art, to repeat, and the meaningfulness of
talking of given works, require a grasp of their historical context.
And I think it is in the ablest among the apologists of artistic modernism, Mr Harold Rosenberg, that the views I oppose find their
reductio ad absurdum. Among such apologists Rosenberg, along with
other assets, enjoys the great advantage of a sense of humour; for
what could be more out of place than solemnity over a species of
art – or as he himself seems to see it, so to speak, of post-art, that is,
a movement that has superseded art – that perhaps chiefly thrives
on self-caricature? Only read the opening chapters of *The Anxious
Object*, however, but imagine its emphasis slightly shifted. The author,
it is hard not to feel, is in danger of dropping into ridicule, of seeing
the whole scene as a gigantic farce. He notes, very accurately, our
terrorised generation of critics; who, faced with works ten times
more outrageous than any that shocked Dickens or Ruskin, dare
not breathe the least murmur of protest. One may search the journals
or the 'quality' weeklies: 'pretentious', which appears just now and
then, is, I think, the boldest expression of condemnation you will
find. Since their predecessors came so frightful a cropper over the
Post-Impressionists and *The Waste Land* it is all changed. And in all
seriousness the point may be worth dwelling on: it is hard to imagine
any object, an object of any sort whatever, whose presence in an
art gallery would move them to the mildest point of exclamation.
True, they generally fail to take notice of attendants, who after all

may have been sent there by Mr Rauschenberg; one is to see them, in Rosenberg's Pickwickian sense, as objects of art. Rosenberg sees too the compulsive novelty of the perpetual revolution with its effects on our artists themselves, and on dealers too who assiduously promote each new mutation. Yet none of this apparently disturbs him. In this climate serious art is supposed to germinate; which, to put it mildly, seems unlikely.

My own heritical views I have, I fear, already betrayed all too clearly. I take a good BBC series serial, say *Z Cars* or *Softly, Softly*, to be doing, with unpretentious commitment, something at bottom far more serious than half those producers of artefacts who claim the prestige and, like Rosenberg, repudiate the tradition of the artist. But *Softly, Softly*, you may say, is mere entertainment not art; which is probably true. But the line between art and entertainment is one I find harder to draw than some aesthetic theorists, who make it absolute – Collingwood for one. Besides, one may notice that Ben Jonson, similarly devoted to high ideals, was disdainful of the popular stage, which he had happily to write for none the less; and produced masterpieces like *Volpone* and *The Alchemist*. 'Our dungy earth alike / Feeds beast as man.' Such, it will be found, are the lowly conditions that have time and again manured the potentiality of art.

Rosenberg, I said, emphatically repudiates the tradition – emphatically if not very consistently. He has, I suspect, Hegelian longings in him and remains a romantic at heart. What he tells us explicitly however is that you kill the new art by looking at it in terms of the old. The very concept is seen as misleading, whence my suggestion that we should speak of it rather as post-art.

He quoted, in the preface to the 1970 edition of *The Tradition of The New*, a comment of Miss Mary Macarthy's made, apparently, when the book first appeared. 'You cannot hang an event on the wall,' she wrote, 'only a picture.' I have failed to find the original review; she seems however, not uncharacteristically, to have put her finger on the precise point. For, we gather, she went on to accuse Rosenberg of what she called 'a weird contradiction'. Now as to Rosenberg, his first love was Action Painting. The picture is what one hangs on the wall; the event, then, is the action of painting it. That action expresses, for Rosenberg, the anguish of the artist, perhaps also of the age, or both at once. For the *Zeitgeist*, along with other left-overs of romantic aesthetics, make spectral appearances in his pages. As to that troublesome spirit, uttering its ominous noises from the cellarage, like the ghost in Hamlet – *hic et ubique* – one might have thought that serious scholarship had long since exorcised it, long since laid it to rest. But the point here is this: we have before us an object, the product of a speculative event. Now either, the *ne plus ultra* of romanticism, you think of the artist's spontaneous gesture as imprinting itself meaningfully on the canvas; or you look at the latter itself, the object as it actually is. Rosenberg vacillates, I think: but his real wish, one suspects, is indeed to look at the object – what else could one do, after all? – yet, looking at it, to see an event: 'a weird contradiction' indeed.

My interest however is in his answer, which is as follows. It is, he says, a contradiction only if,

> through the habit of looking back to other times, we forget the multiple existence which a painting now enjoys in separation from its physical body: its ghostly presence through reproduction in books and magazines that carries it *as picture* far from its durable being of paint and canvas; the intellectual character it takes on from interpretations irremovably tacked on to it by critics, art historians, psychiatrists, philosophers of culture . . . the power of transformation it wields over its own creator through the energy it accumulates in its passage through the social orbit.[1]

What puzzles me is how all that, a brilliant verbal barrage as it is, can even seem to bear on the point at issue – at least to a man so evidently intelligent as Rosenberg – let alone to be a satisfactory answer. What, it seems, Miss Macarthy complained of was the impossibility of responding to an event that is unavoidably inaccessible; to something not there to respond to. Rosenberg answers by referring us to others; events loosely connected with the first, but for his purposes, one would have thought, hardly relevant. Suppose as a patriotic Briton I glory in King Arthur's mighty deeds. But those deeds, I later learn, and even the king himself, are all very possibly mythical. In fact, I suspect, in most cases at least, the same holds for the fine frenzy of action painters. Well, I am told reassuringly, I can respond instead to the subsequent accumulation of legend – the only trouble being that a different response, antiquarian curiosity rather than fervid patriotism, might now seem more appropriate.

For the rest, those processes certainly occur; I mean the processes that Rosenberg speaks of. We can add others too, which belong to the passage of time. Pictures fade, statues get chipped. They also are photographed and reproduced, better or worse, and students often study only reproductions. It is true, too, that later developments, in art and elsewhere, may serve to obscure what preceded them. We can no longer see what contemporaries saw. None of this is likely

---

[1] Op. cit., pp. 10–11.

to be disputed. But all I maintain, to repeat, is the possibility of historical scholarship, which remains an intelligible enterprise; it remains one, whether or not it can ever quite attain its goal, it may progressively approximate to it. And its goal, it would seem, is precisely to reverse the processes in question; to undo, so far as possible, the work of time. The historian of ideas strives to grasp, say, the original thought of Machiavelli, to see it as he himself saw it; and the same holds of the art of his contemporaries. Reviewers too persist in commenting on the quality of reproductions in art books, as though they took it to be important to get as near as possible to the original – a strange practice, nor, on Rosenberg's principles, easy to understand. His position, to repeat, amounts to this, the denial of the possibility of history. And that, incidentally, consistently carried through, leads to much larger consequences; it leads to general denial of the whole possibility of thought.

For the rest, my own heterodox view of the present condition of the arts will, I fear, be sufficiently plain. I shall not speculate as to how it came about. But as to what, speaking very broadly, it represents, I tentatively offer the following notion. What I think we see is some sort of general loss of confidence; which seems at least to tell us more than another somewhat similar concept sometimes appealed to, that of self-criticism. For instance it helps us to relate such seemingly disparate phenomena as the compulsion that drove architects, some fifty years ago, to strip all ornament from the face of their buildings – a phenomenon, I believe, unique in history – with those empty canvases of Rauschenberg which, in the lecture I mentioned previously, Mr Forge spoke of; and again with the reduction of so much literature to a sort of a confessional monotone – though sometimes, one must add, a confessional becomes more like a shriek, a shrill noise of self-vindication. Or take the modern dogma, introduced in the last generation but now very widely upheld, in at least visual art, of truth to the medium; it seems connected with an equally inhibiting dogma in the novel, namely the dogma that condemns telling in favour of showing. The object of each is the same; it seeks, I think, to cling to some failing plank. Indeed it is happily true, as to the latter, that novelists more recently appear to be widely in revolt against it; but modernism is a hard thing to keep pace with. Why is so much recent art, even *qua* art, paradoxical? From time to time some illusory formula releases a new burst of energy; it seems to open the way that was closed, to reveal the possibility of something that both is and isn't art. And new art form survives as long as the illusion survives. Both more and less significant work in recent decades seems to me largely to answer to this pattern.

But suppose this conjecture is right: one must still ask what brought it about. I said I should not speculate. As to the forces that make and unmake cultures, that channel and swell human energies, that disperse and undermine them: of all this, if one wants succinct explanatory generalisations, they are plentifully available. But having wandered too far from my subject and doubtless given provocation enough, I shall leave the issue for others to pursue.

9

AESTHETIC OBJECTIVITY AND THE ANALOGY WITH ETHICS

Oliver Johnson

OF all the kinds of arguments that philosophers use to support their conclusions, the one type that I find personally to stick longest and most vividly in my mind is the verbal pictures they occasionally draw. Whether this is a result of the fact that I myself think best in pictorial terms or, as I would rather like to believe, is a tribute to the verbal artistry of the writers themselves, it remains true that, for me, the history of philosophy is punctuated with pictures, some pleasing and others perplexing. I need hardly mention Plato; with the Allegory of the Cave, the Myth of Er, the Charioteer of the Soul, and countless others he is beyond question the supreme master of the art. But other examples easily come to mind. I see Descartes seated in solitude before the fire in his dressing gown, suddenly to be surprised by a malignant demon, who appears at his shoulder to whisper insinuatingly into his ear that 2 plus 2 does not equal 4 at all. Or William James on a camping trip with friends trying to decide whether one of their number who keeps circling a tree on which a squirrel clings – and in turn circles the tree at equal speed, keeping the tree between him and his tormenter and never permitting the latter to get into a position behind his back – does or does not circle the squirrel, as he undoubtedly does circle the tree to which the squirrel clings. Or, I see G. E. Moore – and it is this picture that gives rise to the present paper – carefully contemplating two complete, independent, and quite different worlds, trying to decide which of the two is intrinsically better than the other.

Since one of my purposes in this paper will be to examine the conclusion that Moore reaches about his two worlds, perhaps the best way to begin would be to let him paint the picture himself. The passage in which the illustration appears, and with which I am sure you are all acquainted, occurs in Chapter III of *Principia Ethica*, as a part of his criticism of Sidgwick's theory that value can reside only in the conscious states of sentient beings. Moore writes:

> . . . Prof. Sidgwick tries to limit the range of objects among which the ultimate end may be found. He does not yet say what that end is, but he does exclude from it everything but certain characters of Human Existence. . . . Now is this exclusion justified?
>
> I cannot think it is. 'No one,' says Prof. Sidgwick, 'would consider it rational to aim at the production of beauty in external nature, apart from any possible contemplation of it by human beings.' Well, I may say at once, that I, for one, do consider this rational; and let us see if I cannot get anyone to agree with me. Consider what this admission really means. It entitles us to put the following case. Let us imagine one world exceedingly beautiful. Imagine it as beautiful as you can; put into it whatever on this earth you most admire – mountains, rivers, the sea; trees, and sunsets, stars and moon. Imagine these all combined in the most exquisite proportions, so that no one thing jars against another, but each contributes to increase the beauty of the whole. And then imagine the ugliest world you can possibly conceive. Imagine it simply one heap of filth, containing everything that is most disgusting to us, for whatever reason, and the whole, as far as may be, without one redeeming feature. Such a pair of worlds we are entitled to compare: They fall within Prof. Sidgwick's meaning, and the comparison is highly relevant to it. The only thing we are not entitled to imagine is that any human being ever has or ever, by any possibility, *can* live in either, can ever see and enjoy the beauty of the one or hate the foulness of the other. Well, even so, supposing them quite apart from any possible contemplation by human beings; still, is it irrational to hold that it is better that the beautiful world should exist, than the one which is ugly? Would it not be well, in any case, to do what we could to produce it rather than the other? Certainly I cannot help thinking that it would; and I hope that some may agree with me . . .[1]

Like other philosophical arguments drawn with pictures, Moore's two-worlds illustration has caught the imagination of most readers of *Principia Ethica*. But it has exerted an unusually strong impression for a reason beyond its pictorial qualities themselves. For one does not have to reflect long over the example before he begins to recognise

[1] G. E. Moore, *Principia Ethica* (Cambridge: Cambridge University Press, 1903) pp. 83–4.

that Moore has dropped a formidable conundrum into the laps of his readers. Consider: One is asked by Moore to choose between two worlds, one beautiful and the other ugly. But the stipulation is made that no human observer will or can ever enjoy the beauty of the first world or hate the ugliness of the second. The problem confronting anyone asked to make a choice under such conditions is all too apparent. Either he visualises, in his imagination, the two alternative worlds – as Moore in fact requests him to do – or he does not. Let us consider his options in reverse order. Suppose he is able – and this is a moot point psychologically – seriously to consider which of the worlds he should choose, without imaginatively picturing the one in its beauty and the other in its ugliness. Recognising intellectually that the aesthetic qualities of neither will be appreciated by any observer, he nevertheless faces the task of choosing one of the two. On what possible grounds could he make his choice? He would have no reason to prefer one to the other. But here Moore would almost certainly disagree, arguing that he indeed does have a reason: his choice, if he made the correct one, would bring into existence a beautiful world, with its intrinsic value. But such an answer does not seem satisfactory. For a person to justify a choice he makes, it is necessary that he be himself in possession of some value grounds to offer in support of that choice. In the present case, he must be able directly to apprehend and appreciate the value of the beautiful world in order to justify his claim that it does in fact have any value. Otherwise, the words applied to the two worlds, 'beautiful' and 'ugly', are to him no more than that – mere words. My point is that it does seem impossible for anyone to recognise the value of a beautiful world without (at least imaginatively) contemplating its beauty. For, if he does not contemplate its beauty and find in that beauty something of value, on what grounds could he possibly base his conclusion that the world in question is intrinsically good?

The other alternative is that the person make his choice on the basis of an imaginative comparison of the two worlds, choosing the former because he finds the value of the beauty he apprehends in it greater than that of the ugliness he apprehends in the latter. But on this alternative, the beauty and ugliness of the respective worlds do not go unnoted; they are imaginatively contemplated by the chooser himself. And that seems to be contrary to Moore's hypothesis. But once again Moore might object, arguing that the chooser, with his imaginative contemplation of the worlds, has to be 'bracketed off' from the issue. The situation, as we are asked to consider it, is this: The chooser must, after contemplating the two worlds, decide which ought to come into being, *at a time later than his contemplation*, and, having come into being, never be observed by anyone. On this analysis both of the objections I have raised to the illustration can be met. On the one hand, the chooser, by imaginatively contemplating the worlds, can gain grounds, in his observation of the aesthetic values of each, for making a choice; nevertheless, neither of the worlds, once it has actually come into being, will ever be seen by anyone.

This would be an ingenious response but once again I do not think that it will do. For the chooser has still not been shown to have made his selection on the basis of a value intrinsic to the worlds, in the sense that it is possessed by them out of any relationship to an observer. Consider: The world of his choice, when it comes into being later, either will or will not have the qualities that he imaginatively pictures in it. If it has the qualities, then it is a world that has been viewed by an observer, even though only by means of imagination. If it does not have these qualities, then we have no grounds on which to attribute any value to it at all, since we have no idea what it is like.

To sum up these somewhat intricate points and counter-points, I think that the root difficulty with Moore's two-world illustration is that he asks the person who is to choose between the worlds to perform a task he simply cannot accomplish – to imagine the unimaginable, to visualise two worlds with certain aesthetic qualities and at the same time to choose between these worlds without allowing that visualisation to affect his choice. But even if Moore could find a way of successfully resolving the dilemma in which he has trapped himself, I think his illustration and argument would still have to face a different, even more serious, difficulty.

According to Moore, the beauty and ugliness of the worlds are intrinsic to them in the sense that they would possess these qualities even though they were never observed by any human eye. But in what, we might ask, are the beauty and ugliness to be found? What qualities of the one world make it beautiful, and of the other make it ugly? In his illustration Moore answers these questions, at least in his description of the beautiful world, by referring to a number of specifics, including 'mountains, rivers, the sea, trees and sunsets, stars and moon.' Most of us would, I think, agree that in this list Moore has cited many of the greatest sources of natural beauty that we find in our own world. Let us take one of them as an illustration and examine in closer detail the nature and status of its beauty. I shall choose what is certainly one of the most beautiful sights in nature of which I have had experience – a flaming sunset over the

Pacific viewed from the shores of my home state of California. I cannot possibly capture in words the glory of such a spectacle – the almost infinite gradations of hue, the extreme differences in brilliance of colour, the subtle changes that occur almost imperceptibly in the visual panorama with the gradual onset of darkness. A sunset needs a poet or artist – and not a philosopher – to describe.

As a philosopher I should however raise a question. Granting that a sunset is almost indescribably beautiful, I ask: In what does its beauty consist? The answer is clear: It consists in the visual spectacle the sunset affords. Take away the colours of a sunset – their changing hues, shapes, and relationships – and you take away its beauty as well. And I need hardly point out that these colours are dependent for their existence on the conscious experience of a certain kind of mind. What, one might ask, does a sunset look like to a dog and how much beauty does it have?

The point I have just made can be generalised. Beauty, whether it be of a sunset, a mountain, or the starry sky, whether it be natural or man-made, depends for its existence on sensory qualities which in turn may be visual as in a sunset or painting, auditory as in the song of a bird or a piece of music, tactile as in the feel of a stone or a woven garment, and so on. These sensory qualities themselves are mind-dependent. There is no colour unless someone sees it, no sound unless someone hears it.

I realise, of course, that the statements I have just been making can be challenged. Epistemologists, who have called themselves 'realists', have maintained the view that the so-called secondary qualities, like sights and sounds, exist in the object viewed in exactly the same form as they are experienced by an observer. To discuss this type of realism adequately would involve me in a digression into the intricacies of epistemology that would not only carry me away from the main thesis I hope to develop in this paper but would eat up many more hours than anyone would care to spend here this afternoon. So, with your indulgence, I shall state my case dogmatically. Realism, considered as the view that secondary qualities exist in their objects in just the way they exist in the experience of a conscious observer, is a hopeless position. It can easily be entangled in absurdities and contradictions from which it simply cannot extricate itself. Although I will not attempt to justify this judgment here, I think it is one in which almost all philosophers concur.

But if the qualities that produce beauty are mind-dependent, then beauty cannot exist outside of a relationship to minds. A world that was never contemplated by an observer, because it would not possess any of these qualities, would be equally bereft of beauty – or, for that

G

matter, of ugliness. Hence, when Moore talks about his two alternative worlds, one beautiful and the other ugly, but neither ever the object of conscious contemplation by any observer, he is describing things that cannot exist as he portrays them.

I should like to turn now to the main thesis that I wish to pursue this afternoon, for which the remarks I have just made may be considered an introduction. Moore's position, which he tries to support with his two-worlds illustration, may be given the label 'aesthetic objectivism'. This view concerning the status of aesthetic qualities, I need hardly add, is one that Moore shares with many other philosophers, although few would defend it in the manner in which he did in *Principia Ethica*. I should like to begin the main argument that will occupy me in the remainder of my paper by asking, and then trying to answer, the question: Why do philosophers cling to aesthetic objectivism, despite the objections that can be raised against it?

A curious fact emerges if one looks more broadly into the philosophical views of aesthetic objectivists. If, like Moore, they have turned their attention to moral philosophy, they tend strongly toward objectivism there as well; certainly Moore himself was an unqualified ethical objectivist.[1] Furthermore, this parallelism between ethics and aesthetics is not a contingent fact; rather I think there is an explanation for it. Briefly put, many moral philosophers have concluded that, for reasons which I shall explore in a moment, ethical values *must* be considered to be objective; when they have turned to aesthetics they have assumed that analogous kinds of reasons apply to its values as well and, as a consequence, have become aesthetic objectivists too. To understand both their concerns and their arguments, and to test the cogency of the transfer they have made from ethics to aesthetics, it will be necessary to examine at some length the kind of reasoning that has compelled such philosophers to accept ethical objectivism.

To begin, it is important to note, and to account for, the vehemence, sometimes amounting to fervour, with which many of them embrace ethical objectivism. Perhaps the best way to do this is to consider its alternative, ethical subjectivism. For a classical statement of the subjectivists' thesis, I turn to Thomas Hobbes. In *Leviathan* he writes:

---

[1] In the case of Moore a further complication arises, in the distinction he makes between value as 'objective' and value as 'intrinsic'. Cf. G. E. Moore, 'The Conception of Intrinsic Value', in *Philosophical Studies* (London: Routledge and Kegan Paul Ltd, 1922) pp. 253–75. Since recognition of this distinction would complicate my argument unnecessarily, I shall disregard it.

But whatsoever is the object of any man's appetite or desire, that is it which he for his part calleth *good*; and the object of his hate and aversion, *evil*; and of his contempt *vile* and *inconsiderable*. For these words of good, evil, and contemptible, are ever used with relation to the person that useth them: there being nothing simply and absolutely so; nor any common rule of good and evil, to be taken from the nature of the objects themselves . . .[1]

Although the revolt against the Hobbesian philosophy, which began in the seventeenth century, waxed in the eighteenth, and still throws out occasional sparks, concentrated on his political philosophy with its advocacy of absolutism, and on his metaphysics with its implicit atheism, it was not limited to these fields. For ethicists too joined in the outcry. What disturbed them most about Hobbes was his subjectivism regarding values – illustrated in the passage I have just read – and its implied ethical relativism. To combat these they emphasised the absolute objectivity of values. To quote one of the leading early critics of Hobbes, Ralph Cudworth:

. . . that common distinction betwixt things, things naturally and positively good and evil, or (as others express it) betwixt things that are therefore commanded because they are good and just, and things that are therefore good and just, because they are commanded, stands in need of a right explication, that we be not led into a mistake thereby, as if the obligation to do those thetical and positive things did arise wholly from will without nature. . . . The difference of these things lies wholly in this, that there are some things which the intellectual nature obligeth to of itself, and directly, absolutely and perpetually, and these things are called naturally good and evil.[2]

The primary fault that moral philosophers find with ethical relativism is easy to appreciate. If the goodness or badness of anything is determined by the response, either favourable or unfavourable, given to it by the individual who contemplates it, then the object itself possesses no value of its own. From this situation awkward consequences follow. The same object may be good today and evil tomorrow as my attitudes toward it shift and, should two people simultaneously respond to it in opposite ways, it automatically is rendered both good and evil at the same time. It is understandable that many moral philosophers should find such consequences of

---

[1] *Leviathan*, bk I, ch. vi.

[2] Ralph Cudworth, *A Treatise Concerning Eternal and Immutable Morality* (1731) bk I, ch. ii.

relativism intellectually unpalatable. For they appear to destroy the possibility of providing a rational foundation for the support of ethical evaluations.

Nevertheless such academic, philosophical considerations are hardly sufficient to account for the heat Hobbes generated by his relativistic subjectivism. The full explanation lies elsewhere – in the practical, rather than the theoretical consequences philosophers have believed to follow from relativism. If nothing is good or evil in itself, then we have no independent, objective standards against which to judge our conduct. Rather, anything goes. To claim, as Hobbes does, that we bestow on it all the value anything possesses simply by desiring it is to imply that, if we then actively seek it, we are pursuing the good, regardless of how others may view our action. Under these conditions human life is in serious danger of degenerating into a scramble on the part of each individual to satisfy his own desires, without regard to the consequences of such action to others. As Hobbes himself believed, life becomes a war 'of every man against every man'. That this, viewed as a description of human affairs, might be accurate is in itself more than a sufficient cause for dismay; that it should be condoned on moral grounds, as it seems to be by subjectivistic relativism, is, in the eyes of many ethicists, grounds for outrage. In their repugnance to such practical consequences that they saw in relativism lies the principal reason for the continued attempts made by ethical objectivists to find an answer to the subjectivism of Hobbes and his followers.

I think – and this is the assumption with which I justify the fairly lengthy analysis of ethical reasoning to follow – that philosophers who have been interested in both ethics and aesthetics have tended to take over from the former to the latter field conceptual frameworks and modes of argumentation without sufficient consideration of whether the two fields are sufficiently analogous to support the transfer. I shall turn my attention to this issue directly later in my paper but I must, before I can consider it, raise a preliminary question: Are ethicists who reject the relativism of values on the grounds of its dire consequences for moral conduct justified in doing so? To find an answer to this question we must examine more closely into the logic of their reasoning.

The goal of the ethical objectivists is to establish an independent standard against which human conduct can be judged, a standard that will permit us not only to assess the rightness or wrongness of the acts we do but also to stipulate certain acts or types of acts to be our moral duties. There are a number of different ways in which one might try to accomplish this result; however, for our purposes –

to examine the analogy between ethics and aesthetics – only one is relevant. That is to derive the standard of moral action from an objectivistic conception of value. Historically, the paradigm case of such a line of argumentation is found in the teleological or utilitarian tradition, with its roots in classical Greek thought and its most eminent twentieth-century spokesman, at least in the English language, is Moore himself. The logic of utilitarian reasoning is simple and well-known: A person confronted with a practical moral decision, in which he has to make a choice between alternative courses of action, must calculate the amount of goodness in the consequences that will follow from each alternative act open to him and, if he is moral, choose to perform that act which will promote the best possible results. If he then so acts, he will have done his duty.

That the utilitarian procedure for determining our duties, if it is sound, provides an answer to Hobbesian moral anarchy is evident. Since values are objective – independent of the wills and desires of everyone – there are, for any possible situation in which we have to act, some consequences that follow from an act we may perform that are at least equal in goodness to the consequences that would follow from any other act we might do.[1] Since, furthermore, the act that we ought to do is that which will realise these consequences, there is always, in every situation of moral choice, theoretically some act that is *the* right act for us to perform. The rightness of the act in question, like the goodness of the results to which it will lead and which determine its rightness, is completely objective. No desire of ours – no fiat of our will – can alter the situation, making right wrong or wrong right. We have thus a standard of moral conduct, based on the objectivity of values, that enables us to reject the morally unacceptable consequences of relativistic subjectivism.

To justify its objectivistic appraisal of moral conduct, the utilitarian theory offers an argument resting on two quite different assumptions: (1) That values are objective and (2) that our duties can be derived from an evaluation of the consequences of our acts. To most utilitarians – and again Moore is a good example – the first is the crucial assumption. If a strong enough case can be made for the objectivity of values, it is assumed, the objectivity of duty easily follows. Consequently, little attention is given by most utilitarian writers to the second assumption. Yet this assumption, I shall argue, is indefensible and, because it is, the utilitarian theory

---

[1] Although we may not always be successful in discovering the consequences that will be best. However, this is a problem of human finitude, which does not significantly affect the cogency of the utilitarians' line of reasoning.

of moral obligation, viewed as a way of insuring the objectivity of right and wrong in moral conduct, completely breaks down. Let us see why this is true.

Since my concern is only with the second assumption the utilitarians make, we can disregard the first. So let us assume that values are, as the utilitarians claim, objective. They are qualities of certain *objects*,[1] which possess them because of their own natures and regardless of the response made to these objects by any observer. The problem we must now face is this: Are the utilitarians correct in claiming that our duties can be derived from the objective values of the universe, in the way I have outlined just above? The critical word in my question is 'derived'. What condition must be met in order for us to be able to *derive* our duties from the goodness of the consequences of our actions? Clearly we can accomplish such a derivation only if it follows from the fact that an act will have better consequences than any other act we could perform that it is our duty to do that act or, to state the case in negative terms, that it should never fail to be our duty to do the act whose consequences will be best. On only two interpretations of the nature of the relationship between values and duty would it seem possible that the satisfaction of this condition could be guaranteed. I shall consider each in turn.

(1) The relationship between the two concepts with which we are concerned – value and duty – could be one of logical identity. If this were the case, a proposition of the form 'One ought always to maximise the good' would be necessarily true because a tautology. For it could be rendered without alteration of meaning into either 'One ought always to maximise what he ought to maximise' or 'It is good always to maximise the good.' Utilitarians who have made use of this interpretation have, understandably, favoured the second of these two renditions. That is to say, they have reduced the concept of duty to that of value. Moore offers a clear example of this form of reduction in *Principia Ethica*, where he writes '. . . when we assert that a certain action is our absolute duty, we are asserting that the performance of that action at that time is unique in respect of value'.[2]

It is not, I think, necessary to spend much time with this interpretation. That the concept of duty has a meaning quite distinct from that of value and therefore that its meaning cannot be reduced to that of the goodness of the consequences of our actions, can be

---

[1] I italicise 'objects' here because I am using the term very broadly, to refer to anything that might possess value.

[2] Moore, p. 147.

quickly shown. Consider any act. Let us assume hypothetically that the act is both my duty and an act whose performance will have uniquely good consequences. Now if the concept of duty is indistinguishable in meaning from that of good consequences, it follows that the characteristic of the act, that it is my duty, is identical with the characteristic, that its consequences are good. But the act is my duty *before* it is performed and it has no good consequences until *after* it is performed. Thus, on this interpretation a characteristic that is applied to the act is identified with another characteristic of the act that does not even exist when the first characteristic must be applied. But if one must exist when the other cannot exist, the two cannot be identical with each other.

(2) The second relationship in whose terms the constant conjunction of value and obligation could be guaranteed is that of logical entailment. This is a less tight connection than the one we have just considered, logical identity, and for that reason apparently more defensible. Let us see if it will do.

To begin we need to be clear about what we mean by the relationship of logical entailment, as we are making use of it here. Since the theory we are examining is utilitarianism, what we need to do is to understand how the utilitarians who defend this relationship between value and duty themselves picture it. As they see it, the entailment runs from value to duty. Admitting that it is one thing to say of an act that we have a duty to do it and quite another to say that it will have good consequences, they nevertheless maintain that an act's possession of the second characteristic entails its possession of the first. If it be true that an act will produce better consequences than any other act I could perform, then it follows logically that I ought to do that act.

Although it takes a slightly longer argument to reach the conclusion, I think it can be shown that this interpretation succumbs to objections similar to those that destroyed the first. Let us suppose that I am trying to reach a practical moral decision. I evaluate the consequences of the two alternative acts I can perform in the situation in which I find myself and conclude that, because those of alternative act A are better than those of act B, I ought to do A. Does the kind of utilitarian reasoning I have used to make my decision represent a valid logical deduction? If it does, it follows that, if one accepts the premises to be true, but denies the truth of the conclusion, he is guilty of committing an elementary logical fallacy, of the order committed by one who agreed that all men are mortal and that Socrates is a man but then denied Socrates' mortality. That the two arguments are not analogous in the crucial respect of the logical relationship between premisses and conclusion, although not perhaps immediately evident, can be shown. To see this let us expand the argument of the utilitarian into ordinary syllogistic form. As major premiss we might put: 'Such and such consequences are the best I can produce by any act I can now perform.' Our minor premiss then would be: 'My performance of act A will produce these consequences.' And our conclusion: 'Therefore, I ought to do act A.' But that is not the conclusion that follows, on the analogy of the argument about Socrates' mortality, from the premisses A. What is entailed logically by these premisses is only the conclusion: 'My performance of act A will lead to the best consequences I could produce by any act I might perform.' And that conclusion says nothing about my duty to perform act A at all. We can conclude, therefore, that the conclusion the utilitarian reaches, which makes a claim about my duty to do act A, is a *non sequitur*.

The point I am making could be put in a somewhat different way. Anyone who admitted that Socrates was a man and that all men are mortal and then denied Socrates' mortality would be contradicting himself. He would be rejecting a proposition to which his earlier assertions logically committed him. But one is not caught in the same logical trap when he admits that a certain set of consequences are the best possible and that performance of a given act will lead to these consequences, but then denies that he has any duty to do that act. His denial that he has such a duty may be mistaken – but that is not the point. All that I am contending is that such a denial is in no way logically inconsistent with his earlier admissions, in the way that the denial of Socrates' mortality would be.[1] And if that is correct then the conclusion the utilitarian draws regarding our duty is not logically deducible from the premisses that he offers, which concern the goodness of the consequences to which performance of the act would lead.

Some utilitarians, at least, would recognise that, because of the objections I have just raised, no attempt to derive our duties from the goodness of the consequences of our acts by a process of logical deduction can succeed. They have concluded, as a result, that the derivation in question must be accomplished by extra-logical means.

---

[1] It might be noted in passing that many moral philosophers would admit that, even though a certain act would produce better consequences than any other act a person could do, it is not true that the person has a duty to perform that act. It would be beyond the scope of this paper to discuss their reasons for taking such a stand but surely it can be said that their view is a logically possible one, which it could not be if the utilitarians' deductive argument were cogent.

A number of such means have been suggested. Some maintain, for example, that we have direct intuitive insight into the invariable connection between goodness and duty; others that we appreciate the connection by means of feeling; still others that it is guaranteed by the way we use language, etc. Because a critical examination of such views would take me too far afield, I shall not undertake it here but shall content myself with simply saying that it can be shown that none can succeed. Although their specific deficiencies vary, all share one unavoidable shortcoming. When challenged they can defend themselves only by a line of argument that always begs some crucial question. That this should prove to be true is a consequence of the fact that a logically unbridgeable gap yawns between the premises to which utilitarians appeal in their attempted justification of duty and the conclusion they reach. If the propositions 'I can maximise the good by performing act A' and 'I have no moral obligation to perform act A' are logically consistent with each other – and it follows from the arguments I have offered above that they are – then the utilitarian or teleological tradition, considered as providing a theory of moral obligation, no matter how it is construed, must be judged a failure.

The conclusion I have just reached may be misunderstood. If it is sound, the attempt made by utilitarians to avoid the moral anarchy of the Hobbesian philosophy by the device of grounding the objectivity of our duties on the objectivity of values cannot succeed. It does not however follow from this, nor do I believe, that Hobbes is correct. The conclusion we must draw, rather, is that, if we are to establish the objectivity of duty, we must do so by some other means than those employed by the utilitarians. Since, once again, pursuit of such a possibility would take us far beyond the scope of the present paper, I shall leave the subject here with only the additional comment that I think the enterprise can be brought to a successful conclusion.

To summarise this somewhat lengthy argument on ethics, we began with the view that philosophers have assumed an analogy between aesthetic and ethical value. If the latter kind of value is objective, they have argued, so, too, must be the former. In order to find the reasons that might have led philosophers to seek such an analogy between the two disciplines, we turned to ethics to determine why ethicists have been so insistent in their claim that goodness is objective. Here we found that their concern has rested on their belief that only by supporting such a claim could they offer a basis for the practical conclusion that our moral actions can be judged on objective grounds. Their argument, we have concluded, is not successful. Hence it cannot be transferred to the realm of aesthetics, and the main reason philosophers could give for accepting the analogy between ethics and aesthetics regarding the objective status of their respective types of value disappears.

But the time has come to look directly at that analogy itself. Just how good is it? Granted that many ethicists have been convinced that, for practical reasons, they must cling to a belief in the objectivity of ethical value, can aestheticians offer any sufficiently analogous reason for claiming that beauty must be objective? These questions resolve themselves into two issues: first, whether the denial of the objectivity of aesthetic value would destroy the possibility of establishing satisfactory standards of beauty and, secondly, whether it would result in a kind of aesthetic anarchy comparable to and as repugnant as Hobbesian moral anarchy. I shall consider these issues in reverse order.

Philosophers have, from Plato onward, made a serious mistake regarding ethics and aesthetics. By categorising the two together as 'value disciplines' they have been led to assume without sufficient further investigation that both are structured in similar ways so that each can be understood in terms derived from the other. As a result they have drawn analogies from one to the other that break down under examination. The case we are now considering is, I think, a clear example of such an unwarranted analogy. For the fact is that ethics contains a crucial dimension that has no counterpart in aesthetics – the dimension to which we apply the concepts of right and wrong, duty and obligation. I do not deny that the terms I have just used can be applied, and properly so, to the realm of aesthetics but I would insist that when they are so applied they stand for concepts substantially different in meaning from those appropriate to ethics. Let me elaborate.

Ethics is a practical inquiry, in the most profound sense. When Plato wrote in the *Republic*: 'Our subject is no trifling matter; it is the question what is the right way to live,' he was both describing ethics and assessing its practical significance. Because our actions affect not only our own lives and well-being but those of others as well, questions of how we ought to act take on a unique urgency and importance. On this point no analogy holds between ethics and aesthetics. Whatever else the two disciplines may have in common, they do not share the feature that we refer to when we speak in ethics of duty or moral obligation. It is simply missing from aesthetics. It is not necessary to my thesis, nor would I claim, that aesthetics is totally lacking in a practical dimension. Quite the contrary. My only point is that, however we may legitimately talk of aesthetic obligation, no elaboration of what we mean by these terms conveys the urgent practical significance that lies in the counterpart terms, moral obligation. Thus, the reason that ethicists have believed themselves to have had for insisting on the objectivity of ethical value is lacking in the realm of aesthetics. It follows as a result that, even had the arguments of the ethicists regarding value and duty proved to be cogent, they could not have been transferred over to aesthetics. For the analogy in whose terms the transfer would have been justified cannot be sustained.

I turn finally to the first of the two issues I raised a few minutes ago: Does the denial of the objectivity of aesthetic value destroy the possibility of establishing standards of beauty? I should say at the outset that I shall not attempt to answer this question in detail here. The most I can do in the time I have is to set the issue before us and suggest the lines that a solution to it might follow. Nor do I claim any originality for the general position I shall assume; my remarks will be concerned mainly with relating the view to the context of the argument I have been pursuing in this paper.

Moore and others have maintained that beauty is objective, in the literal sense that it is an attribute of the 'object' we call beautiful. This position, I have argued, runs into insurmountable epistemological difficulties. What then is the alternative? It might seem that the only other explanation possible would be to hold that beauty is subjective, existing only 'in the eye of the beholder'. Although I do not think these two alternatives to be exhaustive, my primary concern here is not to locate beauty but only to offer some answer to the question of whether any stable standard of aesthetic value can exist if beauty is denied to be a quality of the objects we call beautiful. For purposes of discussing this issue, then, let us assume a subjectivistic interpretation of the status of beauty and see if it may not still be possible to avoid in aesthetics the kind of Hobbesian anarchy we faced earlier in connection with subjectivistic ethics.

A clue to a possible answer to our question can, I think, be found in a consideration of the so-called secondary qualities – colours, sounds, smells, etc. These, we saw, form a large part of the basis on which our evaluations of beauty rest; its colour makes the sunset, its sound the symphony, its scent the rose all beautiful to us. Yet these visual, aural, and olfactory qualities, it is generally agreed, have no status in the objects to which we attribute them. Rather they are subjective. In spite of this we do not find ourselves abandoned to anarchy in relation to the secondary qualities. On the contrary, stable standards exist. In general everyone agrees that red is quite different from green; if this were not so, our mechanical traffic control system would break down in chaos. So too of sounds and all the rest. Naturally, exceptions exist. Some people are colour blind; some are deaf or, possibly, just tone deaf; I myself suffer from a deficient sense of smell. That we can recognise these deficiencies in individuals in itself indicates furthermore that we possess standards of normality in terms of which we can make our judgments.

To account for the fact that we can set standards for the secondary qualities, I think we need to make at least two assumptions: First, that some basis exists in the objective world making possible the appearance of these qualities in the experience of observers and, secondly, that the receiving apparatus, both physiological and psychological, of individual observers is sufficiently similar in general that they interpret the stimuli that they receive from the outside world in similar ways.

Because a rough – although by no means an exact – analogy can be drawn from our experience of secondary qualities to that of beauty, we can, I believe, use parallel reasoning from the one to the other in order to establish stable standards for the beautiful. For this purpose we require, on the one hand, some basis in the objective world as a source for our experiences of beauty; this source however need not be any objective beauty in the sense in which Moore described it in his two-worlds argument. In addition, we require mechanisms in the individual observers that interpret the received stimuli in similar ways, leading us to make stable judgments of aesthetic quality.

That the analogy I have suggested is not perfect must be granted. Clearly our standards for the secondary qualities are much more secure than those for beauty. As a result we can never expect to develop a 'science of aesthetics' that will approach the exactitude of the science of sense perception. That this should be true is not only compatible with but implied by the relationship between our apprehension of secondary qualities and of beauty. We cannot appreciate beauty without apprehending a minimum of one secondary quality – some colour or sound, etc. And in all but the most primitive instances we must apprehend a wide variety of qualities, woven together in highly complex patterns, whether these be purely visual as in a painting, purely aural as in listening to recorded music, or a combination of the two, and indeed sometimes more as in attending a symphony concert or watching a drama or an opera. To create the experience we call the apprehension of beauty, we must ourselves bring into play a 'mechanism' of a higher order of complexity than we need for simple sense perception. Thus, many more variables, both in the object and in the observer, contribute to the experience than occurs in the apprehension of a sense quality. The result that we should naturally expect from the vastly greater complexity of the aesthetic experience is that agreement among observers about aesthetic values is much harder to obtain than equivalent agreement about sense perceptions. We are in no position, therefore, to be rigid or dogmatic about judgments of beauty. Neither however are we justified in going to the opposite extreme of abandoning ourselves to despair. *De gustibus non est disputandum* need not, on the interpretation I am suggesting, be the ruling maxim of aesthetics. On the contrary, we can establish objective – i.e. stable – standards of aesthetic value and we can do so without postulating any quality 'beauty', as an attribute of the world as it exists independent of our aesthetic appreciation of it.

10

ARE BAD WORKS OF ART 'WORKS OF ART'?

Cyril Barrett

1. SOME years ago I came across the following question thrown out almost casually in the course of discussion: How many of us, it was asked, want to call a 'bad work of art' a 'work of art'?[1] The question was clearly rhetorical; the author quite obviously did not consider that anyone in his right mind would suggest that a bad work of art was a work of art. This struck me as rather odd. Surely there can be good and bad works of art, just as there can be good and bad apples or good and bad men. An apple does not cease to be an apple just because it is bad, unless perhaps it has become thoroughly rotten; but the gardener who says 'The Coxes are bad this year' does not mean that they have grown rotten on the trees, much less that they are not apples at all. Moreover, if so-called bad works of art are not works of art, what are they? You may not think highly of the works in the Royal Academy Summer Exhibition but they are not totally dissimilar to some works in Bond Street next door which are highly regarded.

However, there are certain terms which do not readily admit of the epithet 'bad' (or 'good' for that matter). It is odd to speak of a 'bad saint' (though it is conceivable that a saint who did not answer one's petitions might be so described). It is also somewhat odd to speak of a 'bad gentleman' (unless in the now obsolete sense of a member of the landed gentry). Such terms have goodness built into them, so to speak. They are honorific terms. To qualify them with the epithet 'bad' is to be guilty of a contradiction: to take with one hand what one gives with the other.

[1] Sonia Gregor, 'Presentational Theories Need Unpacking', *British Journal of Aesthetics*, vol. 9, no. 2, p. 159.

Is the term 'work of art' like that? Is it an honorific term, used exclusively honorifically, so that to speak of a bad work of art is to involve oneself in a contradiction?

We undoubtedly use the term 'work of art' honorifically. 'You wouldn't call *that* a work of art, would you?' or, more briefly: 'But is it *art?*' are common expressions. On the other hand, we also use 'work of art' in what seems to be a non-honorific or neutral sense. We speak in a non-committal way of works of art being auctioned at Sotheby's or of the National Gallery housing works of art or of thefts of works of art, but this does not commit us to saying that all these works are works of art in the honorific sense.[1]

Indeed, so far from it being obvious that 'work of art' is an exclusively honorific term, it is almost a commonplace among philosophers today that 'work of art' admits of a neutral as well as an honorific use. John Kemp writes:

> I am using both 'artist' and 'work of art' in a neutral sense, so as to include . . . bad and indifferent paintings, poems, etc. as well as good ones; I am not using them in an honorific sense, although they are frequently, and quite properly, so used.[2]

And Morris Weitz implies the distinction when he says:

> Thus, if one chooses to employ 'Art' evaluatively, as many do, so that 'This is a work of art and not (aesthetically) good' makes no sense, he uses 'Art' in such a way that he refuses to *call* anything a work of art unless it embodies his criterion of excellence.[3]

Haig Khatchadourian makes the same point when he says: 'work of art', with emphasis on 'art' is also used as a value term, as equivalent to '*good* work (of art)'.[4]

The most uncompromising statement of the opposite view (the view implied in the rhetorical question with which this paper started) was made by Collingwood in his *Principles of Art*:

---

[1] There is also the neutral sense which is more or less synonymous with 'visual art' or what the French call an *objet d'art*. We are not concerned with this here.

[2] J. Kemp, 'The Work of Art and the Artist's Intentions', *British Journal of Aesthetics*, vol. 4 no. 2, p. 147. Cf. R. F. Racy, 'The Aesthetic Experience', ibid., vol. 9 no. 4: 'The point which one wishes to make is that good art and bad art all come under the classification of art, just as good machines and bad machines are all machines' (p. 350).

[3] M. Weitz, 'The Role of Theory in Aesthetics', *The Journal of Aesthetics and Art Criticism*, vol. 15, p. 34.

[4] H. Khatchadourian, 'Art Names and Aesthetic Judgments', *Philosophy*, vol. 36, p. 31 n.

The definition of any given kind of thing is also the definition of a good thing of that kind: for a thing that is good in its kind is only a thing which possesses the attributes of that kind.[1]

This is a more sweeping claim, too sweeping to be discussed here. It seems possible to maintain that the definition of *certain* kinds of things is honorific without having to maintain that the definition of *every* kind of thing is honorific. The question which we are concerned with is the limited one: is the term which we apply to the kind of thing we call a 'work of art' exclusively honorific?

In the face of common and philosophical usage it would seem a piece of arbitrary verbal legislation to suggest that there is only an honorific use of the term 'work of art'. Common usage, however, is not conclusive. The fact that we may appear to use a term neutrally as well as honorifically is not proof that we in fact do so. We speak of 'bad coins'. A bad coin is one which for some reason or another cannot be accepted as coin of the realm or legal tender. To call a coin 'bad' may simply be another way of saying that it is not coin of the realm. Because we use the term 'bad', it does not follow that there is a neutral sense of 'coin of the realm' which admits of good and bad. In the same way, it might be argued, the term 'bad work of art' in common usage may be interpreted as meaning false, seeming or putative work of art; something which is not really a work of art at all.

But our use of the phrase 'bad work of art' is varied. Some works so described may indeed be false or putative. Works which we also describe as *kitsch* or *schmaltz* (the Germans seem either more prolific in producing this sort of thing or more perceptive in detecting it) are obvious candidates for this category. But not all bad art is pseudo-art. Moreover, when we say of a particular work of art – the Leonardo cartoon, perhaps – 'Now that is a *work of art*', we do not imply that the other works in the National Gallery are not works of art. This, however, might be taken care of by saying that our use of 'work of art' allows for two tiers or degrees of honorificity. To call something a 'work of art' at all is to honour it, but further honour can be conferred by the use of italics or a certain tone of voice. C. S. Lewis's tutor used to say of some of his ideas that they had risen to the dignity of error – that is, above the level of gibberish – and required only to be refuted.

Yet even if common usage can be taken care of in this way, philosophical usage will not succumb so easily. To establish the thesis

[1] R. G. Collingwood, *The Principles of Art* (Oxford, 1938) p. 280.

that 'work of art' is exclusively honorific, it must be shown either that the so-called neutral use is in reality crypto-honorific or that any attempt to define 'work of art' neutrally leads inevitably to some absurdity. In spite of my initial doubts and hesitations, I believe that such an attack on the neutralist position can succeed. In other words, a neutral definition of 'work of art' which is truly neutral, i.e. is not crypto-honorific, is inevitably driven to absurdity.

2. This can be demonstrated by beginning with the definitions of those who confidently assume that a neutral definition can be given. In every case some honorific or positive evaluative term or terms are included in the definition. But before discussing specific cases, I must determine more specifically what I mean by an honorific term. I consider a term (or the use of a term) to be honorific if, among its defining characteristic, there is one or more which commits the user to a favourable judgment of it, as a member of its kind, on pain of contradiction. Thus to say of a Stakhanovite that he is work-shy is contradictory, since calling him a Stakhanovite commits one to saying that he is a good worker. Similarly, to say of a gentleman that he is dishonourable, ungallant to women, etc., is self-contradictory, since such a bounder is no gentleman. The case of 'work of art' is slightly different, since it has already been suggested that its honorificity is two-tiered; one can say: 'Now that is what I call a *work of art*'. Nevertheless, there are certain works which are not just bad works but not works of art in any sense, and no neutral criterion will differentiate them from dull, mediocre, inept, pretentious or downright bad works of art.[1]

It would be impossible, and unnecessary, to examine all attempted definitions of 'work of art' in order to show that they are crypto-honorific; one will suffice to demonstrate the way in which honorific terms get included in so-called neutral definitions. Morris Weitz provides the following instance of what he cautiously describes as 'criteria of recognition' of a work of art:

> when we describe something as a work of art, we do so under the conditions of there being present some sort of artefact, made

---

[1] There are various necessary conditions for something being a work of art: it must be man-made or at least chosen and displayed, it must be proposed for aesthetic enjoyment, etc. But if these alone were accepted, we would have to admit that every parlour mantelpiece, shrine and grave was a work of art, since they are intended as, and believed to be, objects of aesthetic delight. I am assuming that they would not be called works of art, much less bad works of art. If I am wrong in this, then my whole thesis falls to the ground.

by human skill, ingenuity and imagination, which embodies in its
sensuous, public medium – stone, wood, sounds, words – certain
distinguishable elements and relations.[1]

Although he denies that a set of necessary or sufficient conditions
for describing something as a 'work of art' can be forthcoming, it
is hard to see how we could withhold that description from something which fulfilled all Weitz's conditions. However, that is not the
point at issue. The question is: is this a neutral definition? Clearly
it is not. We may have neutral tests for deciding what is an artefact
or what is a sensuous, public medium and possibly, though this is
more doubtful, whether human skill has been used; but when it
comes to such things as ingenuity and, still more, imagination we
are committed to passing a favourable judgment on the work. The
work may be faulted on certain counts, but if it displays ingenuity
and imagination (as these terms are ordinarily understood when
applied to the arts), it cannot be utterly trite and banal; a host of
pejorative epithets are ruled out.

Every other definition which I have come across, with one
exception, which I shall come to later, contains honorific terms. I
now wish to show that this is necessarily the case. One reason in
support of this is that if a neutral definition of work of art could be
devised then certain sections of the community would long ago
have devised it. I am referring chiefly to officers of the Inland
Revenue and Customs and Excise. Brancusi's *Bird in Flight* was
refused entry into the United States as a work of art on the grounds
that it bore no resemblance to a bird. 'What hunter', one official
asked, 'would want to shoot a bird like that?' An expert had to be
called in to assure the officials that, despite appearances, it was
indeed a work of art. It is said that William Scott managed to get
his semi-abstract pictures admitted into Ireland duty-free on the
grounds that they were unfinished works of art – hardly even begun,
as the customs man remarked. At the opposite extreme, it is reported
that at an exhibition in the Hayward Gallery, where pieces of dyed
hessian and piles of sand were on show, the cleaners were reluctant
to remove some polythene sacks of rubbish for fear that they might
have been part of the exhibition.

It might be objected that the reasons for these mistakes, if they
were mistakes, was that the term 'work of art' is open-textured
or open-ended, not that it necessarily involves favourable evaluation.
That it is open-textured in some sense of that word I don't deny.

[1] M. Weitz, p. 32.

New forms of art such as abstract and semi-abstract art, and whatever one may wish to call Barry Flanagan's dyed hessian and piles of sand, call for continual revision of our criteria for calling something a work of art. But the decision to include such objects within the category of works of art is not a purely intellectual one as was the decision to regard $\sqrt{-1}$ as a number, albeit an imaginary number. That is, it is not based solely on the similarity between such works and accepted paintings and sculpture, because it is precisely this similarity which is denied. It is only where people are persuaded that the qualities which they admire in accepted works of art are present also in these *outré* works that the latter are accepted as works of art. What makes things difficult for customs officials and cleaners is that the term 'work of art' fluctuates with the fluctuations of taste. Until a neutral account of value judgments can be given, that is, until it can be shown that some set of qualities non-evaluatively described, imply a value judgment, no neutral definition of 'work of art' will be forthcoming. I have reason to believe, however – though it would require another paper to argue the case – that such an event is not likely to take place in our lifetime.

The same point can be made by adapting an example offered by Professor Kennick. Let us imagine a storekeeper being sent into a warehouse and asked to bring out the works of art stored there. What is he likely to do? Unless he is an exceptional storekeeper he will probably bring out all the paintings, statues, tapestries and ornaments. He will probably leave behind the posters. He may be puzzled by the photographs but will probably leave them behind too. He may also be puzzled by the furniture, glass, ceramics, needlework, cutlery, etc., but will probably be guided by two principles: if it is (1) old or (2) ornamented, bringing it out; otherwise leaving it behind. The garden roller, the Swedish or Japanese functional crockery, cutlery and furniture, and the moleskin trousers will be left behind. (I might add, in parentheses, to simplify matters, that there are no works of literature, no scores or gramophone records, no films, etc., in the warehouse; only works of the visual arts.) It is also probable that Claus Oldenberg's outsize tube of toothpaste, Jim Dine's washbasin, Yves Klein's monochrome painting and Tinguely's auto-destructive machine will be left behind. On the other hand, the storekeeper might well bring out the china ducks (including Donald Duck) and the garden gnomes. (An advanced critic might have brought out the moleskin trousers and left the Raphael.)

I agree with Kennick that none of the existing definitions of 'work of art' would have helped the storekeeper, but this is not because these definitions are more obscure than what they define, but because the use of the term 'work of art' calls for an exercise of aesthetic judgment which we do not usually expect of store-keepers, customs officials and cleaners.[1]

At this point I should like to introduce a distinction which might make a neutral definition of 'work of art' possible, a distinction between what I shall call the *assertive* and the *acquiescent* use of the term 'work of art'. By the *assertive* use of 'work of art' I have in mind a *claim* made by the speaker that some work is or is not a work of art. The clearest expression of this use would take the form: 'Now *that* is what I call a work of *art*' or 'It simply is *not art*, whatever else it is'. The claim can also be made by exhibiting or giving serious critical attention to or by rejecting or pointedly neglecting a work. I take it that this is roughly what Professor Gallie has in mind when he calls 'work of art' an essentially contested concept.[2] On the other hand, one is using the term *acquiescently* when one makes no special claim that a work is or is not a work of art, but simply goes along with accepted usage in so far as this can be ascertained. This is presumably the way in which the term is used by government officials, particularly officers of the Inland Revenue and Customs and Excise, by cleaners, storekeepers and so on. But it may also be used in this way by those who have a very definite idea of what is and what is not a work of art. They acquiesce out of courtesy so as not to give offence or arouse acrimony.

The acquiescent use obviously does not commit the user to a favourable judgment. One may agree to call something a work of art even if one would not so describe it oneself. Hence, it is not honorific. Thus the way is open for a neutral definition. But what form would such a definition take? Clearly it would be unsatisfactory to define a work of art as anything which is *regarded* as a work of art, since the definition would contain that which is to be defined. But for 'work of art' one might substitute 'any work of aesthetic interest, attitude or regard'. Yet even assuming that some meaning

---

[1] Citing the difficulties of the customs or inland revenue is only partially frivolous. Practical legal tests often give an edge to philosophical discussion. In this instance philosophical discussion might have practical fruit. For administrative convenience it has been decided, for instance, that 'multiples' shall be subject to tax on the grounds that they are commercial products (which is true). Yet not only are they original works of art (they are not copies or even prints) but they are by eminent artists, such as Vasarely, Le Parc, Soto (all of whom have won international prizes). (The fear is, presumably, that the manufacturers of garden shears will claim that their products are works of art too.)

[2] W. B. Gallie, 'Essentially Contested Concepts', *Proceedings of the Aristotelian Society*, 1955-6, pp. 167-98.

can be given to this formula,[1] it would not be entirely satisfactory, since everything can be regarded aesthetically, but not everything is a work of art. But if one adds some such modifications as 'anything which is considered to have aesthetic value and is offered as an object to be regarded aesthetically' this difficulty could be partially overcome.[2] The puzzlement of the customs officials faced with Brancusi's *Bird in Flight* and of the cleaners at the Hayward Gallery could thus be explained, not as an aberrant aesthetic judgment, but as being due to ignorance of the fact that the former was rated highly and offered as an object to be regarded aesthetically and the sacks of rubbish were not.

But such a definition would run into some serious difficulties.

First, it seems plausible to argue that when Mozart was composing his Jupiter Symphony or Shakespeare was writing *Hamlet* what they had in their minds were works of art, and they would still have been works of art even if they had never been committed to paper. Oscar Wilde told his publishers that he had completed *Lady Windermere's Fan* even though he had not written a word of it. The notion of a private work of art (*de facto* not *de jure* private) cannot arbitrarily be ruled out.

There are a number of ways of evading this difficulty. The most sensible seems to be to regard this as a limiting case. The artist who is merely contemplating a work of art in his mind is at least offering it to himself, and what he is offering to himself is in principle public, i.e. were he to commit it to paper, canvas, etc., it could be offered in the fullest sense.

A second objection can be put like this. There are in our museums and art galleries a number of objects – medieval or cycladic statues, negro masks, drinking vessels, etc. – which until recently were not regarded aesthetically but now are. According to the definition given above they were not works of art; they have only recently become so. This gives rise to the objection: either they were always works of art or they are not works of art now. Merely offering something for aesthetic consideration cannot make it into a work of art if it was not one already. Something cannot wait to become a

---

[1] It is not within the scope of this paper to determine the meaning of the terms 'aesthetic interest' or (below) 'aesthetic value'. In the discussion which followed this paper, Miss Ruby Meager, the chairman, suggested that one could say that 'what accredited and paid critics regard as works of art are works of art' and this would be an acquiescent, neutral definition of 'work of art'. I agree. But the trouble is that accredited and paid critics do not agree among themselves, and if they did, it would still be open to a budding critic to disagree with their verdict (description) and win support for his views.

[2] Gallie, ibid.

work of art until it is offered for aesthetic consideration. It seems more plausible to say that we have recognised that it was a work of art all the time than to say that, by displaying it in a museum, we have made it into a work of art. Moreover, recognising it as a work of art can only mean appreciating its aesthetic value. Thus one has to fall back on the honorific sense of 'work of art'.

In reply to this it may be said that such objects were potential works of art but objects with a non-aesthetic function. They become works of art when they are given a new status or function by being placed in a museum. A madonna in a museum has (temporarily) ceased to be a cult object, and a cycladic mother-goddess, which had long ceased to be a cult object, acquires a new role on being placed in the museum in the context of other objects with high aesthetic value and not merely of antiquarian interest. Of course, whoever placed them there and called them works of art presumably had a high regard for them and would have used the term 'work of art' honorifically. But someone else might acquiesce in calling them works of art without sharing this high regard.

There is a third, more serious objection. However acquiescent a person may be, there comes a time when his tolerance reaches a limit. At what point this limit is reached will vary with his taste and cultural background. Few connoisseurs would agree to call china ducks or garden gnomes works of art; the plain man in the street is reluctant to admit that a good deal of what is nowadays exhibited in fashionable galleries is art. This lack of tolerance might be defended, in the case of the gnomes at least, on the grounds that people who like such things have a sentimental or other interest in them, not an aesthetic interest. This is a questionable move at best. What if it could be shown that their interest was genuinely aesthetic and that they regard these things highly? Either such objects have to be accepted as works of art – which is bordering on the absurd – or they have to be excluded from the class of work of art. Since their exclusion would be based on judgment of their aesthetic value, the term 'work of art' would then be used honorifically.[1]

This problem was posed in a slightly different form by Marcel Duchamp's ready-mades. When Duchamp exhibited an inverted bicycle-wheel, a coal-shovel, a moustached print of the *Mona Lisa*, an inverted urinal, etc. he stated specifically that 'The choice was based on a reaction of *visual indifference* with a total absence of good or bad taste'. In other words, he did not value the works highly; nor did he choose them because they were positively ugly, as garden

---

[1] See p. 189, n. 1 above.

gnomes may be; they were, as he said, aesthetically indifferent, neither of high nor low aesthetic value. Now according to the neutral acquiescent definition these would not be works of art, because they were not rated highly. Duchamp's own attitude was ambiguous. As Hans Richter reports in one place: 'These works . . . are not works of art but of non-art' but in another place he says:

> He declared that these ready-mades became works of art as soon as he said they were. . . . When he 'chose' this or that object . . . it was lifted from the limbo of unregarded objects into the living world of works of art: *looking at it made it into art!*[1]

It is possible to alter the neutral acquiescent definition to include among works of art anything that anyone exhibits as an object to be looked at or declares to be a work of art. But this move leads to two absurdities: that of saying that an object not worth looking at is an object to be looked at, and secondly that anything is a work of art if anyone declares it to be one. On the other hand, to rule out works which no one thinks highly of is to make the value judgment that these are not worth being called works of art even acquiescently.[2]

So whichever way one turns in an attempt to formulate a neutral definition of work of art one is forced to choose between some absurdity or other, or introduce some crypto-honorific element.

3. This brings us back to the initial question whether, if 'work of art' is used in an exclusively honorific sense, it makes sense to speak of bad works of art.

The answer to this depends on whether one uses a single fixed criterion or set of criteria or different interrelated criteria.

If there is one fixed quality or set of qualities, the possession of which constitute something a work of art, then to say that a work has this quality or set of qualities and is aesthetically bad seems contradictory. It may be bad in some other respect – technically, morally, socially – but not as a work of art. I have in mind here such qualities as being inspired, imaginative, expressive, formally significant, creative – whatever these may mean. Bad works of art according to this criterion are uninspired, unimaginative, inexpressive,

---

[1] H. Richter, *Dada* (London, 1965) pp. 52 and 88–9.
[2] I do not wish to deny that certain things can be declared *not* to be works of art by applying neutral criteria, e.g., that they are not man-made or not made with the intention of giving aesthetic pleasure or whatever. The point is that these conditions are not sufficient to guarantee that the thing in question *is* a work of art.

non-significant, uncreative, etc. But they are not merely bad; they are, strictly speaking, not works of art.

But if, instead of a fixed quality or set of qualities, one is operating with different sets, is it still contradictory to speak of a 'bad work of art'? Let us imagine, to quote Helen Knight's example, that the term 'tennis player' were used honorifically but that someone would qualify as a tennis player even if his (or her) style was bad but his match-winning ability was good (he won matches), or if he had a perfect style, played all the strokes perfectly, but for reasons of temperament seldom got beyond the first round at Wimbledon. Would it be contradictory to say that these two players were 'tennis players' (in the honorific sense – they both, after all, made Wimbledon), but they were bad because one did not play tennis as it should be played and the other could not win a championship? It seems to me that it would not. From one point of view each is good enough to qualify as a tennis player; from another point of view, they are not good enough – a *really* good player would both play well and win matches.

Might not the same be true of works of art? Take a painter like Blake, a composer like Tchaikovsky, a poet like Kipling or a playwright like Barrie. One might want to say that their works were bad for technical reasons or on account of their sentimentality, jingoism or coyness, yet for other reasons – vision, technical brilliance, insight – one might still want to call them works of art. They pass a certain test, they rise above a certain standard, and yet on other counts they fail. They have risen above mediocrity, trash, pastiche and general ineptitude – and yet have a sufficient number of defects to be called bad. (Even if the phrase 'bad work of art' sounds odd, there is nothing linguistically odd about saying of something that it is a work of art but bad.)

Now it might be objected that even if this were so, such works are not bad *as works of art*. Moreover, in so far as they are works of art they are good; so they are both good and bad works of art. As to the first part of the objection, it may indeed be the case that a work of art is called bad for a reason which is not relevant to it as a work of art. A march, which is otherwise an excellent piece of music, may be bad as a march because it is not easy to march to – the beat is not sufficiently clearly stressed. But if the reason for calling a work bad belongs to the class of considerations which would be accepted as relevant to calling a work good as a work of art, then (assuming that the reason is valid) the work is bad as a work of art. If structural organisation, vividness, freshness, psychological insight, elegance, are reasons for calling a work good as a work of art (or calling it a 'work of art'), then the absence of these may count as reasons for calling it bad as a work of art.

As for the second part of the objection, I do not see any problem about accepting the fact that a work may be both good and bad as a work of art. The alternative is to say that only those works which are without any aesthetic defect whatsoever are works of art. But surely this is going too far. Is there any work which reaches this standard? I can think of none. (It is arguable that to be without any notable aesthetic defect would itself be an aesthetic defect.)

These objections take a curate's-egg view of the value of works of art. It is as though one can hive off the good – the true work of art – and ignore the rest. 'Brahms's symphonies are works of art *in spite of* lamentable lapses into sentimentality.' But I don't think this view can be sustained. For someone who regarded the symphonies of Brahms as turgid, pompous, academic and mawkish – defects which he considered more serious than lack of invention or thinness – and yet who recognised their other artistic merits, it would not be possible to ignore the defects and concentrate on the merits, since the meritorious elements are, alas, used in the service of the defective or inextricably bound up with them. All he can say is: 'Pity about Brahms. Such a waste of talent. If only he could have forgotten about Beethoven and Auntie Flo.' Perhaps of a bad work of art (in the honorific sense) it can be said: 'There but for this defect or that goes a great work' and this is a great deal more than can be said of works which would not even qualify as bad works of art.

Two points remain to be made. If it makes sense to speak of a bad work of art, it is still possible to speak of certain works which one particularly admires in a doubly honorific sense. Thus to say of 'The Stag at Bay', for example, 'That is what I call a work of *art*', is not to say that Michelangelo's 'Creation of Adam' is to be excluded from the august company of works of art, but merely to proclaim the superlative merits of Landseer's masterpiece.

The second point is that if 'bad work of art' should be expunged from the language, so should 'good work of art' since it would be redundant. I have tried to show that 'bad work of art' is not necessarily self-contradictory, even though 'work of art' is used honorifically. A good work of art would then be a work whose merits outweighed its defects, or one whose merits were of an outstanding order; a work of which we might say: 'Now *that* is what I call a work of *art*'.

11

PERSONAL QUALITIES AND THE INTENTIONAL FALLACY

Colin Lyas

In their article 'The Intentional Fallacy',[1] Beardsley and Wimsatt raised problems about the legitimacy of certain critical practices. These problems, raised again in later writings[2] and intensively discussed in recent years, remain unsettled and this lecture is intended to throw light upon them.

1. I shall have more to say shortly by way of clarification of the theses I wish to discuss. Before that I want to mention a couple of distinctions that may need to be made in discussing the legitimacy of reference to artists and their intentions.

First, we may need to distinguish what is called 'the personal heresy' from what is called 'the intentional fallacy'. Thus, in 'The Intentional Fallacy' (p. 3) there is clearly an attack on the relevance of critical references to the author's *intentions*. 'The design or intention of the author', we read, 'is neither available nor desirable as a standard for judging the success of a literary work of art.' To make reference to such intentions is to commit the intentional fallacy. Combined with this, however, is an attack on *any* reference to the author. 'There is a danger', they write (p. 10), 'of confusing personal and poetic studies.'[3] To refer to the author in the course of criticism is to commit the personal heresy. We are never told, though, just what

---

[1] Reprinted in W. K. Wimsatt, *The Verbal Icon* (New York: Noonday, 1966). Page references are to this volume.

[2] Notably in M. C. Beardsley, *Aesthetics* (New York: Harcourt Brace and World, 1959) chs. i and x; W. K. Wimsatt 'Genesis: A Fallacy Revisited' in Demetz and others (eds.), *The Disciplines of Criticism* (New Haven: Yale University Press, 1968) and M. C. Beardsley, *The Possibility of Criticism* (Detroit: Wayne, 1971).

[3] Quite what is being distinguished here is not clear. I shall show however that no radical separation of personal and poetic studies can be maintained.

the relation is between the intentional fallacy and the personal heresy and it is not clear that both are supported by the same sort of arguments. I will discuss later some of the connections between the personal heresy and the intentional fallacy.

Secondly, in 'The Intentional Fallacy' at least,[1] Beardsley and Wimsatt did not distinguish clearly between an attack on those references to intentions and personality made in the course of *evaluating* works and an attack on such references made when *interpreting* works. At the beginning of the article their claim is that intentions are irrelevant as a standard for *judging the success* of a work. As the article proceeds, however, emphasis is switched to the irrelevance of references to intention when various problems of *interpretation* are at issue.

Many of those who have attacked Beardsley and Wimsatt's views have done so on the ground that knowledge of intention and other biographical material *is* relevant to this or that problem of interpretation. In so far as interpretation is a preparation for evaluation this is to suggest that such knowledge may be a prerequisite for, and hence, indirectly at least, relevant to evaluation. There is however far less discussion of the more direct ways in which knowledge of artists and their intentions may be relevant to evaluation. What I wish later to show is not that evaluation may presuppose and so *indirectly* require knowledge of intention and other facts about artists, but that some critical evaluations are directly personalistic and as such require a certain sort of knowledge of intention.

2. As a preamble now to a further clarification of the anti-personalistic and anti-intentionalistic theses that might be proposed, I shall state a number of points about intentions. I have no time to argue these points although they can be, and have been, argued at length.

First, intentions should not be thought of as private mental events totally detached from verbal and other behaviour. They are, rather, connected with such behaviour and can be known only because they are so connected.

Secondly we need sometimes to distinguish between what a person explicitly tells us about his intentions prior to, during or after his actions, and what we know from his other words and deeds about his intentions. These other words and deeds can cast doubt on, and even falsify, a person's explicit claims about his intentions. Moreover if no such explicit claims are made or are available, it is through these other words and deeds that our knowledge of intention must and does come.

[1] But see Wimsatt's later article in Demetz, p. 222.

Thirdly we must distinguish between an intention in the sense of a plan or design formed *prior* to an action and an action done *intentionally*. Not every action done intentionally is done with prior intent. A complication here is that Austin and others have claimed that we do not anyway call an action 'intentional' unless there is something 'special' about it.[1] I shall, however, allow myself the use of 'intentional' to describe any action we can attribute to a person as his responsibility, as within his control or, more widely, as something *he* did. And then not every intentional action need be done with forethought, prior intent or design.

In the light of these remarks some anti-intentionalist theses may be distinguished. Since I am interested in problems about evaluation, I shall concentrate on versions of these theses that relate to critical evaluations.

First it might be argued that in critical evaluations no attention need be paid to what artists *say* about their intentions before, during or after the completion of their works. Since their claims that they intended to put certain merits in their works will always have to be checked against what they have done, i.e., the work itself, one can always start there and dispense with quite separate enquiries into the artist's statements of intention.[2]

This first thesis rules out only the need for knowledge of and reference to *statements* of prior intention. It does not establish the dispensability of knowledge of prior intentions where this knowledge is gained in ways other than by study of *explicit* statements of intention. A second, stronger, thesis might therefore be offered. According to this thesis, knowledge of intentions had by the artist prior to producing the work, however this knowledge is obtained, is unnecessary in criticism. At best such knowledge can suggest to us things we should look for in the work. Again, however, since these things will eventually have to be found in the work itself, one can always start there. Moreover, mere successful completion of these prior intentions could never constitute the standard by which the merit of the work is determined. For the work to be meritorious the intentions would have to have been worth having, and this is to say that there must be independent standards in terms of which the intentions, and anything produced by their successful completion, can be judged.

This second, stronger, thesis would, if true, show only the dispensability of knowledge of and reference to *prior* intentions. It does

---

[1] For more on the debate over this matter see the papers collected in my *Philosophy and Linguistics* (London: Macmillan, 1971).

[2] Which is not to say that *in practice* (as opposed to *in principle*) we need dispense with such references. See Wimsatt in Demetz, op. cit., p. 211 § 4 (*b*).

not, as such, rule out reference to our knowledge of the fact that the work and some of its effects are *intentional*. For, as we have seen, this knowledge may not involve reference to prior intentions at all. Hence a third thesis might be added, namely that critical evaluations presuppose no knowledge that a work or its effects are intentional (in the wide sense of 'intentional' adopted above).

To assert the strongest form of anti-intentionalism would be to assert all the theses I have mentioned. This would constitute a total elimination of reference to intention from critical talk about art and would have an interesting consequence. For since the only differences I can see between a work of art and a natural object stem from the fact that intentional human activity is involved in the making of art, so to deny the relevance of *any* knowledge of intention would be to deny the relevance of knowledge that one is dealing with *art*. If a knowledge of intention is totally dispensable in criticism then, from the point of view of evaluation, works of art are on the same footing as natural objects.[1]

In order to maintain that knowledge of intention has some relevance it is not, of course, necessary to claim that all the theses so far mentioned are false. For my part I think that the first two theses mentioned *do* have some plausibility but that the third is false. Since, as I shall show, it *is* false, no comprehensive anti-intentionalist position can be argued.

Beardsley and Wimsatt certainly subscribe to the first two theses, i.e. they certainly wish to attack references to prior intention and references to statements of prior intention. The third thesis is never *explicitly* advocated in their writings and this means that contrary to popular impression they have never argued (and possibly have never wished to argue) a comprehensive anti-intentionalist position. To show this may be to go some way to make their views more palatable to some of their critics.

3. So far I have discussed only anti-intentionalist positions. I turn now to anti-personalist theses. I shall consider two of these. First there is the strong line that *all* references to the artist (including references to his intentions) are eliminable from critical evaluations. This thesis, approached by Beardsley and Wimsatt in their distinction between personal and poetic studies, turns the intentional fallacy into a sub-species of the personal heresy.

Secondly there is a weaker claim. It may be allowed that certain references to artists (particularly if made *in* talking of their works)

---

[1] See §§ 5 and 10 below.

are relevant. At the same time other sorts of references to artists may be excluded. Two cases may be mentioned here. First, it might be said that knowledge of the artist gained independently of a study of the work is not required for knowledge of the work itself. At best it can suggest things to look for in the work. Since this will then involve a confirming scrutiny of the work itself one could, in principle, have made do with this scrutiny alone. The move from knowledge of the artist to statements about his work (where the two are separable) is, strictly speaking, unnecessary. Secondly, knowledge of the artist gained by inference *away* from the work is irrelevant to criticism, although not perhaps to biographical interests. For the critic to move from talking of the work to talking of the artist (where these two things are separable) is for him to move from the proper object of critical study, the work itself, to a study of something else, the work's creator. In general, therefore, *where knowledge of artists and knowledge of works can be distinguished* it is unnecessary for critics to possess the former (even by inference from the latter).

In what follows I shall suggest why a strong, total anti-personalism is false and I shall say what I think is right about a weaker anti-personalism, i.e., an anti-personalism that, without eliminating all references to artists from criticism, nonetheless eliminates certain moves from work to artist and from artist to work.

4. We have therefore some possible theses. How are they to be tested? Here I begin with a general remark about the dispute over the relevance of critical references to artists and their intentions. Those who deny the relevance of such references have claimed that the outcome of the dispute has important implications for critical *practice*. Thus Beardsley and Wimsatt write ('The Intentional Fallacy', p. 3):

> There is hardly a problem of literary criticism in which the critic's approach will not be qualified by his view of intention.

For all that such claims have been made it is critical *theorists*, people arguing about criticism, who have generated the heat in this debate. Those who *practise* criticism have not suspended nor appreciably altered their activities whilst awaiting the outcome of the debate. This suggests that there is, prior to critical theory, a well-founded activity of commenting on works of art in various ways and for various purposes, that the various purposes of the various comments are well recognised and that those who engage in this activity are in principle capable of realising when various sorts of comments are clear and relevant, or obscure and irrelevant.

This in turn suggests a way of assessing critical theories of the type we are examining. Presumably since those who advocate such theories are claiming that certain sorts of references to artists and their intentions frustrate the aims of criticism, we have to ask what in fact these aims are and whether they are frustrated by the sorts of references that are under attack. We decide what these aims in fact are by reference to that well established form of activity I have mentioned, an activity that exists prior to theories about it and which, as I have said, continues uninterrupted even while theoretical debates about it continue. Reference to this activity dictates the shape of my inquiry. Before beginning it, however, I would remark that when one does look at critical practice, one is struck by the ubiquity of references to artists. Critic after critic refers to what this or that *artist* did and to what *his* work was like. Hence presumably the puzzlement felt by those who believe rightly or wrongly that Beardsley and Wimsatt wished to censure such remarks. For if such comments *do* frustrate the aim of criticism, how strange that so many critics should make them and make them so often. I shall make more comments later on the reasons for this puzzlement.

5. In line with a determination to let critical practice govern my inquiries, I begin with a reminder of the enormous vocabulary of terms and phrases by which critics attribute merits and demerits of various sorts to works of various sorts. (They do not, as is sometimes supposed, confine themselves to the terms 'good' and 'beautiful'.) Once certain classifications of this vocabulary are observed we can begin to clarify questions about the role of references in criticism to artists and their intentions.

The task of classification may begin with what I hope is the uncontentious observation that many of the qualities for which we value works of art are also qualities for which we value natural objects, scenes and events. One group of qualities is the following:

> elegance, charm, balance, unity, proportion, grace, richness of colour, sweetness of sound, daintiness.

It is not unnatural to call these *aesthetic* qualities since they are paradigms of the sort of qualities upon which an aesthetic interest centres. Since these *are* qualities of works of art it might be thought that the value features of works of art are the same as value features of natural objects with the difference, insignificant from an evaluative point of view, that in the case of art these features characterise deliberately produced objects. If this were so, then since we clearly need no knowledge of artists and their intentions in order to attribute aesthetic qualities to natural objects, there will be a temptation[1] to suppose that such knowledge is unnecessary when aesthetic qualities are attributed to works of art.

Even if such knowledge *were* unnecessary for the attribution of aesthetic qualities to works of art this would not establish that in general knowledge of artists and their intentions is eliminable from criticism. For there may be other sorts of qualities critics attribute to works of art which *do* presuppose knowledge of and reference to artists and their intentions. I believe in fact that if we are to explain the value and importance of *art* to us we must suppose it to have values additional to any of the aesthetic values that works of art share with natural objects. Critics too have spoken thus. For example, Leavis writes:

> When we examine the formal perfection of *Emma* we find that it can be appreciated only in terms of the moral preoccupations that characterise the novelist's peculiar view of life. Those who suppose it to be an aesthetic matter, a beauty of composition, can give no adequate reason for the view that *Emma* is a great novel.[2]

Whether these additional values, special to art, involve knowledge of artists and their intentions is a matter that will increasingly concern us.

6. I offer now a list of merit and demerit qualities of works of art, qualities special to them as man-made things. We may, first, praise a work of art by using some of the following of it:

> responsible, mature, intelligent, sensitive, perceptive, discriminating, witty, poised, precise, self-aware, ironic, controlled, courageous.

Demerit terms include the following:

> simple-minded, shallow, diffuse, vulgar, immature, self-indulgent, uncomprehending, heavy-handed, gauche, glib, smug.

These terms characterise works of art but not natural objects. I call them *personal qualities* and I want to argue that the presence of these qualities in a work reflects the personality of an artist. Hence,

---

[1] Although possibly a mistaken one. See on this K. Walton, 'Categories of Art', *Philosophical Review*, 1971.

[2] F. R. Leavis, *The Great Tradition* (Harmondsworth: Penguin, 1962) p. 17.

if they are relevant things for critics to mention in talking of works, they become critical remarks about the work's creator.

Clearly the personal quality terms I have introduced need more treatment than I can give them here. Thus, for example, distinctions need to be made within the class of personal qualities. Again we may need to ask how we distinguish works of art which display such qualities from other things that display them, for example things like sermons, political speeches and clinical diagnoses. Here I freely admit that possession of such qualities alone may not be sufficient to make something art, but that these are qualities for which art is praised cannot I think be denied.

A cursory examination of critical writings, particularly on the literary arts, reveals the profusion of attributions of personal qualities to works of art. If anyone now says that although these *are* qualities to be found in works and *are* qualities of the work's producer, none the less it is no part of the *critic's* task to refer to them, then this seems to me merely to be stipulating a definition of 'critic'. I have no idea what argument one could then give to show that reference to personal qualities *is* relevant to the determination of the work's artistic merit. At best one can only draw attention to the fact that critics *do* think the citation of personal qualities is relevant and do often cite them with no widespread feeling of irrelevance. Any philosophy of art must do justice to this fact.

Two remarks by Beardsley and Wimsatt are relevant here. First, in 'The Intentional Fallacy' (p. 5) they write:

> The meaning of the poem may certainly be a personal one in the sense that a poem expresses a personality or state of soul. . . . Even a short lyric poem is dramatic, the response of a speaker to a situation.[1]

In so far as the object of critical study is a response of a speaker, so it is relevant to apply personal quality terms to it. For terms like 'glib', 'smug' or 'perceptive', for example, just are terms we have for characterising human responses.

Secondly, granted that personal quality terms do apply to a speaker-response articulated in and by the work, it is tempting to fall back on the claim that no assumption need be made that the speaker-responder in the work is the creator of the work. Beardsley and Wimsatt certainly did try this. They wrote as follows in 'The Intentional Fallacy':

---

[1] The question 'Response to what?' raises, of course, profound issues in the philosophy of art.

H

We ought to impute the thoughts and attitudes of the poem immediately to the dramatic speaker and if to the author at all only
by an act of biographical inference. (p. 5)

The difficulty here is, as I have argued elsewhere,[1] that for certain
personal quality attributions to the work itself no suitable 'speaker'
other than the author presents himself as the bearer of the personal
qualities of the work. It is worth noting here that in his later work
Wimsatt writes as follows (Demetz, p. 221):

What we meant . . . (in 'The Intentional Fallacy') . . . and what in
effect I think we managed to say, was that the closest one could
ever get to the artist's intending or meaning mind outside his work
would still be short of his *effective* intention or *operative* mind as it
appears in the work itself and can be read from the work.[2]

It does then look as if Wimsatt at least does wish to allow that
the predication of personal qualities to the response-in-the-work *is*
critically relevant and that no harm follows from attributing these
qualities to the artist as he shows himself in the work.

Once it is admitted that personal qualities are qualities properly
predicated of works by critics then certain anti-personalistic and
anti-intentionalistic theses become less plausible. First in order to
be able to attribute personal qualities to a thing at all one needs to
know that that thing was produced by intentional human activity,
rather than by natural causes. Any thesis advocating the total dispensability of knowledge of intention will then collapse.

Secondly, books *qua* ink marks on paper, paintings *qua* oil-based
pigment on canvas, to take but two examples, cannot themselves be
perceptive, intelligent and so on. These are *human* qualities. It is
not unnatural therefore to believe that the referent of these personal
quality attributions is the creator as he shows himself in his work.
If this is so then to attribute personal qualities to a work in the course
of critical evaluation *is* to refer to its artist and any strong anti-
personalist thesis collapses. Moreover we have now found a way in
which critical evaluations are directly personalistic. The only way
to subvert these conclusions would be to show either that attributions
of personal qualities are critically irrelevant or to show that the
speaker-in-the-work should not be identified with the author. I have

---

[1] 'Aesthetic and Personal Qualities', *PAS* 1971–2.
[2] This is surely not what was, even in effect, said in the earlier paper, or less
controversy would have been provoked by it. Note too that Beardsley still seems to
maintain that speaker-in-the-work and the author should be kept distinct. See
The Possibility of Criticism, p. 59.

seen neither of these demonstrated and as far as the second alternative goes, Wimsatt at least seems unwilling to adopt it.

For the remainder of this paper I shall assume that to attribute personal qualities to a work is to speak of its artist.[1] What I want now to do is see what does and does not follow from this assumption and I shall examine this matter by examining two responses that those of an anti-personalist and anti-intentionalist persuasion might make *if* it were established that to make personal quality attributions to the work is to talk of the artist.

7. The first thing an anti-personalist might do, granted that personal quality attributions *are* made to the response articulated by the artist in the work, is modify his position. He might claim that although it is legitimate in criticism to make some references to the artist, *via* the qualities he displays in his work, a wide range of other possible references to him are critically irrelevant. In particular, reference to biographical detail discovered by independent historical research, and reference to the author by inference away from the work, are out of order for critics (although not perhaps for historical scholars).

There is something right about this. Historico-literary scholarship is often confused with, or substituted for, the task of critical judgment. Moreover historical inquiries into biography typically *follow* the completion of the critic's evaluative task. We do not e.g. research into Wordsworth's life in order to find out that his poetry was great but because we already know it is.

Although all this is doubtless true two further points need to be made. First, if I am right, then personal quality attributions characterise the *artist's* response as articulated in the work. It just is a fact about responses however that they may be more fully appreciated as the circumstances of the response are better understood. For this reason we may need extensive literary scholarship in order to reconstruct the social, intellectual and other climate within which the response occurred. Moreover in some cases our appreciation of a response is heightened if we know the circumstances in which it occurred and among these circumstances may be numbered the personal situation of the artist at the time of his writing. To claim this however is not to license the hoarding up of every literary nugget that can be mined by historical biographical inquiry. Rather it is to allow that the kind of biographical knowledge that throws light on the response articulated in the work, and that can be *connected* with the work, is relevant knowledge.

[1] I have *argued* this in the paper referred to above.

The second point I would make is that in opposing the excesses of irrelevant biographism the anti-personalist is objecting to nothing that many notable personalists have not also objected to. Take for example these comments made by E. M. W. Tillyard in the course of his debate with C. S. Lewis:

> Mr Lewis implies that 'personal' as a critical term includes every accident, however trivial, connected with the author. . . . But I should guess that not a few supporters of the 'personal heresy' would simply ignore such trivialities in their conception of personality. They would attach them to the sphere of literary gossip, not that of criticism.[1]

And (p. 34):

> When . . . (Mr Lewis) . . . imagines Keats reading about senators in a little brown book in a room smelling of boiled beef, he attaches these supposed facts to Keats' normal personality. I . . . call them . . . irrelevant to his normal personality. In other words by 'personality' I do not mean practical or everyday personality. I mean rather some mental pattern that makes Keats Keats and not Mr Smith or Mr Jones.

What however is this mental pattern that interests the personalistic critic? Writing of Herrick (p. 47), Tillyard says

> It is not by any laborious process of induction after we have read the poem that we apprehend the qualities of unaffected sensuality, keen observation, sophistication and sense of decorum. We apprehend them from the rhythm, the vocabulary, the word arrangement, the pattern of the poem, in fact from the poem's most intimate poetical features.[2]

What Tillyard here calls the 'mental pattern' is clearly related to particular instantiations of what I have called personal qualities. Although these are qualities of the artist we do not need to discover them by independent historical research, nor do we need to discover them by elaborate inferences away from the work. Hence we can attribute them when, as with Shakespeare, we know very little of the artist's life, or when, as with the ballads, we may know nothing of that life at all.

---

[1] C. S. Lewis and E. M. W. Tillyard, *The Personal Heresy* (Oxford: Oxford paperbacks, 1965) p. 33.
[2] It will be clear how closely this is related to the 'operationalism' allowed by Wimsatt in a passage quoted above, this in spite of the fact that Tillyard appears to be under attack on p. 10 of 'The Intentional Fallacy'.

8. There is a second response that might be made to a demonstration that personal quality attributions are made to the artist's response-in-the-work. Here, although the correctness of some form of personalism may be admitted, it might then be claimed that this entails nothing about the correctness of intentionalism. Personalism and intentionalism, it may be said, are unrelated. Hence the correctness of personalism licenses no reference to the artist's intention.

In order to examine this response we need to look at the relationship between the intentional fallacy and the personal heresy. To begin with, personalism and intentionalism are independent to this extent. When we call a person's responses, say, perceptive or self-indulgent, we often need make no assumption that he had a *prior* intention to exhibit these qualities. To this extent a personalist could go along with those who argue that a knowledge of prior intentions is unnecessary when the work itself is to be studied. It also follows of course that the advice to ignore the prior intention and study 'the work itself' does not rule out personalism. For the qualities found in the work itself may be personal qualities that the artist has, without prior intention, displayed there.

Although the truth of a thesis about the correctness of personalism is independent of the truth of a thesis about the relevance of knowledge of the *prior* intentions of the artist, it does not follow that personalism and other forms of intentionalism are similarly separable. Thus it seems obvious to me that we would not call an artist's productions 'mature', 'sensitive', 'perceptive', 'glib', etc., unless they were done intentionally in the wide sense of 'intentional' I have adopted, that is, unless they were *his* responsibility, in *his* control and attributable *to him*. This being so, application of a wide range of personal terms to a work and many of its effects presupposes that the work and some of its effects are intentional productions.

Does anything that Beardsley and Wimsatt say have any bearing on *this* form of intentionalism? I think not. For they explicitly concern themselves only with questions about the necessity of knowledge of and reference to *prior* intentions and *statements about* prior intentions. Sometimes they argue that these statements are unhelpfully precise. This may well be so. A statement of intention before the composition of something like *War and Peace* might be a pretty vague thing. Sometimes it is argued that knowledge of prior intentions is unavailable to the student of the work itself and is to be had only by leaving the work and conducting some separate inquiry. I doubt that this is so even for knowledge of prior intentions. These, as I said earlier, can be known from behaviour and the work itself is often a substantial and revealing piece of behaviour.[1] However even if prior intentions could not be known from the work, it does not follow that knowledge that the work and some of its effects are intentional, knowledge needed for the critically relevant attribution of personal qualities to the work, cannot be had from the work itself. Intention can be revealed in the work equally as well as in any other piece of human behaviour.

The form of intentionalism that I am advocating survives Beardsley's 'conclusive' argument against the appeal to intention. He writes (*Aesthetics*, p. 458):

> We can seldom know the intention with sufficient exactness independently of the work itself, to compare the work with it and measure its success and failure. Even where we can do so the resulting judgment is not a judgment of the work but only of the worker.

This makes it clear that Beardsley and Wimsatt are opposed to an appeal to intention that takes us away from the work or which makes mere successful fulfilment of intention the standard of success in art. The personalism and the related intentionalism that I have in mind is not of this sort. First, this personalism does not require *any* knowledge independent of the work itself. Rather the intentional effects to which the personal qualities are attributed are found in the work itself. Secondly, I do not want to say that mere successful fulfilment of prior intention is the standard of success in art, nor do I want to give the artist a privileged voice in the assessment of his work. Rather I want to claim that certain human merits are merits of the art that humans produce. To attribute these merits to a work is to suppose that the work and at least some of its effects are intentional. However, whether these intentionally produced works and effects have merits worthy of praise in personalistic terms is not a matter on which the artist has a privileged voice, no more than I have a privileged voice as to whether this 'intentional' lecture is self-indulgent, precious, glib, pretentious or a host of other things.

9. I have argued so far that some forms of personalism and intentionalism have not been shown to be improper in criticism. I want now to conclude with some reflections on why Beardsley and Wimsatt may have arrived at their separation, however unclear, of personal

---

[1] See Wimsatt in Demetz, p. 210, and John Kemp, 'The Work of Art and the Artist's Intentions', *British Journal of Aesthetics* (1964).

and poetic studies and with some suggestions as to why their writings have proved, for many, so disturbing. First then, some reasons why personal and poetic studies were separated.

The first consideration applies particularly to Beardsley. There is, in his writing on art, a strong tendency to stress the aesthetic. Thus very early in his *Aesthetics* he identifies the work of art with what he calls 'the aesthetic object'. He writes (p. 17):

> Statements like 'the play is tragic' seem to be about something . . .; let us call that something an 'aesthetic object'.

The danger in identifying works of art and aesthetic objects is one of thinking that the aesthetic qualities of art are the only important ones and of concentrating on these to the exclusion of other non-aesthetic qualities of art.

These aesthetic qualities are, as I have said, qualities that both works of art and natural objects may display. This being so, once they are made central there will be a temptation to concentrate on what works of art and natural objects have in common, indeed to put works of art and natural objects on the same footing for the purposes of evaluation. We can find some evidence of this way of thinking in Beardsley's *Aesthetics*. He writes (p. 17):

> Aesthetic objects are perceptual objects, but so too are other things, e.g. cows, weeds.

Once this stage is reached it becomes tempting to believe that since in perceiving value qualities in natural objects no knowledge of or reference to a creator is needed, so in attributing these features to works of art no such knowledge or reference is needed. Further, claims about the illegitimacy of references from knowledge of the qualities of the work to statements about the qualities of art are more plausible when *aesthetic* qualities are used as examples.[1] Inferences from the elegance of Pope's writing to the elegance of Pope *are* of dubious critical relevance.

I suggest therefore that one reason why Beardsley at least was led to separate talk about artists and talk about works was that he concentrated on the *aesthetic* qualities of works. For these qualities such separation has some plausibility. Since however these qualities are only a sub-set of the qualities of art no general separation of artist and work can be argued from them. Indeed, such a separation

---

[1] As a case in point here, note the terms used as examples in the argument on p. 20 of Beardsley's *Aesthetics*.

becomes far less plausible when the personal qualities of works are singled out for study.[1]

The second reason Beardsley and Wimsatt may have been led to separate personal and poetic studies was, I think, because of a *dualistic* view of the relation between mental and non-mental phenomena. The author's personality, and in particular his intentions,[2] are 'private'[3] events lying 'behind'[4] the public entity, the work, so that 'inferences'[5] or probabilistic inductions about the artist's mind are the best that the work would 'indirectly'[6] allow. On the one hand there is the public object, the work, on the other the 'private' mind of the artist.[7] Once given this inclination to dualism it follows that the critic who must concentrate on what is public, the work itself, must ignore the private mind of the artist.

It is obvious that all the recent discussions in philosophy of the privacy of experience are relevant here. Although it would take me beyond the scope of this paper to demonstrate the matter it seems to me that at this point the philosophy of art and the philosophy of mind come together. In particular the claim some have argued, that persons are seen *in* their behaviour (rather than inferred from it), is highly germane to our present inquiries. For if it is possible to replace a dualism of persons and behaviour with the monism of 'persons behaving', it may be possible to replace the dualism of artist and work by a monism of an artist showing himself in the response articulated by the work. If this is so, then *in* talking of the work itself we may well be talking of the artist. The separation of artist and work upon which the separation of personal and poetic studies depends may turn out to be untenable. If so, anti-personalist theses will have to be modified so as to rule out only those references to the author that are not related to a study of the work itself.

---

[1] Beardsley says very little about what I have called 'personal qualities'. Where he does touch on them the discussion is not happy, as in the following example: 'Many of the regional qualities we find in art are most aptly, but of course metaphorically, named by qualities taken over from the moral aspects of human nature: they are "disciplined", "decisive", "decorous", "calm", "controlled", "sound", "strong", "bold", "healthy", to cite only positive terms. But an analogy is not a causal connection. To prove that decorous music makes us behave decorously, it is not enough to point out the similarity between the music and the hoped for behaviour.' (*Aesthetics*, pp. 565–6.)

[2] 'The artist's intention is a series of psychological states or events in his mind' (*Aesthetics*, p. 17). See, though, Wimsatt in Demetz, p. 220.

[3] Wimsatt in Demetz, p. 194.

[4] Ibid.

[5] 'The Intentional Fallacy', p. 5.

[6] *Aesthetics*, p. 20.

[7] Note here the whole of Wimsatt's first section in Demetz, pp. 193–7.

10. Why, finally, did the Beardsley-Wimsatt approach seem so disturbing? I think it was assumed that they wished totally to separate the work from the response of some actual person, so that *all* references to persons and their intentions were to be eliminated in some large scale dehumanisation of art.

I am not sure that Beardsley and Wimsatt ever intended this.[1] The temptation to believe that they did may have many sources. I mention three. First, there is Beardsley's concentration on features that works and natural objects share. This might well lead people to assume a belief on Beardsley's part that the artist is as irrelevant to the assessment of his work as he would be to the assessment of a natural object. Secondly, we have Beardsley and Wimsatt's apparently total distinction between personal and poetic studies. Thirdly, those who wished to defend intentionalism never gave a clear enough catalogue of the various possible theses about the relevance or irrelevance of appeals to intention. In consequence many seem not to have realised that Beardsley and Wimsatt argued only a relatively narrow thesis about the irrelevance of reference to prior intentions or statements of intention. They have never argued the dispensability of knowledge of other sorts of intention where this knowledge is gained from the work itself.[2]

Why however, even granted an assumption that Beardsley and Wimsatt *did* wish to argue the total eliminability of references to artists, would this seem so disturbing? One reason I think is that the belief that some works are, in part at least, important as documents of actual human responses, is deeply embedded in the concept of art as we have it. This belief is reflected in the ubiquity of references by critics to artists, that I have referred to above. To assert, as Beardsley and Wimsatt certainly did originally, that the response articulated in the work need not be thought of as some actual person's response but might be treated as the response of a dramatic speaker, a quasi-fictional *persona* detected in the work, was, for many, to urge the elimination of a centrally important feature of art.

It is perhaps relevant here to note the beginning of a possible divergence between Beardsley and Wimsatt on this matter. Wimsatt, as we have seen, does not appear to object to critical references to the mental quality shown by the artist in the work. Beardsley, on the other hand, is still exploring ways in which a wedge can be

[1] 'A poem does not come into existence by accident. The words of a poem . . . come out of a head, not out of a hat.' 'The Intentional Fallacy', p. 4.

[2] Nor do they say much that is positive about such knowledge. See, e.g., Wimsatt in Demetz, p. 210.

driven between the artist and the dramatic-responder-in-the-work. In his latest work he writes

> The writing of a poem is, as such . . . the creation of a fictional character performing a fictional illocutionary act. (*The Possibility of Criticism*, p. 59.)

Given that there is a divergence here I am inclined to say that, without recanting his attack on irrelevant and unnecessary references to artists and their intentions, Wimsatt has come closest to recognising what an interest in art (an interest that becomes most articulate in criticism) *actually* involves. For he seems to recognise that an interest in the value of some art may be in part an interest in the response articulated by an artist *in* his work. As such he may have done more justice to 'the form of life' of criticism as we have it.

12

GENRE AND THE EXPERIENCE
OF ART AND LITERATURE

Martin Dodsworth

LIKE most topics in aesthetics, that of genre is far from simple and for the literary critic has an uninviting air. The questions which arise from its consideration fall under two heads: first, what *is* a genre? and second, what does it contribute to our understanding of a work of art that we can describe it as belonging to this or that genre? A clear answer to either of these questions is not readily forthcoming: the literary critic who is content to be a critic here very properly hesitates where the philosopher is perhaps inclined to go further. If he does so he will find that the two primary questions about genre have many ramifications, some of which may be suggested by a quotation from René Wellek and Austin Warren's book, *Theory of Literature*. They ask one question about genre and then re-phrase it: but as they re-phrase their original question it is quite transformed.

> Does a theory of literary kinds involve the supposition that every work belongs to a kind ? . . . We might try a series of re-phrasings such as give our question sharper focus. Does every work stand in close enough literary relations to other works so that its study is helped by the study of other works? Again, how far is 'intention' involved in the idea of genre? Intention on the part of a pioneer? Intention on the part of others?[1]

Questions of genre are, perhaps, peculiarly pressing for the literary critic because since Aristotle it has been traditional to invoke conditions of genre in judging the merits of literary work. But these questions are by no means the peculiar property of literary critics and theorists. They are felt to be just as relevant to other art-forms –

[1] René Wellek and Austin Warren, *Theory of Literature*, 2nd ed. (New York: Harcourt Brace and Company, Harvest Books edition, 1956) p. 216.

music, painting and architecture, for example. It may be that some
reflections on the role of genre in literary discussion can throw light
on the extent to which the idea is relevant to other arts. This is the
more to be hoped for in that Richard Wollheim in his book *Art and its
Objects* allots an important place to genre in a context which implies
that it is generally relevant to the consideration of any work of art,
literary or not.

He is discussing the 'Presentational' theory of art: 'that a work of art
possesses those properties, and only those, which we can directly
perceive or which are immediately given'.[1] Part of his argument
against this theory (which I have no intention to defend) is that there
are certain concepts 'essential to a proper understanding or appreciation of the work' which nevertheless 'cannot be applied to a work
of art solely on the basis of what is presented'; it is in this category
that he places genre,[2] although in concluding his discussion of this
topic his language is less than unequivocal:

> I have not stated the argument against, therefore I shall not
> consider the argument for, genre-criticism in so far as this relates
> to the adequacy of this traditional classification. It would be
> enough if it could be established that some such classification is
> intrinsic to literary understanding: and certainly the 'radical of
> presentation' strongly suggests that it is.[3]

Professor Wollheim's reliance on the 'radical of presentation' very
much reduces his notion of what a genre is. The term is taken from
Northrop Frye's *Anatomy of Criticism* where it is used to describe
the way the words in a given text are to be taken – as spoken or
sung, for example, or as distributed amongst different imagined
characters in drama or as addressed by a single speaker to his
reader perhaps imagined present with him, perhaps not. But
Wollheim is not prepared to go as far as Frye in his adoption of the
'radical of presentation'. The distinction 'intrinsic to literary understanding' which is denoted by the term in his usage amounts simply
to that between what is drama and what is not. He seems to think it a
bit forward of Professor Frye to distinguish further between 'the case
where the poet addresses his audience (epic) and the case where he is
overheard (lyric)'.[4]

Now this notion of genre is naturally disappointing to someone
like myself particularly concerned with literature. Literary critics

---

[1] Richard Wollheim, *Art and its Objects* (Penguin Books, 1970) p. 60.
[2] p. 82.
[3] p. 86.
[4] p. 86.

have always been under the impression that distinctions in genre comprise the differences between, let us say, tragedy, comedy and tragi-comedy. There are occasions certainly, when we might feel inclined to argue whether a work was drama or not – for example in the case of Byron's *Manfred* or Bailey's *Festus* – but these occasions are marked by their rarity, and in any case have to do with practical problems of stageability on the one hand and the distinctive play of sympathy evoked in the reader or spectator on the other, matters which are of no concern to Professor Wollheim. Consequently it is hard for the literary critic not to look on with a certain wonder at the emphasis laid on the difference between what is and what is not drama.

Perhaps Professor Wollheim's formulation of the inevitability of genre-distinctions is a little unfortunate:

> Starting the problem at its lowest, we might imagine ourselves confronted with the pages in which the lines are printed so that they do not run to the end. One (*Paradise Lost*) is to be read as an epic: the other (*Berenice*) is to be read as a play . . .
> . . . there is nothing in the text that indicates such a distinction unambiguously, nor could there be. There are, of course, certain accepted typographical conventions that distinguish printed plays from printed poems. But as readers of literature we have to know how to interpret these conventions and we must not be like the child who, in learning his part, learns the stage directions as well. And such an interpretation is always in terms of certain aesthetic conventions which the reading presupposes. 'The genre', Frye puts it, 'is determined by the conditions established between the poet and his public.'[1]

I call this an unfortunate way of expounding the problem for it has to do not so much with our interpretation of literature and the words which compose it, as with our interpretation of the printed signs which stand for the words of which literature is composed. Were our literature an exclusively oral literature, and we may assume such literatures to have existed, then he would have nothing to discuss. Even so far as interpretation of a printed text is concerned, surely he is in error to suggest that any 'aesthetic conventions' are involved in the discovery that stage directions are not to be interpreted as part of the speech of dramatic characters. The only conventions involved are printers' conventions, a fact which we can verify if we consider the variety of ways in which a typographer can make the necessary

[1] pp. 85–6.

distinction. 'Aesthetic conventions' would be invoked properly if Professor Wollheim were speaking of the reader's consciousness that the words he is reading were to be *acted*, and even more so if the reader is aware of the stage and other circumstances best calculated to realise this aspect of a text. But a reader might be able to distinguish between what is drama and what is not, in the sense that he sees that in the one the words are supposed to be spoken by a variety of persons with no intervention from the author, or with that intervention taking the form of a kind of brief annotation to his own work, whilst in the other this is not true, without his having the least idea of what a theatrical *enactment* of the drama might be. The reader's consciousness that something is drama does not require a sense of it as *something to be acted* (he may not know what acting is, and yet respond appropriately to the words of the drama). It follows therefore that 'aesthetic conventions' need not be invoked where the distinction between drama and non-drama is concerned. (Indeed, it seems to me erroneous to suggest that 'there is nothing in the text that indicates such a distinction unambiguously'. There is a good deal, I would say, in the play of question and answer to suggest that a given text is drama, though it may not suggest that it is to be acted).

If we wish to establish genre as 'intrinsic to literary understanding' but as something brought to the work by its reader or auditor, then we need a wider view of the topic than any which Professor Wollheim has to offer. The citation of Frye – 'the genre is determined by the conditions established between the poet and his audience' – implies such a view, of course, but it never actually materialises in the pages of *Art and its Objects*.

Wellek and Warren accept the desirability of distinguishing between the 'three more or less ultimate categories' of lyric, epic and drama and the forms developing historically within these categories, such as comedy and tragedy within the 'kind' of drama. They suggest that the word 'genre' should apply only to this latter group of concepts – with reason, as it seems to me, for it answers to the way in which the word is customarily used. Professor Wollheim seems to allude to this usage when he asks how we can distinguish *Paradise Lost*, an epic, from *Hamlet*, a drama, for to say that *Paradise Lost* is an epic is something very different from saying that it is not a drama. (Parenthetically and with deference to Wellek and Warren, it should be noted that it is *also* different from saying that it is not drama or lyric.) The point apparently escaped Wollheim, who treats 'epic' as though it were synonymous with 'non-dramatic narrative', which it is not: try thinking of *The Murders in the Rue Morgue* as epic, and you will see the truth of this. Wollheim's idea of genre nevertheless ought to be that of Wellek and Warren, not just in order to conform to customary usage, but also to satisfy the conditions of his own argument that genre is a concept existing separately from the work of art, not to be deduced from it and yet intrinsic to an understanding of it. This holds true of certain views taken of *Paradise Lost* in its relation to the *Aeneid* and its status as an epic of the Virgilian kind; it does not hold true of our understanding that *Paradise Lost* is 'nondramatic narrative' a fact which *can* be deduced from the text itself, as I hope my previous discussion has suggested.

Professor Wollheim quarrels with the Crocean view of genre, by discussing Croce's arguments on the relation of this topic to that of form and content. On this point his reasoning seems satisfactory, but there is nevertheless a discrepancy between his notion of genre (the distinction between drama and what is not drama) and Croce's. Although he deals satisfactorily with Croce's argument on genre, form and content, he is wrong to suggest that the genre which he discusses is the same idea as the genre discussed by Croce. And in fact Croce's view of genre is worth considering because it reveals a difficulty which Wollheim sidesteps by means of his peculiar notion of genre.

Croce considers concepts of genre along with a great many others in the course of his critique of the so-called 'pseudo-aesthetic concepts'. It is worth noticing that these concepts are all presented by him as adjectives: the list begins:

> tragic, comic, sublime, pathetic, moving, sad, ridiculous, melancholy, tragi-comic, humoristic, majestic, dignified, serious, grave . . .[1]

And so it goes on. Although he is elsewhere content to discuss genre in terms of alternative forms for the same content, his point being that the concept of genre involves a false dichotomy of form and content, Croce here reduces genre to psychological effect: the word 'tragic' appears on the same level of meaning as the word 'moving'. And his point is now that, since genre as a 'pseudo-aesthetic concept' principally has significance of a psychological kind, it is incapable of any certain definition and must consequently be abandoned: 'As is the case with all other psychological constructions, so it is with those: no vigorous definitions are possible . . .'[2]

Now Croce's concern with 'definition' need not in principle concern us, and I have not quoted from him in order to take up arms against him. What *is* worth considering is the link implied

[1] Benedetto Croce, *Aesthetic*, tr. Douglas Ainslie (Macmillan, 1909) p. 142.
[2] p. 146.

between genre and emotion. For this is not an idiosyncrasy of Croce's aesthetics: it has a long and reputable history in literary discourse. Aristotle distinguishes tragedy from comedy in terms of its psychological effects – catharsis by means of the arousal of pity and fear – and many other writers followed him in this practice. Wollheim's reduction of the term genre excludes this consideration altogether; but it should not. For if there is a legitimate association between psychological effect and genre, then genre would be something that we could deduce from our experience of the work in question. We would distinguish between comedy and tragedy by the effect either form of drama had upon us. Genre would not in that case be necessarily intrinsic to literary understanding although it might be so, depending on the way in which the play drew or did not draw attention to the effect it might be supposed to have on its audience or reader.

If we look once more at Croce's arguments however we will see that he does not confine himself to the view that genre is determined by reference to psychological effect, but also that he says positively what genre is *not*: that is, a form separable from the content of a given work. And Professor Wollheim deals very well with Croce here; he reduces the argument to the following general thesis that 'if we say a is f, we must be able to imagine what it would be like for a not to be f but to be, say, g, where g is a contrary of f'.[1] Wollheim points out that this is false over a range of cases

i.e. where we cannot identify a except by reference (explicit or implicit) to f. And it might well be that we could not identify *Paradise Lost* except as an epic or *Hamlet* except as a drama.[2]

This could be a good argument if Professor Wollheim cared to advance it: his 'might well be', however, recalls the hesitancy of 'it would be enough if it could be established' of a passage from his book which we have already looked at. But were he to advance it, one difficulty would have to be met: Wollheim's view that we cannot identify *Paradise Lost except* as an epic (and I think that I am right in attributing this view to Wollheim, for it is certainly not that of Northrop Frye, whose concept of the 'radical of presentation' is used in the course of Wollheim's discussion) – Wollheim's view depends on giving the word 'epic' a different meaning from that which it has in Croce or in ordinary literary discourse, and a meaning which is in conflict with his notion that the description 'epic' cannot be deduced from a reading of the poem alone. We *can* discern that

[1] Wollheim, p. 84.
[2] Ibid.

Paradise Lost is non-dramatic narrative without response to any prior aesthetic conventions.

What does a literary critic mean when he says that *Paradise Lost* is an epic? What tells him that it *is* an epic? I would suggest that he calls an epic an epic for exactly the same reason that he calls a plum a plum: he has been told that that is what it is. But having been told that *Paradise Lost* is an epic could he then recognise that the *Aeneid* is another, in the same way that, having recognised one plum as a plum, he could recognise another? I do not see why this should not be the case. The fact that we are uncertain whether to call this or that work of literature an epic does not complicate the issue necessarily, for we might be equally doubtful about the status of certain fruits: the relation between Victoria plums, golden plums, greengages and nectarines admits of confusion just as does that between the *Aeneid*, *Paradise Lost*, *Jerusalem Delivered* and *Beowulf*. We identify an epic by its similarity to other epics.

In the case of *Paradise Lost* the similarity is hardly accidental:

> Of man's first disobedience, and the fruit
> Of that forbidden tree, whose mortal taste
> Brought death into the world, and all our woe,
> With loss of Eden, till one greater man
> Restore us, and regain the blissful seat,
> Sing heavenly Muse . . .

We notice that this has a similarity to the opening of the *Odyssey*:

> The man for wisdom's various arts renown'd,
> Long exercised in woes, O Muse! resound . . .
>   POPE

and to that of the *Iliad*:

> Achilles' wrath, to Greece the direful spring
> Of woes unnumber'd, heavenly goddess, sing!
>   POPE

as well as to that of the *Aeneid*:

> Arms, and the Man I sing, who, forc'd by Fate,
> And haughty *Juno's* unrelenting Hate;
> Expell'd and exil'd, left the *Trojan* Shoar:
> Long Labours, both by Sea and Land he bore;
> And in the doubtful War, before he won
> The *Latian* Realm, and built the destin'd Town:

His banish'd Gods restor'd to Rites Divine,
And setl'd sure Succession in his Line:
From whence the race of *Alban* Fathers come,
And the long Glories of Majestick *Rome*.

DRYDEN

These similarities might be classified as follows: like Homer in both
his epics, Milton begins with an invocation to the Muse which names
the subject of her song before she is asked to sing it: like Homer in
the *Iliad*, Milton takes as his subject an action with large consequences for others as for the man who performs or (as it were) undergoes it: like Homer in the *Odyssey* and Virgil in the *Aeneid*, Milton
stresses the human quality of his subject ('The man for wisdom's
various arts renown'd . . .', 'Arms, and the Man I sing . . .', 'Of
man's first disobedience . . .'): and like Virgil, he begins with a
statement of the whole scope of the poem's action. The significance
of these similarities is suggested by the following passage from Alastair
Fowler's annotation to the lines:

> Milton's particular overlapping arrangement of the opening parts
> traditional in epic combines the Virgilian and Homeric plans; so
> that, without the interruption of direct allusion, *Paradise Lost* is
> silently related to its three principal analogues. A metaphorical
> comparison is set up between Adam and Achilles, Odysseus and
> Aeneas, and between the loss of Paradise and the loss of Troy . . .[1]

It is because there is a reasonable consistency of such reference to
other epics that we call *Paradise Lost* an epic. As Fowler's note makes
clear, the identification of Milton's poem as an epic does affect the
way we respond to it, encouraging us to compare Adam with
Achilles, and so on. The question now arises whether such a response
is 'intrinsic to literary understanding' of the poem.

Now if this question is applied to the opening lines of the poem
which I have quoted, then the answer must surely be that there is
nothing 'intrinsic to literary understanding' of them in such an identification with epic. The lines allude to Virgil and to Homer, but they
make perfectly good sense even if we fail to take the allusions into
account. It might be objected certainly that it is not enough to
satisfy 'literary understanding' that the lines should merely make
sense; it could be argued that the lines owe their literary quality to
something other than the mere fact of saying something. In order to
advance this kind of argument it is necessary to have some clear idea

[1] *The Poems of John Milton*, ed. John Carey and Alastair Fowler (Longmans,
1968) p. 458.

of what constitutes 'literary understanding'. In the context of *Art and its Objects*, this is surely the specific form of the 'aesthetic attitude' directed towards words:

> in art there is a further constraining influence of greater authority [than practical considerations], in the person of the artist who has made or moulded the work of art according to his own inner demands. It is the imprint of these demands upon the work that we must respect, if we are to retain the aesthetic attitude.[1]

'Literary understanding' then would be consciousness of 'the imprint of the artist's inner demands' on *Paradise Lost*. Can there exist such a consciousness of the opening lines of the poem apart from a consciousness that these are 'epic' lines?

Surely there can, at least in this limited respect that we can be aware of the author's part in shaping his utterance grammatically and syntactically. The inversion by which the poet names what the Muse is to sing before he calls to the Muse to sing it is distinctive in terms of the English language (and, we might add, the English *poetic* language too) and is used distinctively. We might point, for example, to the way in which 'fruit' seems first to have an abstract significance as fruit or consequences of man's disobedience, and then takes on a literal meaning:[2]

> Of man's first disobedience, and the fruit
> Of that forbidden tree . . .

We might similarly point to the double function of the phrase 'all our woe' which may be read either as a further object to the verb 'brought' in

> Brought death into the world, and all our woe . . .

or as a further, independent item in the list of subjects which the Muse is to sing: man's first disobedience, the fruit which brought death into the world, and 'all our woe', all the woe that accompanied the expulsion from the garden and that is to characterise our life until we are restored to God's favour by Christ's intercession on our behalf at the Last Judgment. This double function of 'all our woe' produces a syntactical uncertainty in the description of human suffering corresponding to the uncertainty of its duration and contrasted with the certainty of its final alleviation: 'till one greater Man/Restore us, and regain the blissful seat'.

There is no need to extend this account of the language used in

---

[1] Wollheim, p. 118.
[2] Noted by Fowler, from Daiches.

these perhaps over-familiar lines. I hope that enough has been said to show that *some* kind of literary understanding of the passage is possible without reference to the genre to which the poem belongs. I would argue further that, since this understanding is of the relation of what is said to the means of saying it, although it leaves out of account one dimension of the poem's meaning (that which invites comparison of the action of this epic poem with that of other epic poems), it is nevertheless an understanding of what is *essential* to the poem. It is an understanding of qualities unique to this way of saying what is said.

I have said that 'literary understanding', according to Professor Wollheim, would be consciousness of the imprint of the artist's 'inner demands' on a work of literature, but it will be seen that in discussing the lines from *Paradise Lost* I have made no reference to 'inner demands'. Instead, I described the reader as being aware 'of the author's part in shaping his utterance'. This is not really a satisfactory formulation, but I used it because I did not want to part company with Wollheim before I had illustrated what literary understanding might be like. In the light of my example it is surely evident that there is no need to invoke a consciousness of this or that person making choices. The choices have been made; our task is to comprehend the significance of those choices, and there is no compelling reason why that should be found within the artist's nature. On the contrary: in illustrating the literary understanding of the grammar and syntax of the opening of *Paradise Lost*, we interpreted idiosyncrasies such as the double syntactic function of 'all our woe' by reference to what the words meant in their alternative groupings.

It does not follow that the 'inner demands' of the artist play *no* part in the shaping of a work of art, but in so far as they result in the work's being of *this* character rather than another, the elements of the work in which they are reflected take on a functional aspect, and in this way their origin ceases to be a matter of importance to the reader. The phrase 'and all our woe' might have assumed its function in response to the inner demands of the artist, but this function is expressive in relation to the entire sentence in which it figures, and no reference to the artist's 'inner demands' (which can in any case never be more than hypothetical) is necessary.

I have tried to show that it is not necessary to perceive that the opening lines of *Paradise Lost* are the opening lines of an epic in order to have a literary understanding of them. I would like now to argue that the same is true of the poem as a whole: that we can have a perfectly adequate literary understanding of it without identifying

or being able to identify it as epic. This might seem to be a paradoxical position, and I admit the implausibility of the case in
practical terms. It arises from the fact that the poem is never
described as an epic within its own compass; it follows that we do
not need to know what an epic is in order to see what the poem is
about. It is true that when the narrator of the poem describes himself as

> Not sedulous by nature to indite
> Wars, hitherto the only argument
> Heroic deemed, chief mastery to dissect
> With long and tedious havoc fabled knights
> In battles feigned; the better fortitude
> Of patience and heroic martyrdom
> Unsung . . .,

it is hard for the reader with some knowledge of literary history not
to gloss the word 'heroic' which here receives such an emphasis, as
meaning 'epic'. But he does not need to do so. The circumstantial
evidence that he is meant to do so is strong, of course, but it imposes
no obligation. Indeed we may reflect that Milton's central place in
English Protestant culture is due, in part at least, to the tact with
which he alludes to such things as the epic tradition. Had an understanding of epic been mandatory to an understanding of his poem,
Milton's importance within our culture would have been greatly
diminished because of the necessary restriction on the audience
which in fact he found. We may regard this as at least an interesting
corollary to the ambiguity of allusion and reference to epic in
Paradise Lost.

In this discussion of the genre classification of Milton's poem I have
been aiming at a general point. I have wanted to show by a particular
examination the falsity of Wollheim's argument against the Crocean
view of genre. According to Wollheim there is a range of cases
(which 'might well' include *Paradise Lost*) 'where we cannot identify
a except by reference (explicit or implicit) to *f*'. It is my view that
this range must be limited, as far as genre is concerned, to works of
literature where it is made an issue within the work itself what genre
it belongs to, and the issue needs to be expressed unequivocally as it
is not in the case of *Paradise Lost*. Indeed since genre terms are so
closely associated with certain kinds of feeling as well as with certain
kinds of art object – a fact for which we have the testimony not only
of Aristotle and Croce but also of the everyday use of such terms as
'tragic' applied to domestic distress or 'epic' applied to some feat of
human endurance such as Sir Francis Chichester's voyage round the

world – it may well be that even had the word 'epic' appeared in the text of Milton's poem, we would still not need to *identify* it as an epic.

However, before going on to the general conclusions to be drawn from this concerning the argument of *Art and its Objects*, I want to consider the extent to which it is possible to apply what has been said on the subject of genre in literature to other arts. I said earlier on that Professor Wollheim's consideration of the subject might suggest that the issue of genre was not simply a problem in the study of literature. I would base this on his associating with the genre question the question of 'expectancy' in music and architecture and his endorsement of Panofsky's contention that 'there are cases where our understanding of a work of (visual) art and its stylistic peculiarities depends upon reconstructing the artistic intentions that went to its making'.[1] We might further note Wollheim's involvement with and general approval of the work of Ernst Gombrich, whose essay 'Tradition and Expression in Western Still Life'[2] applies arguments about the importance of genre to the visual arts.

Professor Gombrich opens his essay with a description of a sculptural still life by Manzù, a chair with a bunch of vegetables spread on it, the whole done in bronze. He points out that the sculpture functions in the tradition of the *paragone* as a challenge on the part of sculpture to the art of painting:

> Sculpture too can delight and surprise the eye by celebrating the beauty of humble things, sculpture also can conquer the still life. It is a fair guess that the purpose of this comparison can be narrowed down even further. Manzù would hardly have conceived of this challenge had the painted genre of the still life not included, among its possibilities, the famous chairs of Van Gogh. Without these elements of recognition and comparison, the discovery of the familiar in the unfamiliar, Manzù's chair would lose most of its meaning.[3]

But *would* it indeed lose 'most' of its meaning? It seems to me that, as in the case of the opening lines of *Paradise Lost*, if we discount the allusion to Van Gogh, if we ignore or are ignorant of the tradition of the *paragone*, if we do not even recall that the subject of the sculpture would have made a suitable subject for a painting, then there

---

[1] Wollheim's summary, op. cit., p. 87. Erwin Panofsky's essay 'The History of Art as a Humanist Discipline' will be found in his *Meaning in the Visual Arts*, 1955.
[2] Ernst Gombrich, *Meditations on a Hobby Horse* (Phaidon Press, 1963) pp. 95–105.
[3] Gombrich, op. cit. p. 95.

is still a good deal left for us to contemplate in Manzù's vegetables which are over-life-size, cast in bronze, and arranged immovably. There is still before our eyes an object which conflicts with our ordinary sense of things and which may, because it does so conflict, enhance that sense. Professor Gombrich is an art historian and naturally values art history highly: when he looks at a work of art such as Manzù's vegetables he sees an interesting piece of art history. It does not follow that art-historical understanding is *intrinsic* to an 'artistic understanding' of the sculpture: irrespective of art history, the sculpture still invites us to experience by looking, and perhaps touching, vegetables that are and are not vegetables – to experience, that is, another way of imagining objects and our relation to them.

Professor Gombrich develops his argument by reference to the necessity of seeing art in terms of a context:

> Within the context of medieval art Manzù's chair would have lacked any meaning. Even for us, of course, its 'meaning' is not that of a 'message' investigated by engineers, but in so far as it has a message it must and does relate to a number of alternatives which it denies.[1]

Professor Gombrich allows that expression and communication in art depend on unlearnt as well as acquired reactions. Critics like to talk largely in terms of the former, of 'loud' and 'subdued' colours and 'violent' or 'melodious' tunes:

> it is dangerous to underrate the distance between such natural reactions to forms and their articulated meaning in the contexts of a culture. Even an art of pure form such as music, needs a background of expectations to become understandable. The same must be true of the still life.[2]

For Professor Gombrich then, genre becomes the context within which we are able to make sense of the artist's choices. The genre sets up certain expectations, these are either confirmed or denied by the artist, and we understand the artist by providing a rationale for the choices he has made.

The solidity of this argument is however only apparent. For if we recognise that the artist may choose to do this or that within a certain genre, it must also be remembered that the artist chooses what to do within a certain medium. As Gombrich himself puts it, 'the unexpected transformation of the medium is at least as expressive as the unusual transformation of the motif'[3] and he cites 'Manzù's way

[1] p. 97.   [2] p. 98.   [3] p. 99.

with bronze' in support of this. So much then for 'most' in the 'most' of the sculpture's meaning that we lose if we fail to identify it as belonging to a certain genre. Gombrich uses this word to slur over the difficulty of saying whether we need to perceive that the sculpture is in a certain genre at all. The analogy with *Paradise Lost* suggests that it is not necessary to do so, as of course does the fact that we can recognise the sculpture as having a subject-matter without reference at all to the concept of genre. We have, in that, context enough to render meaningful the artist's choices in the handling of his medium.

This is not of course to deny the validity of Gombrich's general sense that the work of art is amongst other things socially determined. But he wants to draw the wrong sort of implications from this. He says that 'within the context of medieval art Manzù's chair would have lacked any meaning'. What he means surely is that, viewing that sculpture from within the context of medieval art, the spectator would have had to overcome a complex of social inhibitions to realise what the sculpture 'meant'. And whilst such inhibitions might *in practice* prove insuperable, it would be wrong to suppose that they were so in principle. The sculpture would have retained its 'meaning' in the context of medieval art, but the 'meaning' would in practice probably have been unseizable. Professor Gombrich is closer to the truth of the matter when he describes the consequences of the lack of a frame of reference when we view exotic art:

> we can still project expressive characters into these works but we are usually aware of our uncertainty as to whether our meaning is indeed the intended one, whether anything like communication has taken place.[1]

This could well be an accurate account of a usual feeling about exotic art, without at all demonstrating the *necessity* of a frame of reference. Our uncertainty may be caused because exotic art may *require* us to see clearly, where within our own culture we are able to protect ourselves from seeing by interposing a 'frame of reference'. Again, many exotic works of art are *more* than works of art, functioning within a ritual framework which may indeed limit the choices of the artist even as they affect the medium within which he works. The medium may for example be subject to valuations other than aesthetic which forbid it to be used in certain ways. We might reasonably feel uneasy about our ignorance in such a case, once it had been pointed out to us, without deciding either that we had previously had *no* 'artistic' understanding of the object concerned or

[1] p. 96.

that we had to argue from that uneasiness the necessity of 'frames of reference' of a kind represented by genre or 'aesthetic convention'. Thus I do not feel that any significant modifications of the argument are required when we apply what has been said of genre in literature to other arts.

We might ask then of what use genre terms are to us. The answer seems to be that they permit us to compare one sort of experience with another. By putting *Paradise Lost* in the class of 'epic', we imply that it is comparable with the *Aeneid* and the *Odyssey*. It could be categorised as a work narrating the story of the Fall, inviting comparison with Dryden's adaptation *The State of Innocence* and the first part of Shaw's *Back to Methuselah*. It could be categorised as a work narrating the story of the world, inviting comparison with, for example, Joyce's *Finnegans Wake*. If we think that genre classification is more important than the sort of classification represented by my two latter examples, the reason is only that we feel that to compete with Virgil and Homer is a more honourable thing than to compete with Dryden, Shaw and Joyce. And if genre classification seems to the literary critic a matter of ever diminishing moment, the reason may well be that as we know less of Homer and Virgil we value Joyce and Shaw the more, and look for different likenesses in the things we value. That is to say no more than that genre terms are socially conditioned and belong not so much to our experience of literature but to the way we describe that experience. They do also have to do with that experience directly: the artist himself is liable to be affected by the way people talk about literature and to conceive of what he is doing in terms of that talk. *Paradise Lost* is a case in point. We do not need to take 'heroic' in the sense of 'epic' but we cannot overlook the availability of that sense and its congruence with much in the poem, if, that is, we have a certain acquaintance with the literary tradition within which Milton wrote. But it is excessive to suggest that we do not 'understand' the poem if we cannot, as doubtless a number of his readers in the past could not and today cannot, see that it sets itself up as an epic in emulation of and in opposition to Virgil's. That would only be true were we required to have a complete understanding of the poem in order to have an understanding of it at all.

Professor Wollheim presses the case of genre for much the same reason as Professor Gombrich: he is anxious to emphasise the socially determined aspect of art. But it seems to me that he gives it a false emphasis. He asks for example, 'to what extent do we need to be able to locate the work of art in its historical setting?' but offers in reply this rough principle – that the more 'original' the work of art, or rather, the more radical the transformation of existing rules for art in a given work, the more necessary it will be to be aware of the rules transformed. He illustrates this by the following example:

> Merleau-Ponty suggests that much of the dramatic tension of Julien Sorel's return to Verrières arises from the suppression of the kind of thoughts or interior detail that we could expect to find in such an account: we get in one page what might have taken up five. If this is so, then it would seem to follow that, for the understanding of this passage, the reader of *Le Rouge et le Noir* needs to come to the book with at any rate some acquaintance with the conventions of the early nineteenth-century novel.[1]

But does this follow? Surely not. We don't need to think of a specific kind of novel where the passage would have been longer in order to observe that in Stendhal it is shorter than it might have been. We don't need to because we have ourselves a sense of what is and is not worth recording, and a sense of what may or may not be done with language, which exist irrespective both of any specifically literary training and of whether or not we are well read in the early nineteenth-century novel. In any case, the passage discussed by Merleau-Ponty is consistent with the style of narration throughout *Le Rouge et le Noir*: having got so far in the novel, we would not expect any significantly longer account than we get of the return to Verrières. But it is on this point rather than the one raised by Professor Wollheim that I would wish to quarrel with Merleau-Ponty; for *he* says nothing about the 'conventions of the early nineteenth-century novel' at all.[2] That is entirely Professor Wollheim's addition.

We have here a mistake very much like that which he makes about genre. He mistakes as something necessary to an understanding of the novel a phenomenon that could only be necessary to an understanding of the historical circumstances of its composition. There is no identity between these two concepts. Similarly, genre is part of the way we talk about art, but not a necessary part of the way we experience art. Wollheim tells us that

> it would certainly seem as though there is one element that we must bring to our perception of a work of art, which is quite incompatible with the Presentational theory: and that is the recognition that it is a work of art.[3]

[1] Wollheim, p. 163.

[2] See Maurice Merleau-Ponty, *Signs*, translated with an introduction by Richard C. McCleary (Evanston, Illinois: Northwestern University Press, 1964) p. 76.

[3] Wollheim, p. 89.

But if this recognition is exemplified in the 'necessary' identification of *Paradise Lost* as an epic or the 'necessary' knowledge of early nineteenth-century fiction for a reading of *Le Rouge et le Noir*, then it is hard for a literary critic to agree, and I have suggested that the grounds for his reluctance apply where other arts are concerned also. Rejecting the idea that we should 'regard the concept "art" as part of the conceptual framework with which we are required to approach art',[1] Professor Wollheim argues that 'art' is 'a concept of such complexity that it is hard to see how it could be fitted into an argument designed with merely descriptive or rhetorical concepts in mind'. We may agree with Professor Wollheim that art is a complex concept, and yet feel that he adds unnecessarily to its complexity.

Note

On p. 225 I distinguish between 'a complete understanding of the poem' and 'an understanding of it'. It should be obvious that the former is hypothetical. Roland Barthes argues that it would be undesirable even if it could exist. M. Barthes does not always command immediate assent, but on this point he seems to be right. See his *S/Z* (Paris: Éditions du Seuil, 1970) pp. 16–18.

On genre and intention, see Michael Black, 'Reading a Play', *The Human World*, 1 (November 1970) p. 17. On difficulties associated with the genre model, see Ralph Berry, 'Shakespearean Comedy and Northrop Frye', *Essays in Criticism*, XXII 1 (January 1972) p. 33.

[1] p. 90.

13

ART/NATURE

Andrew Forge

EIGHTEENTH-CENTURY country gentlemen would carry small amber-coloured reducing lenses on their evening walks, and with their help they would transport themselves from Derbyshire or Kent into the Roman campagna or into the ideal campagna they had learnt from the paintings of Claude or Gaspard Poussin.

I am on the top deck of a bus and I look up to find myself facing a plane tree. It is still in full leaf, but on the turn so that some leaves are dark green, others yellow, others brown, the whole flooded with sunlight. I think 'Pissarro!' Not that a particular picture comes to mind or that I think of the kind of tree that he might have painted. I am too close to see it like that. The sensation is not of a picture picked out at a distance but of being in the centre of one. I am wrapped round by Impressionism and the leaves look like brush strokes.

I am in the bath. Ahead of me is the window. A net curtain is drawn over it and daylight filters through. A single vertical fold makes a darker stripe from top to bottom of the rectangle of light. I find that I am looking at the window in the frame of mind that I have learnt from looking at the pictures of Barnet Newman. The bathroom is forgotten. I explore the field of the curtain. The vertical stripe seems 'right'; it seems even to have meaning and intention, and although I reflect that this is absurd, the impression remains. I focus on the edge of the stripe. It has a kind of vibration, neither vague nor clean as if cut by a knife. I reflect that this quality is the consequence of the structure of the fabric that it is made from, acted upon by gravity and light. At the same time I cannot exclude the memory of Newman's edges, and the patient gradual way with which they are found by the brush, a brush that had been groping for such edges for twenty years, against all sense. . . .

One more. A few streets away they are digging the road for new drains. The drains are square and they come in sections like concrete boxes with open ends, about four feet by four feet by six. All along the road where the trench has not yet been dug these boxes have been arranged in a neat level row. The intervals between them are irregular, but their axes are regular. If somebody told me that this row was a major work by some minimal sculptor, a follower of Robert Morris or Don Judd I can think of no reason for not believing him.

When I was invited to read a paper to you on the subject of Art and Nature (one of the suggested titles was *Nature in the light of Art*) these were the kind of experiences which at once came into my mind. They are examples of how art focuses attention and charges one's experience of certain aspects of the world which then blossom out into something far richer and more resonant than the things or scenes in themselves would warrant. It seems to me that there is quite a clear-cut difference between the first of my examples and the rest. It is this difference which I want to discuss.

In the eighteenth-century example we can be fairly clear about the boundaries within which the nature into art game was being played out. 'Art' was a certain kind of painting, painted in Rome during the preceding century, mostly by non-Italian artists who were themselves looking at the campagna with a certain nostalgia. 'Nature' was the natural world – the land, the trees, the sky. The pictures in question were warm in tonality and their varnish was getting old; that was why the cold blues of nature needed to be seen through an amber-coloured glass. The pictures were being used to give a face, an image to all that countryside. The countryside was being used to yield up a kind of cultured entertainment. 'Did you see that Colosseum?' asks the woman tourist in the cartoon. 'Why, no honey, I was flat out of film.' We are tempted to laugh at the tourists who put their postcards before, rather than after the tour, but we all know that there are circumstances when any of us will turn to an image in order to know what we are looking at in 'the raw', an image which will articulate our experience and without which we can hardly say whether we have seen anything or not.

But is this exactly applicable to the other examples, the tree, the bathroom curtain and the drains? The sense of being transported into an Impressionist painting did not depend upon the fact that it was a certain kind of tree that I was looking at. It could have happened through the fall of light on water, or on a brick wall or on people crossing a pavement. It did not depend upon casting my mind back to a certain type of picture whose features I could list and combine in my mind. It depended rather on a special way of seeing, which, once understood, could be applied to almost anything. Does this mean that art is something that I carry in my eye, irrespective of what I fasten on out there? Or, if it doesn't matter what I look at, does it mean that 'nature' is in the way that I look too, and that the contrast art – nature has somehow broken down? Looking through a Claude glass at a landscape is a kind of game that I can snap out of at any moment, returning art to art and nature to nature. But the business with the concrete boxes is more serious. Once I have started to look at them as though they are sculptures I can no longer discriminate between my experience of them and my experience of a row of metal boxes in Don Judd's recent exhibition at the Whitechapel art gallery. Having seen the Judd boxes could have focused my attention in a certain way, but I cannot be sure of that. It could just as easily have worked the other way round. Is the boundary between Judd's 'art' and the Lewisham Borough Council's 'nature' then simply a matter of labelling? 'Don't use that. Use this!' says one's hostess, leaning forward sharply, and at once the ashtray that one was about to knock out one's pipe in turns into a Bernard Leach or a nice piece of Chelsea.

If at this point I seem to be heading for the question What is Art, I must take another tack. But the fact that I seem to have come close to it underlies the general point that I am trying to make, which is that the boundaries have shifted in such a way that one can't talk about art and nature as if they were two separate domains.

Let me remind you of some earlier attitudes to these boundaries. Here is Joshua Reynolds – his Third Discourse. Beauty – the object of Art – was contained in nature, but only in a general sense. Students of art should be warned against copying nature because 'A mere copier of nature can never produce anything great'. For 'All the objects which are exhibited to our view by nature, upon close examination will be found to have blemishes and defects. The most beautiful forms have something about them like weakness or minuteness or imperfection. But it is not every eye that perceives these blemishes. It must be an eye long used to the contemplation and the comparison of these forms; and which by a long habit of observing what any set of objects of the same kind have in common, has the power of discerning what each wants in particular.' This artist 'being enabled to distinguish the accidental deficiencies, excrescences and deformities of things from their general figures, makes out an abstract idea of their forms more perfect than any one original'.

It seems to me that in reading Reynolds – or any other statement of Ideal Beauty – one has an extraordinary sense of remoteness and distance, and this is not so much because the idea of art that it is putting forward is so foreign or remote, but because that way of seeing is so foreign and remote. Somehow the idea of nature as some kind of ore from which the precious metal has to be smelted is impossible to relate to any experience. It's just not like that. Perhaps it is the juxtaposition of Beauty and flawed nature. The two go hand-in-hand. Certainly it is easier to feel at home with Constable, forty years or so later, when he says 'I never saw an ugly thing in my life'. The centre has shifted. Nature is allowed some of the attributes of art. 'The sound of water escaping from mill-dams, willows, old rotten planks, slimy posts and brickwork, I love such things. . . . Painting is for me but another word for feeling, and I associate my careless boyhood with all that lies on the banks of the Stour; these scenes made me a painter and I am grateful. . . .'

The letter from which these much-quoted lines are taken was written in 1821. The position that he was affirming was to be an ingredient in almost all the most vital painting of the next sixty years, and what happened after, although it seems in contradiction, grows out of it too.

What is Constable saying? He was affirming an intense attachment to a place. His friend had been on a fishing expedition and had written describing it. His letter must have triggered a flood of memories and associations of childhood, and perhaps a longing to be in the country. Then he is affirming the emotional role of his painting, which puts him daily in contact with these memories. Through painting he can do something about those ancient loves, could re-make the circumstances of childhood and perhaps re-make not only the appearance, but also something of the quality of his recollection – the freshness, the unspoiltness of nature (for which we can also read 'the freshness and unspoiltness of his youth') – and also the darkness, the turbulence and the sense of change which we can associate with the regrets and apprehensions of middle age. But what does he mean by 'these scenes made me a painter'? Obviously this is a figure of speech. What made Constable a painter was painting pictures. If he had spelt things out at length he would perhaps have said: 'I learnt to paint from painting pictures modelled on the pictures by Claude and Rubens and Ruisdael which appealed to me and which I modified as I learned more about my own abilities. But these scenes gave me a sense of direction and a belief that what I was painting was mine alone. Thanks to that I was able to hold to a completely uncharted path, which included a tonality that no painting had had before mine, an abruptness of handling, a vividness of light and an accuracy in certain transitory effects that was unprecedented. Thanks to these scenes I learned what to look for, and had the spirit to risk altering painting to include my observations.'

The reason why I have put words into Constable's mouth in this unhistorical way is because I want to bring out two lines of thought in his original words. One, his relationship with Nature as an inner experience. The other, the processes of observation and description which painting involved him in. I want to follow these two lines separately for a while and then try to bring them together at a later point.

These two lines reappear side by side in a letter by the French painter of landscapes and peasant subjects, J.-F. Millet. It could be matched by quotations from Corot, Rousseau and several others of his generation.

Whatever the temperament of the artist, and whatever the impressions he is open to, he should only be prepared to receive them from Nature. You must believe that Nature is rich enough to provide for every experience. Whatever you love with the greatest passion and rapture becomes your embodiment of beauty and conveys itself to others. Each painter must confront Nature on his own. Impression determines Expression, above all it insists upon the medium which will convey it with the greatest force.' Again we find this expression of faith that Nature can 'teach': 'Impression determines Expression'. Millet was even more deeply steeped in the Old Masters than Constable. His utterance here is a claim for 'truth' and 'simplicity' against the artifice of the studios, an artifice which we knew well and rejected. The project of an art which was based on first-hand experience, supported by belief in Nature's richness, was to guide at least two generations of painters in this stand against the dominance of Salon painting and bourgeois philistinism. There are parallels with the political ideals of Proudhon, and with his faith in first-hand experience over against the dead weight of institutions and with his rejection of formal programmes.

The revolution in painting brought about by Impressionism really stems from this. Instead of turning to nature for separate items of information, for props to be assimilated into a framework determined in the studio, as earlier art had done, you look at the whole view in front of you with the idea that the whole view is potentially a picture. This in turn leads to the experiment of painting the whole view from observation and trying to reconstruct it feature by feature on the canvas, instead of submitting it to the selecting and stylising processes which are part and parcel of the traditional studio procedures. Working directly from observation brings a whole train of consequences. In the first place, it induces a quite new awareness of what is seen at any one time; this in turn induces a different idea of drawing.

If you are faced with a flat canvas (your picture to be), and a view – say a typical Impressionist subject of a road running away in perspective with trees on either side – and working under the discipline of 'Impression forces Expression' you can hardly fail to project in your mind the view on to the canvas and the canvas on to the view. The canvas looks empty, ready to be filled right up with what you see in front of you. This is a radically different way of looking to the normal way, when one is continually separating objects out from their backgrounds, seeing them as more or less free-standing, their backgrounds vague and unimportant. (Here I am not just contrasting useful, everyday vision with the way a painter looks, but that, and the way of looking implied by traditional art with the way of looking implied by impressionism.) Until Impressionism, drawing had always had this meaning. It had been a kind of separating out of form from background, of figure from field. And until the Impressionists, all painting had, in one way or another, been based on drawing.

But working from all-over observation in the Impressionist way gives a new bias. I think that most accounts of Impressionism neglect the practical consequences of setting out to fill a canvas with what is in front of the eyes, and consequently miss the endless circuits of feed-back that connect and modify vision, technique and subject-matter. The Impressionist emphasis on light, for example, is often discussed as though it had been introduced almost arbitrarily as a new subject. But once one is attending to the whole visual field and not selected features in it, all-over light comes to take the place of the figure-field discriminations that one had relinquished. There is no avoiding its action. Attention to light in this context leads to technical discoveries such as the colour value of shadows. This in turn leads to certain motifs, to snow scenes, where the colour effects of light and shade can be observed at their maximum purity, or the effects of light on water or filtered through leaves, where the interpretation of light and surface reduces figure-field relations to the minimum and the whole can be observed as a continuous web. These subjects in turn – once rendered into paint – suggest new ways of painting. The picture itself yields new sensations leading to even purer colour or even more broken touches or even less continuous profiles. The challenge of reading the picture stimulates new responses to the subject. In a sense the Impressionist brush

I

stroke 'is' a leaf or a ripple or a figure crossing the bridge. In a sense, the vision of a Pissarro or a Monet was such that there was a picture whichever way they looked.

This being so, Nature is no longer limited to trees and skies, pigs and rocks. It is no longer limited to some concept of 'natural' life. Nature becomes what is 'out there'. Railway bridges, people in city suits, pavements, buildings, street lamps. To paint from nature came to mean to paint from observation, not necessarily in the forest of Fontainebleau.

Compared with more traditional ways of drawing, the Impressionist vision was introspective. This paradox is best explained in the actual experience of drawing. If I draw a single form – a cup, say – and try to describe its shape with outline I have the sensation of trying to reach out for it. This sensation will often be just as vivid if I am drawing out of my head. On the other hand, if I am trying to paint an extended scene in front of me, this outward movement of my attention will alternate with a more inward sensation, where I am trying to grasp how I see. I will be withdrawing attention from discrete forms. I will be scanning across them, trying to balance background and foreground shapes so that one does not take precedence over the other. I am looking inwards, trying to discern the way I see (I put it that way; I know that one can never see how one sees – although I dare say that some painters get closer to it than some psychologists would allow) and in doing so, I am aware of a cutting down of attention to what it is specifically that I am looking at.

It was this all-over attention, coupled with the most demanding sense of pictorial structure that any painter has ever had, and an irreducible grasp of the subject that made the late works of Cézanne what they were. Here, as nowhere before, the thing seen out there and the sensation of scanning across it, the modelling of the picture surface and the scanning across it, come together in a single structure. Impossible to say where the outward form stops and sensation begins: or where the boundary lies between looking at 'nature' and looking at the picture. If we had to name the subject of a Cézanne water-colour once and for all we might perhaps call it *Cézanne looking at a pine tree under the conditions of painting it*. 'We must render the image of what we see,' he told Emile Bernard, 'forgetting everything that existed before us.' Where then is Nature? In the pine tree? In the artist's nerves and eyes and finger tips? Both, surely.

Because the essential feature of Cézanne's presence in the picture is that it is revealed through his sensations. His presence is not by virtue of his culture. It is not a projection of any hierarchy which we can extrapolate outwards from the picture on to other spheres, unless in the most indirect way: unless via his unique sensations and his unique awareness of them. The paths that connect him with his motif are so many and knotted, and the traffic on them so complex that it is impossible to picture any kind of threshold or gap of which one can say: on this side is the artist; on that side is his subject.

I want to make a rather large leap forward to that notorious episode during the First World War when Marcel Duchamp invented the Readymade. You will remember that he took ordinary objects, a bicycle wheel, a shovel, a bottle rack, a porcelain urinal, and presented them as sculpture. The urinal was entered for an exhibition in New York and when it was rejected Duchamp wrote an anonymous defence of it in which he said that it didn't matter whether the urinal was a work of art or not because the 'sculptor' had *chosen* it and by doing this had created 'a new thought for the object'. This episode has been commented upon endlessly since and interpreted as a gesture of anti-art, of the absurd, or as demonstrating the primacy of conception over execution. I only want to add a small point, which is that if we think of it as a comment made about art, it seems an extremely reasonable one. It matches a train of thought which might go as follows: an artist can paint anything; the reason that he can paint anything is that it is his perceptions and his selections that give value to his picture, not what he perceives. First he chooses what to paint (i.e. transform), then he transforms it. But he can't transform it unless he has first chosen it. Why not apply that choice directly, skipping the rest? That is, *choose an object*.

It is a train of thought that only makes sense against the background of the kind of painting that I have been describing up to now; that is, painting based on the direct observation of nature. We are left looking at a piece of 'nature' (i.e. the outside world) to which a 'new thought' has been attached: it is presented as art. Looking at it we are left with our own perceptions. We are looking at the real world as art.

I said earlier that there were two lines of thought in the Constable letter which I wanted to follow. It is now time to pick up with his relationship with Nature and his acknowledgment of her influence. I know that this side of the subject spreads out into the general history of ideas where I am not able to follow. I don't know whether a study has been made of the way in which this aspect of Romanticism contributed to and was itself affected by the developments in science. Constable talked about painting as a branch of natural science, and it is striking how frequently science and landscape painting are linked at this time. Goethe's scientific interests had a vast influence on his views about painting and the combination was passed on to the new school of landscape painters in Germany and elsewhere. Carl Carus's letters on landscape painting are an example. Nature calms, he says: 'The change of time, of day, of year, the passage of the clouds . . . the ebb and flow of the sea, the slow but inevitable advancing change of the earth's surface, the weathering of naked cliffs whose crags, soon washed down produce fertile soil, the welling-up of springs whose waters follow the direction of the mountain chains . . . everything obeys quiet and eternal laws by whose power we ourselves are of course controlled. . . .'

'Go up to the top of the mountains, look over the long range of hills, observe the flow of the rivers and all the splendours that open before your eyes, and what feeling touches you? It is one of quiet devotion; you lose yourself in boundless space; your whole ego vanishes; you are nothing; God is all.'

What interests me about that passage is the sense it gives of the writer being carried out of himself, letting himself drift, so to speak, on a tide of natural process. He is released from his human scale; he sees himself as part of a system whose horizons he can't begin to discern from a human point of observation. There is implied a distrust, even a hatred of the human scale. Such a feeling comes over strongly in the nature worship of Ruskin. Nothing is more telling from this point of view than the following passage from the *Elements of Drawing*, where he is advising his readers on how to tackle landscape subjects: 'Passing then to skies, note that there is this great peculiarity about sky subjects, as distinct from earth subjects – that the clouds, not being much liable to man's interference, are always beautifully arranged. You cannot be sure of this in any other features of landscape.' And he goes on to list all the ways in which human interference can spoil nature's perfection.

Ruskin's absolute love of nature goes wrong at a certain point. Nature turns her face away from him. He is haunted by the thought that she is spoilt. Was this a feature of his impending illness, or was it the consequence of the shock he underwent as the implications of Darwin sank in on him: that man really was part of a larger natural process and that he was not a favoured onlooker? If that was so, it would clearly be harder to keep up the picture in one's own mind of 'vile' man and 'perfect' nature. That picture was after all an illusion, the result of standing in the wrong place.

This changed viewpoint was implicit in Impressionism as it was in the literature of realism. And when, during the 'eighties, the re-action to realism sets in, it comes to the fore in the guise of all sorts of irrational and mystical attitudes. The railing against 'mere' naturalism, 'mere' description of the outer skin of things that is the accompaniment of the emerging art, seems to contain an attack on the fact of observation itself and the human scale it implies. Art must deal with larger issues than that. Art must 'penetrate the surface of things'. Such slogans fill the air during the birth-pangs of abstract art. The shift from representational to abstract art can be seen as a shift in viewpoint. But where was the new viewpoint to be? The traditional grand subjects were dead and gone. Perhaps art could claim a place nearer to the processes of nature herself. This at any rate, seems to be the thought in a great deal of Expressionism, from which abstract art derived. Paul Klee made no bones about it in his lectures and his teaching notebooks at the Bauhaus between 1921 and 1930.

The idea was of an art which would develop its own organic processes, using the bare formal elements of line, shape, area, colour, tone and so on. These were considered like elements which are explored first by themselves, then in combination, following the internal logic. A structure grows; an image emerges. In trying to characterise the new art, Klee repeatedly invoked the image of a tree. The artist was the trunk. His roots spread deep into the ground – they represented the artist's contact with nature. The crown of the tree represents his work unfolding 'in full view of the world'. Nobody would expect the crown of a tree to mirror its roots, Klee says, and yet this is what is expected of the artist by people who can only accept naturalism. 'And yet, standing at his appointed place, the trunk of the tree, he does nothing other than gather and pass on what comes to him from the depths. He neither serves nor rules – he transmits. . . . The beauty at the crown is not his own. He is merely a channel.'

I think that a lot goes unexplained in twentieth-century art if we overlook the mood expressed here, this mood of surrender, this nostalgia for a force larger than the artist's own talent. Anything that promises a release from the human scale of naturalism. This is partly behind the force that mathematics has for certain artists, mathematics at different levels, sometimes quite sophisticated, sometimes extremely simple, sometimes not applied literally at all but present as a background inspiration. Both Klee and Kandinsky delighted in discussing the formal properties of their art as though discussing the theorems of some cosmic geometry. *Gestalt* psychology held out another path away from the limits of self. If seeing itself was a kind of form-recognition – if, that is to say, the involuntary processes of perception had at their centre a response to wholeness and pattern, then here was another link that bound the artist into the world of nature. His structures and harmonies could be talked about in a much broader context than mere self-expression, and art need not come into it.

'Dada is for nature and against art!' Hans Arp declared in one of his notes, and in his biography he says 'I remember a discussion with Mondrian in which he distinguished between art and nature, saying that art is artificial and nature natural. I do not share his opinion. I believe that nature is not in opposition to art. Art is of natural origin. . . .' This is the background to Arp's use of chance, perhaps the most significant of all the paths that artists were to explore outside a human viewpoint. Arp had been working for several years with pasted paper, using it as a medium for abstract designs of a more or less geometrical kind. Then around 1918 he began to arrange them by chance. He would prepare the coloured papers, tear them at random and allow them to flutter down on to his drawing board as they would. 'The forms come, pleasing or strange, hostile, inexplicable, dumb or drowsy. They are born of themselves. It seems to me that I have only to move my hands. These lights, these shadows that chance sends should be welcomed by us with astonishment and gratitude. . . . [They] give us access to mysteries and reveal a profound sense of life.'

This, it seems to me, is the most striking change of all in the relationship between artist and nature. The collage arranged by chance 'reads' as a design. But the design is not the upshot of 'work' in the sense of constructing a harmony within a formal framework given by art. No effort is spent in realising an intention within the bounds of a restricting form. The leaves flutter from the tree; the coloured papers flutter to the floor. The formative process extends from the forest to the studio and the artist's own participation is simply a 'reading', gathering up and passing on what comes to him. 'The beauty at the crown is not his own. He is merely a channel.'

But the characteristic of his function as channel is that he defines the limits of the work. He makes a claim for an art attitude on its behalf. He makes the arena within which we recognise what has come to him as art, and not as a mere section of unbounded nature. This seems to have brought us back to the place we were at when we were considering Marcel Duchamp's readymades.

Neither Duchamp's readymades nor Arp's use of chance are conceivable except through the heritage of naturalistic painting *en plein air*. In the intense dialogue based on the principle of 'Impression forces Expression' the frontiers between art and nature that had once been so clearly defined spill over into each other. No

painter who had worked for long periods from observation would be likely to think of nature as limited to organic things. In a Cézanne still-life, nature doesn't end with the apples, but includes the napkin and the coffee-pot too. But then neither is the boundary between what he sees and how he sees it clear cut. The cubists introduced untransformed material into their paintings in an attempt to clarify and articulate the new and more complex boundaries. The framework of the painting is broken open. Other frameworks are juxtaposed. In a Braque or a Picasso collage painting we contemplate more than one framework side by side. We switch from one to the other, reading newsprint or wallpaper as paint, as illusion, or paint as matter, or both as factors in a description or a structural idea.

Viewpoint was no longer fixed. The introspective focus that *plein air* painting had brought to perception, disclosed the relativity and the shiftingness of perception. Cubism deals, among other things, with multiple viewpoints and several levels of perception, not just optical ones. Other lines in twentieth-century art tried to transcend a human viewpoint altogether, and to enlist nature directly into the arena of art. Let me remind you of some of the ways in which this has been done:

Max Ernst made numbers of pictures in the 'twenties in which the forms were the result of rubbings made from natural surfaces, such as wood, bark, leaves or unravelled fabric.

Henry Moore, having spent much of his working life drawing ideas from natural objects like bones and pebbles, started at a certain point to use them, either modified or unmodified, as the models for his sculpture.

Dubuffet, at various points during the 'fifties, used such materials as butterflies' wings, earth, stones, twigs, banana-skins, rhubarb, burdock, sponge in the construction of paintings, some of which look so like a stretch of earth that one could easily step on them if they were placed flat on a well-dug bed.

Yves Klein made paintings in the late 'fifties using fire, in which the 'composition' – form, colour, everything – is determined by the play of flame and smoke on the picture surface. He also made a series of nudes in which the 'figure' consists of the imprint on the canvas of a girl's body, naked except for a coat of paint.

In 1952 Robert Rauschenberg exhibited a series of canvases which were white all over. In a sense there was nothing in them to see. As pictures they were completely empty. However, like any white surfaces they were exceptionally open to the light. A person looking at them could hardly fail to be aware of his own shadow looming up as he moved, or the shadows of other people, or a slant of sunlight, or the change of colour when the lights were switched on. At least, he could hardly fail to be aware of all this, *once* he had relinquished the idea that these were pictures of the expected kind in which everything that the picture presented was contained in a stable form within the bounds of the frame. Up until that point the picture was empty. But once nature was allowed to participate, then the canvas became a real object on level terms with other objects and subject to natural occurrences, as other objects are. Its identity as canvas and its place in an art gallery serves simply to focus aesthetic attention on to it. This was perhaps the boldest invitation to date, to deploy aesthetic awareness on to life.

Rauschenberg's demonstration was exactly parallel with John Cage's 'silent music'. Cage's aphoristic question 'Is a truck passing by music?' gives the key. He set up the framework of musical attention – an audience sitting in rows, a particular point in time for the 'performance' to begin – and then filled the framework with whatever sound happend along. Organisation is in the ear of each listener. Art is decentralised, dispersed, given to all in the form of a certain focus of attention, brought to bear on the world as it is.

In the twenty years or so since Rauschenberg's white paintings and Cage's silent music, the shock effect has somewhat dispersed. The re-drawn boundaries, which they drew attention to so dramatically, have been taken as the point of departure by many of the liveliest artists. With them there is often an extreme unwillingness to accept that the work of art is a bounded container for or example of aesthetic qualities. Rather they prefer to think of it as merely one item in a relationship which includes the onlooker and the natural conditions in which he encounters the work. This has been the background to the so-called Minimal Sculpture, of which Robert Morris has been one of the most articulate exponents.

'While the work must be autonomous in the sense of being a self-contained unit for the formation of the *gestalt* . . . the major aesthetic terms are not *in* but *dependent upon* this autonomous object and exist as unfixed variables which find their specific definition in the particular space and light and physical viewpoint of the spectator. Only one aspect of the work is immediate: the apprehension of the *gestalt*. . . . The experience of the work necessarily exists in time. The intention is diametrically opposed to cubism with its concern for simultaneous views in one plane.' Instead it looks for 'A more emphatic focusing on the very conditions under which certain kinds of objects are seen. The object itself is carefully placed in these new conditions to be but one of the terms.'

Since making these pieces – which include the boxes that I thought about when I was looking at the square drains in the street – he has made sculpture in which blocks of wood, stone, and scaffolding have been deployed over large areas. These materials have not been consumed by the work but have been used for other purposes after the occasion of the work. 'Art' has been merely one phase in their life-cycle. He has also used trees, steam, earth, rocks, and like many others in the last few years has worked over quite large areas of landscape. The eighteenth-century connoisseur with whom I started would have been quite likely to have employed a landscape gardener in his park, planting here, channelling there. I leave you to reflect on the relationship between him and the earth sculptor of our own time.

14

NATURE IN THE LIGHT OF ART

R. W. Hepburn

1. ART is without doubt a powerful agent in determining how nature appears to us. Andrew Forge describes seeing tree leaves in sunlight, and 'thinking Pissarro'. 'I am wrapped round by Impressionism and the leaves look like brush strokes'.[1] To Harold Osborne, once one has been impressed by Van Gogh's painting of certain objects, 'it is difficult ever again to see the objects uninfluenced by Van Gogh's vision of them'.[2]

Nelson Goodman recently wrote: 'That nature imitates art is too timid a dictum. Nature is a product of art and discourse.' A picture can 'bring out neglected likenesses and differences, force unaccustomed associations, and in some measure re-make our world'.[3] Gyorgy Kepes makes the central claim as clearly as anyone: 'We see as the painters, sculptors, architects, photographers, advertising designers teach us to see. The social value of the representational image is therefore that it may give us education for a new standard of vision.'[4]

The particular view of nature which a work of visual art mediates is a function of the graphic vocabulary, the repertoire of visual types used in that work. These determine its bondings and separatings of forms, what is merged and what singled out, the distinctive unities-to-perception it facilitates. They determine the all-important analogies or visual metaphors which an artist affirms among normally quite disparate realms of experience.[5] Certain human forms

[1] See above, p. 228.
[2] *The Art of Appreciation* (1970) p. 155.
[3] *Languages of Art* (1968) p. 33.
[4] *Language of Vision* (1961) p. 67.
[5] Cf. P. Rawson, *Drawing* (1969) pp. 246 ff.

of Henry Moore's are also rock, cliff and cave forms.[1] Elsewhere, tree-forms may fuse with flame-forms: human head with animal head. . . . From the contemplating of such works of painting and sculpture something is readily carried across to the perception of nature. We may call that 'something' the work's 'after-effect': but it is slightly more helpful to introduce the phrase '*over*-effect' – for one may be aware of the power of a work to modify one's perception of nature, aware of it while yet in the presence of the work itself.

In some cases we can say that a painting has made us aware of an aspect of nature we would have been unlikely to notice without its help. But since conceivably we might have come to notice the aspect unaided, the painting is contingently instrumental to our noticing it. In other instances, the memory of how the painting presented that aspect through a particular handling of paint is not 'contingently instrumental': we are seeing the world *in terms of* that painting, its medium and style. Still more often, analysis would hover uncertainly between these positions.

'The leaves look like brush strokes.' *Could* we have seen the leaves as we do, unless we had seen Impressionists' brush-strokes? Have they simply enabled us to see the leaves *thus* (and now we no longer require to think of them, since we have learned the lesson); or is the thought of the brush-strokes nearer to being a necessary ingredient in the experience signalled by 'The leaves look like brush-strokes'? In Andrew Forge's case we are in the latter area: 'I think Pissarro' . . . 'I am wrapped round by Impressionism'. He is not just recording a particular feature of the leaves – the feature which is the ground of the possibility of their being painted as Impressionists would have painted them; but recording also a vivid, episodic memory-experience, whereby the presently-perceived leaves are set in a context of a class of paintings. These leaves *look like* brush-strokes: and their looking so goes to constitute the present episode of experience. It is certainly not just a matter of 'What we'd say if asked' what the leaves are like, nor of how we should paint them ourselves. Incompetence with a brush would not discredit our claim. This combination of discerning and projecting makes apt Andrew Forge's statement that art makes of certain aspects of the world 'something far richer and more resonant than the things or scenes in themselves would warrant'.[2]

2. These phenomena deserve a place of importance in aesthetic theory. They are not always given it however. Some theories cannot

[1] Cf. L. R. Rogers, *Sculpture* (1969) p. 231.
[2] Above, p. 229.

easily account for their occurrence at all: others see the relation between nature and art chiefly in terms of art's *assimilation* of natural forms, not of its provision of new perspectives on nature. Consider these in turn.

If experience of nature is to be enlarged and transformed by art, art's mimesis of nature cannot be described as a naïve *mirroring*. No account like the following in Burke will do:

> If I make a drawing of a palace, or a temple, or a landscape, I present a very clear idea of those objects; but then (allowing for the effect of imitation which is something) my picture can at most affect only as the palace, temple or landscape would have affected in the reality.[1]

No more satisfactory are accounts of aesthetic contemplation which see it as an emptying of the mind, an isolating of objects in perception, a suspending of all thoughts about them, including all thought about their interrelationships. Aesthetic experience, whether of art or of nature, does not rest content with everyday categorising of objects; but it is very much a matter of grasping new additional relationships, with the aid of metaphor, simile, analogy.[2] 'Representation', writes Goodman, 'is apt [or] subtle . . . to the extent that the artist or writer grasps fresh and significant relationships and devises means for making them manifest.'[3]

Very far removed from naïve mimetic theories are accounts of art which centre upon the power of the artist to assimilate and transmute nature's forms, so as to make them elements in wholly new structures. To André Malraux, for instance, the 'immemorial impulse of creative art' is to 'build up a world apart and self-contained'.[4] At its best, painting exhibits a 'conquest of the visible world', an annexing, not a celebrating, of external nature.[5] In the autonomous structures which are works of art, natural shapes take on quite new significance and new values. Focillon wrote: 'Organic life designs spirals, orbs . . . stars. . . . But the instant these shapes invade the space and the materials specific to art, they acquire an entirely

---

[1] *A Philosophical Enquiry into the Origin of our Ideas of the Sublime and Beautiful* (1757) pt. II, § iv.

[2] Cf. Andrew Harrison, in *The Business of Reason*, ed. MacIntosh and Coval (1969) pp. 127 f.

[3] *Languages of Art*, p. 32.

[4] *The Voices of Silence* (Eng. tr. 1954) p. 616.

[5] I do not mean to imply that Malraux denies art can set forth a view of the world. He acknowledges this, but eloquently emphasises the other side, the distinctive, autonomous values of painting.

new value and give rise to entirely new systems.'[1] And Roger Fry
writing on Seurat: 'The question of verisimilitude hardly occurs to
one, so little can we refer his paintings to anything outside themselves, so completely does the created reality hold us by the laws of
its self-contained system.'[2]

From the point of view of the present topic, such emphatic statements are a helpful corrective. They properly insist that there exist
in painting kinds of formal unity, textures, colour-harmonies that
do not exist outside painting, and which we should waste our energies
trying to project on to nature.

Achievement in representation itself is not to be analysed simply
as an ability to facilitate 'exportable' new views of nature. For
example: high in this scale of achievement is the power of a painting
or drawing to present a dense, rich portrayal of objects or scenes –
with extraordinary economy of means: often, to use a phrase of
Reynolds, by 'seemingly inadequate means'.[3] The work is prized in
substantial measure because of this power to evoke, say, deep
recession in a landscape, or the massing of foliage, or the movement
of animals, and (crucially) to evoke them by ink- or paint-marks that
are prima facie incompetent to evoke them – being mere undisguised
blobs and smudges. This 'magic' (Reynolds' word) clearly belongs
to the 'effect' proper of the art-work, not to what I am calling its
'over-effect'.

On the other hand, such a work of art may *at the same time* invite
a new awareness of some natural features. We can acknowledge
important sources of aesthetic value that are not a matter of seeing
nature afresh, without ruling out other sources of value that are.
We should have to rule them out only if we were convinced that
there is a single source of value in art. But on the contrary, one of
the astonishing things about the major arts is their power to realise
a rich plurality of valuable goals, simultaneously and by the same
seemingly exiguous means.

An over-simple notion of picturing would suggest that the importance or the hauntingness of what is carried over from art to nature
must be greater the more closely nature evidently conforms to the
feature in art, and less where the artist presents forms discrepant
from natural forms. This is not necessarily so. The most haunting
Samuel Palmer landscapes do not consistently match nature point
by point: they allude to, but transform nature in a visionary way.
Yet the allusion is strong enough for the empirical appearances to

[1] *The Life of Forms in Art* (1934) 2nd Eng. ed. (1948) p. 3.
[2] *Transformations* (1926) p. 196.
[3] *Discourses on Art*, Discourse 11.

come to seem 'on the brink' of responding to Palmer's hints. These paintings may make a lasting impression on one's view of nature, while Palmer's more minutely naturalistic work of later years does not.[1] 'Distortions' of our habitual modes of representing objects cannot, similarly, be taken as indicating that a painting is a 'self-contained system', as forbidding a new view of nature in its light. A distorted form may function in a painting both as a structural designful element and as an invitation to perceive an object anew. Francis Bacon faces may make us see faces outside the canvas as incipiently disintegrating, as betraying a normally veiled potentiality.[2] Of course I am not saying that *all* discrepancy can be taken as insinuating, 'Things can be seen like that!' Fragmented fruit-dishes in Braque neither intimate that Braque saw fruit-dishes so, nor that he expected anyone else to. Fascinatingly ambiguous cases occupy the borderlands between 'pure design' and 'invitation to see nature differently'.

It is easy to understand the pressures upon a writer on art to interpret the history of painting as a gradual progression towards pure construction and away from interest in the world beyond the canvas. Such an account will dwell upon those aspects of painting (even representational painting) whose value is independent of representation. This does constitute an important 'plot' in the history of art. But it does not follow that it is the *only* plot, the exclusively correct interpretation. Repeated encounters with particular paintings and drawings alone can tell us what in them can in fact 'rub off' on our view of nature, and what cannot. Even some forms of abstract art seek their complex correlatives in nature. Instead of competing, alternative theories of art, we are seeing, I suggest, a tension with which art and its appreciators have perennially to live – between a stress upon the internal relatedness of elements in a work of art, and upon their relations to external nature.

3. I want now to take some account of the *diversity* of ways in which nature can be seen, or modified, in the light of art: our examples so far have been unsystematic. First of all, there are great differences in the *range of application* to nature of features in works of art. (i) A painting, say of Langdale, may facilitate a new way of seeing that piece of country when next I visit it. (ii) A painting may sensitise me to a *type* of visual feature, which nature constantly repeats, but whose pervasiveness we might well not perceive, without the

---

[1] See Plate 5, *Study of a Garden at Tintern*. Compare also Lord David Cecil, *Visionary and Dreamer* (1969) pp. 75 f.

[2] See Plate 6.

painting's help. (iii) A painting or style of painting may prompt a new way of looking at virtually any visible object or scene, a way which, although certainly a creation of the artist, is also no less a discovery, since nature 'takes', lends itself to, the approach. (Cf. Andrew Forge on Impressionism, above, p. 228.)

(iv) Still greater range is possible. An art-work or -movement may be seen not only as an invitation to revise our ways of organising our purely *visual* experience but, beyond that, it may suggest an ontology. In Zen art, for instance, a refusal to depict the visual world as a world of enclosed, discrete *things* vividly presents a metaphysical denial that reality is ultimately constructed from such. Ultimate reality is 'without beginning or end, without internal distinctions or separations'.[1] To become imaginatively absorbed in such art can bring about a change in one's total conception of nature. Doubtless some theoretical interpretation is needed to ground or vindicate the application of this vision to the world-as-a-whole: but art may well be the indispensable companion of speculative thought – indispensable for realising the implication of its claims.

(v) Applications of widest scope are not confined to expressions of specific doctrines, Buddhist, Christian or other. A work of art (visual or literary) may modify my view of the world by strengthening or weakening my sense of the propriety or the value of certain very general attitudes – for instance an attitude of openness to mystery, or of openness only to the clearly-defined, clearly lit and comprehensible. Much less specific still, but significant, is the way in which a serious concern with art can invest objects and scenes in nature with a quality hard to label, but hinted at in the phrases 'potentially, or incipiently expressive', 'a possible focus for aesthetic experience, even if not yet developed'. We could apply to nature seen in the light of art what Hegel said about art itself, that it is concerned with divesting the world of its 'stubborn alienation'.[2] To put the point in poet's language: Leopardi said that the 'sensitive and imaginative man' sees 'the world and its objects' in a 'double' way:

> He would see with his eyes one tower, one country; hear with his ears one sound of a bell; and, at the same time, see another country and another tower, and hear another sound through his imagination. In the second category . . . lies all that is beautiful and pleasant about the things.[3]

[1] P. Rawson, 'The Methods of Zen Painting', *British Journal of Aesthetics*, 1967, p. 335.

[2] *The Philosophy of Fine Art*, Introduction.

[3] *Zibaldone*, ed. Flora, vol. II, pp. 1230 f. Cf. G. Singh, *Leopardi and the Theory of Poetry*, pp. 112 f.

(vi) One cannot be sure that a work of art will affect one's view of
nature on a single level only. My first example (a painting of Langdale) simplified; for topographical particularity does not prevent
a work from making a general impact upon our view of other scenes
and places. Once again, a familiar criterion of excellence in art is
the ability of a work to operate on several levels simultaneously:
to be, say, thoroughly concrete but also to set up the widest-ranging
reverberations. I may be able to interpret one and the same wintry
landscape as (1) a self-contained formal system, (2) facilitating my
seeing in nature analogues, perhaps remote in form but close in
expressive quality (e.g. sinister, ominous, desolate), and (3) prompt-
ing an interpretation of nature-in-general in pessimistic, chill terms.

4. Correlative to any general view of nature – as innocent, benign,
hostile or whatever – is a view of the viewer himself. He confronts
nature's hostility with defiance or resignation; he luxuriates in its
benignity. To have one's view of nature part-determined by art is
also to have one's sense of self, one's posture *vis-à-vis* nature determined as well. Seeing nature in the light of art has a *reflexive* aspect.
Some works of art prompt a view of the spectator himself as detached
and distanced, aesthetically dominating external nature, however
precariously. Others suggest that the spectator is immersed in the
scene depicted – as often in Chinese landscape. Art that seeks to
integrate man and landscape can be tragically sombre or mystically
ecstatic. It can be voluptuous and strange: as in that extraordinary
painting of Pavel Tchelitchew's, *Hide and Seek* – a fusing of human
forms and plant forms, the life of nature-and-man presented as one
indissoluble life, the seasonal surging and ebbing of a single creative
energy.[1]

The Dutch philosopher C. A. van Peursen writes: 'the way in
which [the] body is experienced can change . . . according to the
picture men have of the world in which they are living'.[2] To turn
momentarily to literature: we may contrast the view of the world
that carries as its correlative a view of embodied selfhood like that
expressed in Thomas Traherne's *Thanksgiving for the Body*, with
a world-picture that elicits a Samuel Beckett view of the body,
limping and generally malfunctioning. ('So all things limp together
for the only possible.' *Murphy*.)

Moreover, what we call the *'inner'* life is substantially constituted
by the images, metaphors, analogies we draw from external nature

---

[1] On Chinese landscape, cf. H. Osborne, *The Art of Appreciation*, pp. 158 f. For
Tchelitchew, see Plate 7.

[2] *Body, Soul, Spirit* (1966) p. 165.

and re-apply to the articulating of our emotions, feelings, attitudes. And the stock of images of nature on which we thus draw is itself, in part, the product of art or filtered through art. What we internalise is often far from being a 'bare' datum.

For someone who is familiar with G. M. Hopkins it is not easy to think of the turbulence of disordered mental life, its 'peaks' and 'depths' – without an awareness of Hopkins's version of that 'landscape' at its most jagged and vertiginous. 'Mind has mountains; cliffs of fall/Frightful, sheer, no-man-fathomed. Hold them cheap/May who ne'er hung there.'

5. Inevitably my comments on the topics of this lecture have had evaluative implications. These now need a fuller and more explicit discussion. For a start, we cannot assume that the scale of value appropriate to art-objects *as such* will coincide at all points with a scale that evaluates the power of a work to determine a significant view of nature. It is possible for a work of art to be great but not because of any view of nature that it facilitates. Nevertheless the power of a work to facilitate a new view of nature is not *distinct* from its 'properly aesthetic' properties: it can make for aesthetic excellence. We do commend a painting when we say that after viewing it nature seems pervasively to repeat its motifs or its style.

The range of perceptual experience affected by a work is one criterion of appraisal. 'The particular genius of an artist', wrote Eric Newton, 'can often be defined by answering . . . "What things will never be quite the same again now that I have seen his work?".'[1]

Appraisal-questions can be complex. Some works of art are more faithful to the way the world is than others: nature can be 'persuaded' to accept the view of it that they offer – not always a matter of simple naturalism, as we have seen (above, pp. 245 f.). In other cases, nature eventually refuses the proposed view: nature cannot be consistently seen in the light of *this* art. M. C. Escher offers arresting and disturbing graphic works where perspectival laws and limits which we ordinarily think inviolable are very thoroughly violated, and the impossible seems to be shown as possible. But they do not present a new way of seeing nature: nature cannot but refuse the vision: what is 'possible' in the drawings, the ingenious combining of incompatible perspectives in one design, is not *ipso facto* revealed as possible outside the drawings. Two comments on this. The experience of nature 'refusing' to be seen after the manner of some art-work must not (preposterously) be taken in isolation as ground of disparagement; for the work may not be attempting to propose a new

[1] *The Meaning of Beauty* (1959) (Penguin Books, 1962) p. 131.

view of nature, rather an alternative nature (*Autre Monde* – an
Escher title).[1] Secondly, the notion of nature accepting or refusing
a particular view is a less straightforward notion than I have so
far acknowledged. Think again of the Zen paintings (or any other
presentation of a plurality-denying world-view). For such a view of
'ultimate reality' to be acceptable, it would not be necessary that
every incomplete, unclosed form in a painting should match an
incomplete form in nature. It would be enough if we could come,
with the help of the painting, to hold in abeyance our ordinary
division of the world into discrete objects. Because of this possibility
of non-literal, indirect acceptance, the question, 'Does nature
accept or refuse this particular vision?' often cannot be instantly
or easily answered. We have no mechanical procedures for
deciding.

Even if something of an artist's style does rub off on our perception
of nature, we cannot be certain *a priori* that it will be the most significant aspects of his style. To find superficial resemblances in nature
to, say, the geometrical forms of Paul Klee's drawing, is not to see
the main grounds for calling Klee a significant artist – i.e. how he
incorporated such forms in a composition. So we have to ask not
only, 'Can we see a wide range of natural objects in the light of the
work of the artist concerned?' but also 'Are the aspects that do carry
across to nature significant or superficial?'

Further appraisal-questions are these. We may ask of an artist's
work, 'What set of natural objects has this artist brought within
our power to contemplate for the first time: and to contemplate
rewardingly?' The objects may not have been thought worth
contemplating, or emotionally bearable, or morally in order, to
contemplate. 'The Alpine world', wrote Max Friedländer, 'appeared
frightening and savage' to sixteenth- and seventeenth-century men.
It became contemplatable through painting, 'like a . . . conquered
foe'. 'I have no doubt but that the visual arts paved the way for the
enjoyment of reality which came later. . . '.[2]

We have already touched upon another relevant question. 'Could
the view of nature I now have, thanks to a particular painting or
drawing, have been acquired by any other means – verbal, for
instance?' This is a question about the dispensability or indispens-
ability of the medium and particular use of the medium. To answer,
'Only this work done in this medium could make that view available' is clearly to appraise the work highly in respect of distinctive
achievement.

[1] See Plate 8.

[2] *Landscape: Portrait: Still-Life* (1949) pp. 73 f.

In some cases, I know that I have been sensitised by art to particular aspects of nature, although no paintings are explicitly brought to mind as I look at nature: in other cases I am vividly reminded of a painting by some object or scene before me. Now I can be *reminded* of a painting, without my vision of nature being thereby transformed. Certainly, the fact that a painting makes such visual impact as to be readily called to mind is relevant to appraising the painting. It has strong visual impact, the clarity required for being memorable. But these characteristics are different grounds of value from the other characteristics we have been considering – power to reorganise a view of nature, reveal unnoticed aspects etc. I am not implying that either ground is superior to the other, only that they are distinguishable. Often too we confront intermediate cases, where it is chiefly reminding that is going on, but where the reminding carries *some* power, even if of a modest order, to modify the perception of the object or scene before us.

One question traditionally of great importance in the appraisal of art-works themselves has been the following. 'How effectively does the work guide or *control* the responses of the spectator?' Does it provide merely an occasion for self-indulgent free fantasy, for generalised and stereotyped emotion; or has the artist worked successfully so as to lead his spectator to new, precisely determined and un-hackneyed perception? Degree of control remains important in the appraisal of art's power to make and re-make nature. Obviously, in any 'application' of art to perception of nature, some considerable loss of precision, some 'degeneration of the image', is bound to occur, if only because of the spectator's limitations of memory; but the loss will be least where the art-work itself has been highly distinctive in character, economical, clear – aesthetically relevant qualities. The status of this criterion is not one on which there is critical agreement today. How much work does this painting do to ensure that our experience is re-fashioned precisely and distinctively? A great deal of work, if the painting is Cézanne's. Little or none if the object is a canvas white all over. The invitation may be there 'to deploy aesthetic awareness on to life',[1] but no control is attempted of the form that awareness should take. It is tempting to see in this, and to lament, an attenuation of the role of the artist: though in saying that I am perhaps relinquishing the office of philosopher of art for that of critic. In 'silent music', the 'organisation is in the ear of each listener'.[2] This is scant commendation from the viewpoint of an

---

[1] Above, p. 240.
[2] Above, p. 240.

aesthetic theory that sees the conferring of order or organisation as *par excellence* the artist's task and privilege.

6. Aesthetic experience of nature can be meagre, repetitive and undeveloping. To deplore such a state of affairs and to seek amelioration, is to accept an ideal which can be roughly formulated thus. It is the ideal of a rich and diversified experience, far from static, open to constant revision of viewpoint and of organisation of the visual field, constant increase in scope of what can be taken as an object of rewarding aesthetic contemplation, an ideal of increase in sensitivity and in mobility of mind in discerning expressive qualities in natural objects. That ideal could be called 'the maximising of aesthetic reward' in nature. We have noted various ways in which art-experience can be a vital agent in approaching this ideal; and I want, in this section, to gather them together and add further comments.

The maximising of aesthetic reward in nature is dependent on the extent to which one learns to shift attention flexibly from aspect to aspect of the natural objects before one, to shift focus from close-up to long-shot, from textural detail to overall atmospheric haze or radiance; to overcome stereotyped grouping and clichéd ways of seeing. The more flexibility, the greater likelihood of discovering aesthetically rewarding modes of perception of any given subject-matter. My becoming sensitised to a particular art-style may enable me to make out forms in nature that embrace objects which otherwise are quite distinct and separate. An art-style may even cause me to revise or enrich my idea of what constitutes unity of form as such. Any distinctive representational art-style effects a simplification of appearances and may facilitate an analogous simplification, guiding the selection of data, in one's perception of nature itself. What Philip Rawson says of drawing has application to aesthetic experience of nature also.

> ... to see forms we must first have formal ideas. If a good pattern-typology is not provided, [the student of drawing] will simply use a bad one from his experience of inferior popular imagery.[1]

Adapting this: failing a good store of visual art-experience, we are liable to perceive the natural objects and scenes we encounter in the light of second-rate art.

Put it another way. The enemy of the aesthetic is the object of perception that is inexpressive, characterless, null, incoherent,

[1] *Drawing*, p. 298.

unable to sustain attention, full of 'holes' or 'dead spaces'.[1] *A priori* we have no ground for denying that natural objects and scenes may sometimes be irremediably inexpressive, unredeemably character-less and aesthetically null. But the likelihood of remedying and redeeing in many particular context is vastly greater, the greater the range of art-styles and media that are available in memory, even below the threshold of explicit recollection.

In part it is a matter of abstracting and thinking away certain features of objects and of attending to others: thinking away differ-ences of material substance, of distance or scale – so as for instance to take as one form-with-variations a tree-covered hill-top, a cloud-curve, and a curve hinted at by detached rocks or buildings. Or of becoming aware not only of the shapes of objects, but of the spaces between the objects as well.

Even more specific art-factors can further this maximising of aesthetic reward. The media and tools of art strongly suggest dis-tinctive ways of grasping objects outside the canvas altogether. As Max Friedländer put it: 'it makes a difference whether the artist looks [at nature] with a pencil in his hand or with a brush in his hand. *The tool determines the way of looking.*'[2] And, I want to say, having brooded on what the various tools achieve, we are enabled to see as many different views of natural objects as there are tools and ways of handling tools – sensitised to 'branchy' bare trees by thin pointed tools, to broad, object-unifying forms by bold brush-work. For with any tool goes a system of representational possibilities – inclusions and exclusions, distinguishings and mergings.

Maximising aesthetic reward from nature is crucially a matter of imagination's providing what we could call new 'perceptual environ-ments' for the objects and scenes; or of interrogating nature in the light of art in its diversity, so securing a disengagement both from the attitudes of utility and from hackneyed aesthetic attitudes no less.

Some qualifications need to be added however. I have not been claiming that nature can be aesthetically contemplated *only* in the light of art, or that every sort of influence art-experience can have on nature-experience is necessarily beneficial to the latter. There can be aesthetic reward in considering a natural object, a shell or cave or fern, out of all relation to human artifice, in terms of the natural processes that produced them or maintain them in being. Aesthetic pleasure can arise in being aware of the very *remoteness* of those processes from the activities of artists.

[1] John Dewey, *Art as Experience*, pp. 36 ff. R. L. Zimmerman, 'Can Anything be an Aesthetic Object?', *Journal of Aesthetics and Art-Criticism*, 1966–7, p. 184.

[2] *Landscape: Portrait: Still-Life*, p. 87, my italics.

Moreover the interposing of thoughts and memories of art can sometimes mar, rather than enhance, potential aesthetic experience of nature. I noted already that there are some types of formal unity proper to the arts, which we look for in vain in nature. If we interrogate a fine work of art for pervasive presence of formal motifs, for the most thoroughgoing inter-connecting of its elements, it will not let us down. If we make the same demands upon a piece of nature, we may be let down. Again, and I think of Andrew Forge's reference to the eighteenth-century 'amber coloured glass', seeing nature in the light of art may condition a person into having eyes only for frameworthy 'scenes', forming bounded unities. If however we mentally place a frame round a natural scene, as often as not we turn good natural beauty into mediocre quasi-art. An aesthetically important feature of nature is precisely the absence of bounds and frames: endless processions of clouds, ridge on ridge of hills, wave upon wave.

To see nature uncritically and exclusively in the light of art can lure a person into appraising natural beauty by criteria relevant to visual art, but less relevant to nature. Oscar Wilde offers a familiar and happy caricature of this.

> Nobody of any real culture . . . ever talks nowadays about the beauty of a sunset. . . . Upon the other hand they go on. Yesterday evening Mrs Arundel insisted on my going to the window, and looking at the glorious sky, as she called it. . . . And what was it? It was simply a very second-rate Turner, a Turner of a bad period, with all the painter's worst faults exaggerated and over-emphasized.[1]

7. At the most general level of all, two notions determine our thinking on these themes. First, what I shall call the notion of 'struggle'. Taken out of all contexts (including Goodman's), the words 'Nature is a product of art and discourse' could be seriously misleading. They mask the important fact that nature can be aesthetically recalcitrant, that effort, struggle, can be involved both in annexing natural forms for use in art and in perceiving nature aesthetically afresh in the light of art. If nature is a product of art, it is also that with which art *contends*. The seventeenth and eighteenth centuries for instance had to contend with the new sense of the infinity of space, and contend with objects (e.g. the Alps again) that could not

---

[1] 'The Decay of Lying', in *Intention and the Soul of Man* (1891). The whole context is a *locus classicus* on nature seen in the light of art: e.g., 'Things are because we see them, and what we see, and how we see it, depends on the Arts that have influenced us.'

be assimilated by existing concepts of beauty and required the fashioning of new concepts, notably the 'sublime'.

Secondly, over against the notion of 'struggle' has to be set that of the inexhaustibility of types of successful outcome of the struggle. There are inexhaustibly many alternative systems of representation and description: we are enabled to see the world in as many ways as it can be pictured.[1] Since art is an essentially self-transcending enterprise, no limit can be set to the possible styles and treatments of objects in art (and to higher-level organising concepts, like 'sublime'), some at least of which in turn modify our view of nature. And nature itself contains such diversity of individual forms and fluid patterns of organisation, that there is no discernible limit to the possible ways of seeing, grouping and re-grouping open to us. As Dewey put it: 'the aspects of the spectacle of nature are inexhaustible, and . . . every significant new movement in painting is the discovery and exploitation of some possibility of vision not previously developed'.[2]

What is the most reasonable *response* to make to this state of affairs? Among alternatives is a religio-metaphysical response, that sees all our limitless viewings and representings of the world as so many 'filterings' of a wholly mysterious Ground of appearances, that eludes every attempt to grasp and represent it. Or one may repudiate such a 'mystical' interpretation (as does Goodman's article, 'The Way the World Is'[3]) by denying that there is any *one* way the world is. We can achieve a *multitude* of true descriptions and true representations of particular ways the world is; there can be many true views, and no exclusively true view.

I do not myself want to argue that there is some one ineffable way the world is. But I do not think on the other hand that every sort of religiously-toned response is for that reason ruled out. A hint of a possible approach can be found in Gabriel Marcel's *Metaphysical Diary*:

> Consider Being as the principle of inexhaustibility. Joy is bound up with the feeling of something inexhaustible . . . [Contrast the condition of *despair*, the sense that] we can make an inventory. But Being is above all inventories. . . .[4]

I am taking *no more* than a hint from Marcel: his comments could be adapted to the notion of *aesthetic* inexhaustibility; and a claim made for the legitimacy of a religious – if undogmatically religious –

1 Cf. Goodman, *Languages of Art*, pp. 6, 40 ff.
2 *Art as Experience*, p. 235.
3 *Review of Metaphysics* (1960) pp. 48–56.
4 *Being and Having* (Fontana) p. 111.

response to that. We have a proper object of wonderment and a sense of mystery in the idea of boundless aesthetic possibilities, the product of the interacting of non-human nature and human creative imagination. I doubt if we are liable to find ourselves marvelling at a mere truth of logic, at a situation that in no sense could have been otherwise. There is nothing logically necessary either in nature's amenability to perceptual re-interpretation, the power of its forms to furnish endless material for our 'analogising' and quest for expressiveness; or in our own power to invent new ways or styles of seeing and representing. Here too there can be no 'inventory' and hence no 'despair'. Religious feeling could be directed at this state of affairs, even if no inference were attempted *beyond* the phenomena.

8. A paper on Art and Nature could very easily have been devoted to conceptual 'map-work': to plotting the ways in which boundaries have been drawn between art and nature, drawn by some and obliterated by others: and between man and nature, also partitioned, also merged. Some of the grounds for these boundary-disputes will, I hope, have shone through in my discussion; and some of the complexities also. To re-state one point only: we noted how the 'inner' life of man is radically dependent upon his outer experience and power to appropriate forms of external nature; that furthermore these forms, as he perceives them, are very often already perceived in the light of art. Human inwardness is already stamped upon them.

Again, in some plausible accounts of some art, man the artist *triumphs over* external nature, drawing upon its forms certainly, but making a use of them wholly unprecedented in nature. Other types of art are more plausibly described in the language we use to speak of natural objects themselves, like the eastern ceramics which, according to Focillon, 'appear to be less the work of a potter than a marvellous conglomerate created by subterranean fire or accident'.[1]

Do we have a completely free choice where (and whether) to draw these boundary-lines? Think of Andrew Forge on Cézanne and the pine tree.[2] Certainly we can call 'nature' pine tree, canvas, brush and Cézanne himself, all together – if we choose. Or, to make a different point, we can still set Cézanne apart from the rest, in order to mark off the distinctiveness of what Cézanne can do, what the pine tree cannot do nor the brush on its own. We can make our vocabulary mark the continuities between the 'work' of non-human nature and the work of certain artists, e.g. between wave-smoothed pebbles and smooth-carved works of sculpture; or mark the presence of

---

[1] *The Life of Forms in Art*, p. 33.
[2] Above, p. 234.

chance elements in art. We can make the vocabulary mark the *dis*continuities between artist and non-human nature, e.g. contrasting nature's repetitiveness and art's inventiveness.

If we can draw the conceptual boundaries at a variety of places, to bring out various aspects of the artist's enterprise, does it follow that there is no room for unfortunate or misleading stipulations? Not at all. For example: consider a suggestion that the most serious or rewarding art is likely to emerge from random and chance ('natural') effects rather than from the effects of thought and labour. Compare Andrew Forge: 'The leaves flutter from the tree: the coloured papers flutter to the floor',[1] and the words he quotes from Arp 'Art is of natural origin'. In this sort of context, 'natural' is used with commendatory force, and it is also used in opposition to 'produced by purposive activity'. Now, philosophy cannot legislate against the possibility that significant art may emerge, and may have emerged, from non-purposive activities. But it can be pointed out that nothing effective is being done to commend such art on the score of its 'naturalness' in the relevant sense. 'Natural-to-man' is by no means necessarily to be equated with 'natural to the wind, the leaves and the forest floor'. A description of human nature without reference to purposing, designing, appraising, revising . . . is an incomplete description.

When Klee spoke of art as the fruit that grows out of man, rooted in nature, the image he used does not in itself exclude the possibility that *thought* enters the activity of art-creation. The metaphor of the artist as 'merely a channel',[2] however, neither 'serving' nor 'ruling' but 'transmitting', does have power to mislead. If we are to avoid incoherence, there are severe limits to the use that can be made of it. As Andrew Forge is fully aware, the artist cannot abrogate the role of one who chooses, defines the boundaries of what he is to exhibit, even if it is an *objet trouvé* or a 'ready-made'. 'Choosing' and 'defining' are active verbs, and they run against the grain of the metaphor, 'being merely a channel'.

We are continually 'arranging' and rearranging objects during our daily lives, whether thoughtlessly or with various degrees of thoughtfulness, objects on a tea-tray, a workshop bench, a study-table – or wholly at random, as pencil-sharpenings fall or crumbs when we shake out a tablecloth. Only rarely do we *present* the result as having art-interest and -value. Something of *mauvaise foi* enters one's thinking if one attempts to see man as a conduit of natural energies,

[1] Above, p. 238. I have profited here from a conversation with Mr M. J. Hutchings.
[2] Above, p. 238.

as submerged again in unthinking natural processes. Once more we move away from, rather than approach, a realisation of distinctively *human* nature, in letting metaphors of passivity, of oneness with non-human nature, take charge of our thought. The paradoxical human situation is that of a being who, in one aspect, is evidently a transient bit of nature, yet knows that he thinks and acts as well as undergoes, and cannot consistently interpret his own thoughts and actions as predictable natural occurrences. It is not as mere occurrences that art productions are appraised and appreciated.

In a word, the 'channel' metaphor and its cognates do not help us to answer questions about what the artist should *do* with natural forms (represent them, transform them, ignore them in favour of pure constructed forms); nor what he should do with his materials – toss pieces of paper in the air, or carefully place them on his board. The most they can do is to prepare the spectator not for instance to expect a mirroring of familiar appearances in art, and (positively) to look for some continuities between non-human and human productive processes. With the question of how to *appraise* these art-objects, the metaphors and manoeuvrings with the concept of nature give little help.

INDEX